From The Ground Up

1429561 ADKIN, F. From the Ground up.

358.413

-0 SEP. 1984 PR. 10.83 £11.95

Please renew/return this item by the last date shown.

So that your telephone call is charged at local rate, please call the numbers as set out below:

	From Area codes 01923 or 0208:	From the rest of Herts:
Renewals:	01923 471373	01438 737373
Enquiries:	01923 471333	01438 737333
Minicom:	01923 471599	01438 737599

L32b

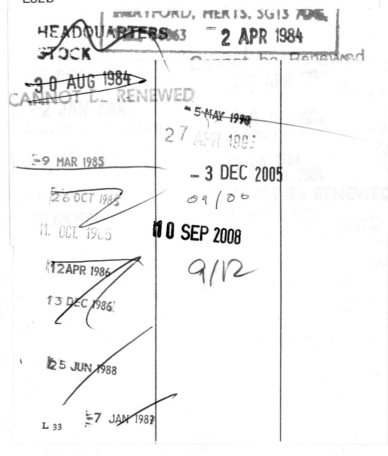

HEADQUARTERS
STOCK

2 APR 1984

3 0 AUG 1984
CANNOT BE RENEWED

-5 MAY 1990

27 APR 1993

-9 MAR 1985

- 3 DEC 2005

26 OCT 1985

09/00

11. OCT. 1985

1 0 SEP 2008

12 APR 1986

9/12

13 DEC 1986

25 JUN 1988

L 33 27 JAN 1987

From The Ground Up

by

Fred Adkin

To Service ground crew everywhere

Airlife
England

Copyright © 1983 F. J. Adkin

ISBN 0 906393 21 3

First Published in 1983
by Airlife Publishing Ltd.

Printed by Livesey Limited, Shrewsbury, England.

Airlife Publishing Ltd.

7 St. John's Hill, Shrewsbury, England.

Author's Foreword

When I retired from the R.A.F. in 1957 a still active interest in military aviation led me to the discovery that practically no standard information was available about service ground crews, and a subsequent decision to try and rectify the omission.

Scores of books have been written about the exploits of service aircrew. The greater majority of these described the parts played by service ground crew in their individual saga in a mere sentence, some in as much as a paragraph. Only two books have been written about airmen, one by an Air Chief Marshal and the other by a wartime clerk.

Aircrew deserved all the recognition they subsequently received, for their profession was at all times responsible, frequently hazardous, sometimes positively dangerous, particularly in time of war. They will, I am sure, agree with me that they enjoyed their flying. A few of them will also agree that they struck up a rapport with their own particular ground crew. But the severe discipline of the inter-war years in the services created a wide gap between officer and man which impeded the understanding of the problems of the other.

R.A.F. other ranks have been among the least publicised of all the services groups. Excepting for the propaganda films of the Second World War what does the public know of the ordinary airman who stood in the shadow of the aircrew for so long ? Very little, judging from the reticence of most airmen. So what was the background of the ground crew? How was the erk trained? What was his life like in the early days of the air services? How did the manifold trades come into being? And not forgetting the ladies, how did their service evolve?

This book outlines the development of service ground crew from the puny beginnings of the Royal Engineer sappers, through the maturity of the World War One air mechanic to the established erk of World War Two, the conditions in which they lived and operated, some of their problems, hardships and lighter moments. Because of the commercial necessity some detail has had to be omitted.

The motto of the Royal Air Force is 'Per Ardua ad Astra' loosely translated as 'Through Difficulties to the Stars'. The ground crew airmen's life is one of continuous difficulties, mostly of a technical nature the overcoming of which has contributed more than is realised to the Royal Air Force reaching those stars.

F.J.A.

Contents

Bibliography

The Balloonatics, Alan Morris, Jarrolds (London) Ltd., 1970.

The Aeronauts, L. T. C. Rolt, Longmans, 1966.

Kites–an Historical Survey, Clive Hart, Faber and Faber Ltd., 1967.

The History of Airships, Basil Clarke, Herbert Jenkins, 1961.

The Aero Manual 1909, The Motor.

R.F.C. Technical Notes 1916, Arms and Armour Press, 1968.

Confessions of a L.A.C. in the R.F.C. and R.A.F., H. Hague, Private Print, H. Sharp & Sons.

Five Years in the Royal Flying Corps, Major McCudden, The Aeroplane and General Publishing Co. Ltd., 1918.

The War in the Air, Vols 1 to 5, Hamish Hamilton.

R.F.C., The Work of the Rank and File, Autocar, September 1915.

Work and Training of the R.N.A.S. 1917, London News and Sketch Ltd.

Women of the Royal Air Force 1921-22, A. Chauncey, W.R.A.F. Old Comrades Association.

Eight Months with the Womens Royal Air Force (Immobile), Gertrude A. George, Hugh Granton, 1920.

Flying Years, C. H. Keith, John Hamilton

The Royal Air Force, F. V. Monk and H. T. Winter, Blackie and Son, 1938.

The Royal Air Force as a Career, H.M.S.O.

The Royal Air Force, Capt. O. A. Pollard, Hutchinson and Co. Ltd.

Royal Air Force 1939-46, H.M.S.O., 1953-55.

ABC of the R.A.F., ed Sir J. Hammerton, The Amalgamated Press, 1942.

Jet, Sir Frank Whittle, Frederick Muller Ltd., 1956.

Book of the W.A.A.F., Amalgamated Press, 1943.

The W.A.A.F. in Action, Adam and Charles Black, 1944.

Air Files from the Public Record Office.

History of Early British Military Aeronautics, P. W. L. Broke-Smith, Cedric Chivers Ltd., 1968.

Trenchard, Andrew Boyle, Collins 1962.

Wings over Westminister, Harold Balfour, Hutchinson 1973.

Empire of the Air, Viscount Templewood, Collins 1957.

Swifter than Eagles, John Laffin, William Blackwood and Sons, 1964.

The Forgotten Ones, A.C.M. Sir Phillip de la Ferté, Hutchinson 1961

Middle East 1940-1942, Philip Guedalla, Hodder and Stoughton, 1944.

The Mediterranean Air War, Christopher F. Shores, Ian Allan, 1973.

Malta, Ian Hay, Hodder and Stoughton, 1943.

Wings of the Phoenix, H.M.S.O., 1949.

Pictorial History of the R.A.F, Taylor and Moyes, Ian Allan 1971.

Acknowledgements

Any work of this nature must, of necessity, be a combined operation. It is the end result of many contributions, unstintingly given. The modesty of the ex ground crew to put their own exploits into print led me to suspect that many could tell more than they put down on paper. Perhaps they considered their own experience too ordinary, too routine to warrant recognition. But without them this book would be a great deal less 'human'.

The patient and helpful staff of the Public Record Office at Portugal Street from whence the factual material of this book was mainly researched.

Mr. D. A. Langdon, researcher for the P.R.O. who, in effect, began the hard work necessary at the beginning of the project.

Mr. J. H. G. Bennett of the Inspector of Recruiting Department, Royal Air Force, who was most helpful in allowing access to the photographic library.

Mr. W. Rigby, librarian of the Imperial War Museum, who gave similar assistance from the photographic section of his department.

Cedric Chivers Ltd. publishers of 'History of Early British Military Aeronautics' by Brig-Gen P. W. L. Broke-Smith, which has been a fruitful source of information.

Mr. C. H. Cole, author of the revised biography of Capt. McCudden, who recommended me to write to the National Press for assistance.

The News of the World who printed my request from which 400 replies from readers amply bore out Mr. Cole's recommendation and the popularity of the newspaper with 'other ranks'.

Lt/Col. F. T. Stear, Royal Engineer Corps Library, for useful basic information on which to build further research.

Mr. Frank S. White, Adastral House Ministry of Defence, for his help in providing further sources to investigate.

The Officer Commanding, Mr. W. S. Revill, and Mr. N. G. Hoskins, Air Historical Branch, and Mr. J. G. Rose, Northumberland House, M.O.D.

Royal Engineers Museum, Mr. R. Simpson R.A.F. Museum, F/O S. Ingold W.R.A.F. Museum, the Fleet Air Arm Museum, Mr. D. Goddard National Maritime Museum and the London Gazette.

To my wife who helped type the text, who suggested many improvements and who suffered the silence of a would-be author at work.

To all who have supplied photographs — these are individually credited after each caption.

Finally Mr. W. Hughes, who tackled the editing of the book with a natural enthusiasm and the accuracy of an aviation engineer.

Chapter 1
The Balloon Dominates

In an effort to keep Britain in the front line of military technical thinking, two Royal Engineers captains, Beaumont and Groves, who were both balloon enthusiasts, tried in 1862 to convince the War Office of the usefulness of the war balloon as an adjunct to the traditional arms. The government and military dozed over the idea for eleven years. In 1873 the War Office asked the Royal Engineers Committee to prepare a balloon for the Ashanti expedition, but as the balloon arrived too late and cost too much the idea was abandoned.

Meanwhile, the Franco-Prussian war had taken place, culminating in the Siege of Paris, surely the best possible example of the efficiency of the balloon. A rash of small foreign wars had spread closer to the Empire and when the Congress of Berlin was signed in 1878 the threat caused the politicans to stir uneasily.

In that significant year of 1878 the War Office decided to begin tentative balloon experiments once more. The development of this new arm and the requirements necessary to sustain it was given to the Royal Engineers, setting that dedicated and efficient regiment on a programme that was to be beset by apathy, prejudice, and very little equipment. Their victory over these man-made obstacles began a tradition of perseverance which has rarely been equalled.

In British history the great event has usually produced the man. The Royal Engineers produced two, Capt. J. L. B. Templer, who was joint founder of the original team of 1878 and Lt-Col. J. E. Capper who succeeded Templer as C.O. of the Balloon Section in 1903.

Captain, later Lt-Col. Templer of the Middlesex Militia, fought against these soporific conditions using conventional and unconventional methods, in addition to his own wealth, in order to keep his command in being and to expand it from a single experimental balloon into four companies. His command served overseas, took an active part in a major war and was a cohesive and very proficient Balloon Company when he handed over to Lt-Col. Capper in 1903.

Lt-Col. Capper carried on the fight. He had served under Templer as a Lieutenant in 1883 and had absorbed his ideals. He faced much the same problems and had the additional hard tasks of incorporating into his command the kite, airship and aeroplane and devising tactical and strategic techniques for their operational use. That he succeeded soon became evident, for the War Office expanded his command into the Air Battalion in 1911. Unfortunately, they also considered the new unit not important enough for a full Colonel and Capper was posted away when his talents were most needed.

The great air commanders who came after were able to build on the solid base these two men had laid. If Marshal of the Royal Air Force Lord Trenchard is known as 'Father' of the R.A.F., then Colonel Templer and Major General Sir John Capper should be joint 'Founders' of British Military Aviation.

The R.E.'s Balloon Equipment Store, as it was first known in 1878 had but one balloon, the 'Crusader' the personal property of Capt. Templer, until an official balloon, the 'Pioneer' was built in 1879.

On a fateful day in that year a party of sappers arrived at the local gasworks, parking their wagons in the yard. Under the command of Capt. Templer a few sappers carried a folded bag from the wagon and laid it out on the ground; others lifted out a net which was placed over the bag, and a wicker basket which they set down nearby. A command had been given that all naked lights in the vicinity were to be extinguished.

At one of the gasholders, officials connected a flexible hose to a valved outlet pipe. The unconnected end led to the inflation trunk of the bag. An air of expectancy pervaded the group of blue and red uniformed sappers. Brushing his great moustache, Capt. Templer gave the order and the official opened the gas valve.

Slowly the gas began to inflate the bag into the typical mushroom mound of flexing cambric. The sappers took hold of the net to prevent the blossoming bag lifting into its natural element. The wicker basket was secured to the ropes which passed through a large grommet from the net and ballast bags were attached. To many of them this was the nearest they had been to an example of man's success in airborne flight, for the sight of a balloon drifting across the sky was still a rarity. This particular balloon gave them a double sense of satisfaction for it was the army's official first; it had cost £71 to produce.

So began British military flying. The balloon was a success and made many flights, both tethered and free-running.

*   *   *   *   *

Technical training in the beginning was merely to acquaint the men with their places in the team, teach them what the balloon was for and how it was made, and in the case of the tradesmen concerned, how to repair it.

Training was adapted from the existing types of wagons in use and a system was evolved for launching and retrieving balloons that was quick and used a minimum of manpower. An operational balloon train at the end of the century consisted of slow, heavy, general service wagons pulled either by mules, horses or steam traction engines in Britain, or oxen in most overseas theatres, especially in South Africa. A number of the wagons carried gas cylinders, one carried the section's equipment, stores, the cable and a spare balloon bag. A few lucky sappers were carried on the wagon; the rest marched alongside, not too arduous a task in view of the slow progress of the convoys. Several years later those on foot were mounted which increased the mobility of the sections.

In 1885 two sections of the Balloon Store were sent overseas: one of eight N.C.O.'s and men to the Sudan, the other of 10 N.C.O.'s and men to Bechuanaland. The trained personnel were so few — the parent unit at Chatham had been denuded as a result of these postings — that untrained men were used to make up the sections. In these two expeditions the first hint of the value of balloon mobility was revealed.

After arrival in the Sudan, and anxious to be active after the restrained and uncomfortable conditions of troopship life, the sappers soon had a balloon flying at 122 metres from its G.S. wagon. Protected by armed escort it was marched seven miles (11.25 km) in seven hours and provided some very useful information as well as having a great deterrent effect on the primitive minds of the enemy. The R.E.'s were always assured of an appreciative audience of British troops.

Despite the initial success of the section the overall net result of their part in the Sudan expedition was negative. When the gas cylinders were emptied there were no more; the gas plant laid down at Suakin could not supply.

This lack of real success had one adverse effect, the War Office cut back the unit's annual estimates from £2000 to £1600. Templer's unit fought back. They were not disheartened for they had proved, despite their inadequacies, that balloon observation overseas was a workable proposition. The years preceding the South African War were spent in applying the lessons already learnt: the need to develop suitable transport, more intensive training for both ground and air crews, better liaison with forward units and a reserve of trained ground crews. In addition tentative experiments were begun with wireless telegraphy and photography from the air. In 1891 the Balloon School moved to Aldershot.

A short distance away, at Baldwyns Park, Bexley, Sir Hiram Maxim was progressing and building his giant flying machine and laying down a track for launching it. His fortunate civilian workers were gaining valuable experience in building and rigging the first real aeroplane of the world. One man's enthusiastic approach to flying, backed by keen technical knowledge and the wealth to put his ideas into practice, was making the efforts of the Royal Engineers look very puny indeed. Of this the R.E.'s were well aware, but the aeroplane was only a design exercise whereas the balloon was an established lighter-than-air craft so, whilst keeping an interested eye on Maxim's project, the sappers kept to the practical job of making theirs a worthwhile operational weapon.

Technical trades in the Balloon sections were urgently required and the first ground crews were selected from the 42 trades available in the R.E.'s, almost certainly from blacksmiths, wheelwrights, farriers, sailmakers, carpenters and fitters. All were required to adapt their skills to the repair and maintenance of the bag and its equipment, and to its wheeled and hooved transport.

With typical Army thoroughness drills were evolved for all contingencies of balloon handling. Operating the new drills an efficient section was capable of filling and launching a balloon in the planned time of 20 minutes, a time only made possible by the introduction of new compressed gas cylinders in 1884.

*   *   *   *   *

The crack of shrapnel shell overhead made the sappers instinctively duck for cover. No. 1 Section had arrived on the sunbaked plains outside Bloemfontein after weeks on the march, including keeping their last balloon inflated for 22 days while the section moved it over 165 miles of hostile land. Starting off with a full complement of balloon equipment, gas cylinders, wagons and oxen they had trudged behind the army to Bloemfontein. All the training and exercises the sappers had endured back at the Balloon School was now to be redeemed.

To cope with the immediate demand for their services the Balloon School was raised from one company in September 1899, to six sections in 1900. No's. 1 and 2 Sections went to South Africa in 1899, followed by No. 3 in 1900. In the campaigning that followed all three sections acquitted themselves with distinction.

No. 1 Section was particularly active, the ground crew launching the balloon frequently during the Battle of Magersfontein against the natural hazards of bad weather and open country and the man-made hazards of heavy shrapnel fire from the Boers which caused considerable damage to the balloons. One was so damaged that it was necessary to transfer its gas to the last balloon.

Eventually, due to the transfer of their oxen to the navy and artillery, the section was rendered immobile. The end of their effective support was due to their inability to replenish their gas supplies. The depots at Durban and Cape Town were too far away; the lessons of Sualkin had not been fully learned. Following the transfer of their oxen, the men who had done so well on their first foray on active service, were absorbed into general engineering duties and the skills and experience lost to the Balloon School. A repeat of 1863.

No. 2 Section did not have a mobile war, as very early in their service they were contained in Ladysmith for the famous siege where they were subjected to heavy shrapnel fire. The Boers would fire at the balloon as it was ascending or descending, the low altitude of attack making the shrapnel fly uncomfortably close. But the ground crew stayed at their post and after the shelling would set to and repair net, bag or rope, topping up the bag from their precious hydrogen supply to have an operational craft ready for the next occasion. When gas supplies finally ran out the men of No 2 suffered the same fate as their comrades of No. 1, being directed to the town's defences as field troops.

No. 3 Section were also blooded in a similar manner to the others, their contribution causing a large force of Boers to evacuate their laager at Fourteen Streams. They kept the balloon continuously inflated for 15 days despite the usual hail of bullets and shrapnel from the Boers. It was the section's only major action and after this, despite efforts to keep it in being, it was placed in limbo with the others. The men were used on railway duties before finally being split up on individual postings.

With such a series of successes to their credit and officers and men blooded by operational experience, their reward had been the disbanding of the three sections which had contributed so materially to the action. It was tragic in the light of the initial devotion and enthusiasm shown at the beginning of the balloon era.

*   *   *   *   *

After the South African War, the lessons learned were analysed and the results put to future use. The ponderous balloon train had been a dilemma in a campaign where mobility had been the key to success; needed fighting troops had been tied up in escort duties. These were lessons which Templer did his best to resolve. The balloon men had proved that theirs was a practical weapon and a vital one, not to be ignored, but the War Office accepting the result, failed to develop it as quickly as they might have done.

Technical training was still largely by word of mouth, generally relying mainly in the fact that the men were already skilled tradesmen. Officers posted to the sections were given a course of technical training on the balloon and its operation; in turn they passed this information on to the men in their own personal way. There was no standard form of communicating technical knowledge so that all benefitted. The approach to operating techniques at this time was that ballooning was additional to the normal military training, not an integral part of it.

The idea of using kites as a weapon of war had been tried with mediocre success over many years by different countries. The type of kite designed to lift a man was a logical development of those originally flown in China many centuries before. So far as Britain was concerned man-lifting kites had finally been successfully designed and flown by Capt.

Baden-Powell in Britain in 1894. At the same time an Australian, Lawrence Hargraves, was also successfully designing and flying kites which formed the basis of man-lifters designed by a Mr. S. A. Cody for the War Office. This system was adopted.

Briefly, a number of kites, up to seven according to wind strength, was attached to a light steel cable. When the necessary pull was achieved on the cable the man lifter was hooked onto the cable and drew a basket up (and down) the cable by a steel trolley to which the car bridle was secured. A brake was fitted and control of lift was achieved by a system of lines.

Operating kites required their own special drills but were able to use existing balloon wagons and winch. The drills were soon organised to the point where a kite could be launched in rather less than the 20 minutes target time for a balloon. One aspect of kite flying that involved ground crew skill was the sensitivity of the craft at low altitudes. Great judgment was needed by a winch operator when raising and lowering a kite near the ground. Kites, unlike balloons, did not fly well in conditions of light air or no wind and if the wind dropped whilst they were still in the air quick action was necessary to haul the flight of kites down before they stalled.

On August 9th, 1907, under War Office letter 34/379 (A.G.7) the Balloon Companies were incorporated into a School of Instruction in Military Ballooning. This Balloon School, as it was known, was no more fortunate than its predecessors in its attempt to expand. Of the original three companies envisaged only two were ever effective.

The move of the Balloon Companies to Farnborough, and the subsequent reorganisation of Balloon School and Factory, proved to be a great step forward in technical progress of the ground crew. The Factory, of which Col. Capper became the first Superintendent, was built to manufacture army balloons and airships and to explore the possibility of eventually manufacturing aeroplanes. This provided the men of the school with ample opportunities to practice their own basic trades and to absorb the new engineering techniques that were now arising as aviation began to develop.

Efforts were made to retain a nucleus of skilled operators by keeping the N.C.O.'s and men under instruction for two years before passing them back to normal units, and a more progressive system for training the newer recruits was organised, based on the necessity of trainees joining during the out-of-season period of field training.

The first of the army's airships was built at the Factory by its own skilled civilian tradesmen and, in order to operate the ship efficiently, army personnel were trained to service and maintain the ship. The School posted its tradesmen to the Factory on a rota system to provide the men with invaluable experience. Skilled men were to become so few in the Balloon School that when a few N.C.O.'s and men went on reserve their absence was acutely felt. Because these men were specialists their loss tended to throw their former section out of phase until new men could be trained.

An account of a typical week's training in August 1909 reveals the great variety of work that was undertaken by the sapper. The beginning of every day was routine. The men were audibly aroused from tent or hut at 0530 and rose from their plank beds for a hurried wash and shave, probably in cold water, performed quite quickly in those mustachioed days. Afterwards they were marched to the stables. The horse took preference to man. Here, in a dark, aromatic and ammonia-laden atmosphere the stables were purged of the night's soil and the horses made ready for the day's work, resplendent in gleaming brass and polished leather. After a very necessary clean up and breakfast, the day's activities began.

Some of the companies began the week by giving ascents to N.C.O.'s and men of the Territorial Army (Balloon) company which had been formed the previous year, and teaching them the latest balloon operations. They showed the part-timers how to read maps and relate what they had seen during their brief spell aloft. Instruction was given on the intricacies of the latest method of communication, the field telephone, together with the need for one of the oldest, writing messages by hand.

The Terriers were distributed among the seasoned sappers and taught the practical side of the business. No. 1 Company went out on a co-ordination exercise, the object being to see if the heliograph signalling from the ground could be received and understood by a balloon operator. The short answer was that it could not; the difficulty of aligning the reflected sun spot on a small, moving and often oscillating balloon was too great. No. 2 Company did a recce around the surrounding countryside. On the open Laffain Plain 'A' Section launched their balloon and after a successful observation the inflated balloon was marched across country on foot to give the men and transport cross-country experience.

Balloon drill was carried out both in launching and 'bagging down', as the term was known for deflating. Two free run balloons, the 'Toronto' and 'Voertrekker', were inflated and given a check test on their internal gas temperature.

Any spare time left over was devoted to fatigues, parades, cleaning the wagons and equipment — a must at the end of the day — and preparing for inspections by the frequent visitors who came to the School. The week passed quickly.

As one would expect in a close-knit small unit where an overall pride in their craft bound them closely together, 'esprit de corps' was practised as it was meant to be. By the very nature of their technical work, in which high standards were demanded and given, the strict impersonal discipline of line regiments was relaxed in the Royal Engineers.

By 1910 the efforts sown in the previous years to systemise training began to bear fruit. A technical training course by then had increased to a period of 32 days, but even if the course was the only one of the year, it was the most intensive in terms of real training, that had been devised so far.

The syllabus was designed for recruit trainees in all aspects of balloon operation. Extensive team practice for balloons and kites were carried out every morning; the remainder of the day was spent in repair practice. It became a feature of most technical training at this time, and for many years to come, that the trainees repaired the actual operational equipment, thus combining the best of both worlds, with the added benefit of an economic saving.

The report for a proposed summer camp in 1910 had actually been dealt with in 1909 and an interesting facet on the over preoccupation with the economic cost of the operation is shown in correspondence of the time. The estimated cost of a balloon company to proceed to Rhayader for a period of 17 days had been costed, to the last penny, and amounted to a total of £148-11-4, (£148.57p).

This summer camp was as intensive as had been the schooling, a total of 72 practices and drills of all kinds being carried out. Although many of the subjects taught were as before, nevertheless the fact that the camp was run as an all-embracing training scheme, and that all the trainees were assembled for it at a set time, was a big step forward in this vital matter of correct trade training. It began to set a pattern for the future R.A.F. practice camps and exercises.

Whilst the balloon and kite had been developed to a state of operational efficiency and reliability, the logical successor to the balloon, the powered dirigible, had appeared on the Army scene. Airships had been built and successfully flown on the Continent, mainly in non-rigid and semi-rigid form for many years before the British Army decided to build. This final decision, although tardy, had one typically British advantage in that the countries developing the dirigible had brought the airship to a practical proposition before the Army gave the go-ahead.

The first Army airship, officially Dirigible No. 1, or the 'Nulli Secundus' as it was generally known, finally flew in September 1907 and was a complete success. On October 5th 1907, Nulli Secundus flew from Farnborough to London, circled St. Paul's Cathedral and by so doing gained the world's long distance flight record for airships. She (to give these ships their accepted gender) was on the return journey when she had to put down in the grounds of the Crystal Palace because of strong winds. The airship was left there under the care of a Sergeant Ramsey who, when the storm increased, wisely made the decision to deflate. Nulli Secundus finished her journey by road.

The Royal Engineers dirigible Nulli Secundus at Crystal Palace in October 1907. R.A.F. Museum.

One of the earliest forms of dual control fitted to training aircraft of pre-1914 era.

The practical success of No. 1 and the others that followed caused an increased demand for motor mechanics, electrical and instrument trades. The majority of the early servicing had been carried out by selected balloon trades at the Factory, as both forms of flight had much in common.

In the construction of these airships the trades gained valuable knowledge and experience in the type of precision engineering required. The airship needed the skills of the established sapper trades who had hitherto not been required for aircraft. The use of the lattice type keel, for instance, which was designed to stiffen the semi-rigid and accommodate her crew and engine, required the use of blacksmiths, coppersmiths, welders, turners and machine operators.

The rigger was the first of the aviation tradesmen. Because of his knowledge of ropes and canvas, splicing and knots, he was the natural selection for balloon servicing. A contemporary tradesman, the sailmaker, was impressed into balloon service for his knowledge in repairing and making sails. Eventually the two trades were amalgamated.

Whilst the standard procedure of filling the dirigible bags was the same as for balloons, for the first time the 'trueing-up' or rigging of a complete structure was a vital factor to flying efficiency. Flying control surfaces and their operating gear was now important. With a heavy structure carrying an engine and fuel, in addition to the flying crew, the rigger had to understand the importance of adequate support and bracing of the structure. The aeroplane completed his apprenticeship and the rigger finally emerged into the 20th century as a senior aviation tradesman in his own right.

Another senior trade that developed quickly was the motor mechanic, or fitter. Aircraft were being propelled no more reliably than the early airships and their designers were trying out different types of engines, which in turn required more maintenance. Skilled motor mechanics were rare and were jealously retained by the motor manufacturers but the R.E. took steps to cure this deficiency. The forcing ground of war eliminated to a large extent the unreliability of the engines but placed a greater demand on the mechanic as the increased reliability brought complexity of design.

Chapter 2
Enter the Air Mechanics

A firm proposal for the formation of an aeroplane branch of an Air Corps — four years after the introduction of the Dunne and Cody gliders — was raised in 1910, which proved to be a year of progress.

Extracts are quoted from an important Air Corps document which was raised to show its intended effect on the training of future ground crew.

Training

'...Probably it will be found best to pass one company through a year, so that each company will obtain aeroplane training.' This last proposal, like the following one, was not taken up, due to the formation of the Air Battalion in the next year and the rapid increase in the size of this new Air Corps.

'It is suggested after recruit ballooning the companies will be passed alternatively to aeroplane and dirigible courses. .... The course may be divided into;
1 Instruction individually in the principles of flight and practical training on the flying ground and in the workshop
2 Instruction collectively in military uses of aeroplanes, reconnaissance and work as a unit in the field.
...The training of officers and men will proceed together, but may be considered under three heads;
1 Pilots. The training of these is well known.
2 Tradesmen.
3 Mechanics and N.C.O.'s i/c machines.

'Tradesmen

The system successfully employed at the School of Mechanical Engineering (S.M.E.) of training men by means of N.C.O. Instructors will be allowed as far as practicable. Generally speaking the early training will consist of continuous employment in the care, maintenance and repair of the machines in their charge.

'They will be given elementary instruction by the mechanist instructor in the principles of flight and the use of the various parts of the machine. The specialist tradesmen of the experimental staff may also be called on to explain the adaptation of their trades to the technical needs of the aeroplane. Beyond this the training will consist of work in the field; the transport, erection and dismantling of the machines and their portable sheds. This will be reduced to a drill and it is hoped to make it a very rapid process with trained men. ....' (Hangar erection was initially taken over as a specialist job by men trained to work as erection teams, after the hangars were eventually standardised to a few practical types).

'When no repairs are required the men will be employed in the manufacture of spare parts, or if necessary, in the later stages of constructional work for the experimental officer.

'Mechanics and N.C.O.'s i/c machines

The military machinists, fitters training for such, and N.C.O.'s whom it is intended to place in charge of machines, will of course require further instruction.

'The ideal to be aimed at is a handy mechanic, with sufficient knowledge of the principles of flight to understand the uses and working of the various parts, and with sufficient experience of the machine to enable him to keep them in good order, adjustment and repair and to make a rapid and accurate examination before a flight with certainty that no important defect will escape him. ...' (Here, in 1910, was laid down the essence of a good mechanic, the basic principles of which have been maintained up to the present day. Throughout the intensive technical development that followed, these basic precepts have never been allowed to lapse by the Royal Air Force). The remainder of the report describes recommendations which were all accepted.

By 1910 there were sufficient aeroplanes in the country to give the Balloon School a representative cross section of constructional methods. Although most of these were 'one-off' types, several others were so successful as to be adapted for military use. Chief among them were the Henri Farman series, Voisin and Bleriot. Practically the entire Balloon School and subsequent Air Battalion ground crew were taught their basic knowledge on the Henri Farman Shorthorn and Longhorn, which became the standard training aircraft in the Royal Flying Corps.

The men were required to know the structure of an aeroplane and its component parts, flying and control surface coverings, the multiplicity of wires. They were taught the properties of spruce, ash and bamboo used in longeron and spars and how to lighten the spars by hollowing out in two halves and glueing. Repairing or renewing the plane surface covering required knowledge of the materials in use, which in 1909 included fine quality canvas, some types with a fine coat of indiarubber or pegamoid; oiled Japanese silk; cotton oiled paper covered with muslin; Egyptian cotton, and aluminium cloth. The various methods of handling the material were taught, including their treatment, which usually consisted of boiled oil, oak varnish or glue.

The structure of an aeroplane of that time was braced internally and externally by straining and bracing wires, the breaking strains of which had to be known, with their different types of connections to the structure; the eye, the twisted eye or Hope rigging eye, the thimble or rigging screw. Allied to the bracing wires were the control wires. The intricacies of wing warping, front or rear elevation rudder and elevator plane controls were assimilated along with the adjustments of the rigging wires. The largest operation carried out by the riggers was the 'trueing-up', 'tuning' or rigging of the complete structure, including the undercarriage. One mistake at the beginning of the operation and the error could be magnified into inoperable proportions, even with the coarse settings allowed by these slow flying machines. To carry out his task the rigger had the aid of the specialist equipment, such as dihedral and incidence boards, straightedges, spirit levels, plumbbobs, trammels and measuring tape.

The mechanics had a large range of engines to care for and considering the state of the art, the engines were matched by their variety of design. Understanding the design performance and servicing of the engines did not present such problems as with the aeroplane structures, because the internal combustion engine had been around since 1885, and in production use for motor cars and lorries for many years. An aero engine was still very much a large car engine.

A pre-war pusher biplane which appears to be based on a Wright design but with a rudimentary fuselage. Clough.

However, the mechanic had to know the engine he would service and he was usually required to remove the engine from the aeroplane, to strip it down, clean and recondition it and where necessary reassemble it. The mechanic learned from the practical side as did most tradesmen of the day. Theoretical knowledge was strictly limited to the basic principles of theory of flight for the riggers and the Otto cycle and magneto operation for the mechanics.

The engines most generally available to the Service in 1909 were the Antoinette (Voisin, Bleriot, Farman, Cody), the Anzani (Bleriot), E.N.V. (Voisin, Bleriot), Gnome (Voisin, Farman) and Renault (Voisin, Farman). The last two became standard engines for instruction.

By the end of the 19th century all the basic manifestations of electricity were known and understood. Electricians, as a trade, were still in the minority and mostly confined to associated industries, such as shipbuilding, general engineering, engine and motor vehicle building. The first aircraft electricians had to understand the idiosyncrasies of engine ignition equipment, the coils, condensers and magneto. No electrical equipment was carried on the early aeroplanes or airships, so the electricians were in at the beginning of aeronautical development. The experienced electricians of the Balloon School quickly applied their trade to heavier-than-air craft requirements.

Photographically, the state of that trade was on a par with the electricians. The skills were well developed, albeit with equipment which was bulky and cumbersome. Army ground photographers accepted it as normal, but air service photographers soon foresaw the need for a lighter camera and equipment. As they gained practical experience so camera weight came down and efficiency increased. The aerial photographier did not really come into his own until W.W.1 increased dramatically the demands for his skills. Prior to that time he had mastered the cameras of the day and experimented with systems for developing plates in the field.

The armourers had a comparatively simple, but infinitely more dangerous task. Theirs was the problem of arming the early aeroplanes with primitive bombs carried on flimsy racks and made live by crude fuses. They took a very real risk every time they 'bombed-up' and although, as experience was gained, bomb armament was made safer to handle, the risks still remained.

This then was the position of the basic aircraft trades at the formation of the Air Battalion. But these were the 'front' men. Equally important tradesmen were working in squadron or depot workshop, ready to back-up any major repair work required. Fitters, sailmakers, carpenters, black-, tin-, copper- and silver-smiths, turners and machine men were all ready to apply their skills to keep the aircraft serviceable, as their successors have done ever since.

The years 1911-1914 were formative years for the air arm. The Balloon School was now expanding rapidly and becoming too specialised to be just one part of an army regiment. The final severance came on April 1, 1911 when the Balloon School was reorganised as the Air Battalion, still under the normal control of the Royal Engineers and largely officered by them. On its formation, the establishment of the Air Battalion, which remained in being for one year, consisted of a H.Q. unit and two companies with a total strength of 190.

*   *   *   *   *

To evaluate the potential of the aeroplane for mobility in the field, Captain Fulton visited the French Army aeroplane trials in late October.

In his report he attributed the failure of a Clerget engined Deperdussin as '. . . the failure of this machine to pass the tests should be attributed to the fact that the mechanics were at first unfamiliar with the type of engine. . .'. Quite a responsibility rested on the shoulders of the mechanics, whose apparent inability to master an engine could have lost the manufacturers of that aircraft the chance of a Government contract. Captain Fulton goes on '. . . the 100hp Gnome ran well and consistently throughout the trials as did the 80hp Anzani engine. . . The salient difference between these two engines was that;

1.   The Gnome engine requires to be taken down and completely overhauled after, at the outside, 12 hours running. This work requires to be be done by mechanics who have had considerable experience of Gnome engines.

2.   The Anzani engine can be run for 30 or 40 hours before it needs an overhaul and when this is needed it can be carried out by any good mechanic who is accustomed to petrol engines'.

Captain Fulton's report ended with a short paragraph on the type of aeroplane sheds which the French were using, which were subsequently to be purchased by the British in large numbers and became hangar, canteen, bedroom and workshop to a generation of air mechanics. '... Bessoneau portable hangars are considered to be very good. It is said that 20 men can erect one in 8 working hours. They are made in two sizes: 25 x 25 metres price

12,000 francs and 20 x 20 metres price 8,000 francs. There are at least 20 of these portable hangars standing at the Rheims ground alone. I saw no other make of portable. . .'

Efforts were made to improve the meagre instrumentation of the aircraft. The most fully equipped aircraft could boast only an engine revolution counter, an aneroid barometer for altitude measurement and a maritime compass. When compasses had to be swung the Navy was called in to give instruction to the instrument mechanic. The trades of instrument mechanic and electrician were soon combined, but because of the shortage of these skilled trades the maintenance of instruments was often carried out by the rigger and fitter. It was not until the 1930's that the instrument trades really came into their own.

Towards the end of the year Major Sir Alexander Bannerman issued his training schedule for 1912 which required that for every two aircraft a military machinist be detailed and there should be one rigger per machine. All the ground crews should have a manufacturers course as early as possible in the year. The major requested that several 30 cwt. lorries be supplied to the new establishment for modification to fit them for use as aeroplane and airship tenders, gas wagons and travelling workshops.

From this report, and others that follow, it will be seen that the Air Battalion was in good hands and that those who controlled it were completing the substantial foundations that were necessary to support the units which eventually would be formed. Most of the basic organisation, methods and systems of the R.F.C. were laid down during this period. Some of the recommendations that were adopted have lasted through to the present day in a modified form, as a report issued by Captain Burke reveals.

Captain Burke was asked to give his definition of technical and military aviation and submitted a report in which he defined factors that are now accepted as commonplace. It took a war to make them so, unfortunately, because only in that state was there sufficient men and money available to implement some of his suggestions.

'1.   At present aviation can be divided into two branches, technical and military aviation.

'2.   The study of the former would mean a long engineering training, practical work in aeroplane workshops, and a course at an institution such as Ecole Superieure d'Aeronautique at Paris. Such a study would be necessary if construction is going to be embarked on. ...'

Prophetic words indeed, for The Aircraft Factory was still in the future. It is now standard practice to send selected R.A.F. officers to University for aeronautical degrees and specialist qualifications.

The Captain concluded '... The employment of aeroplanes requires skilled military pilots and what is *equally important,** efficient staffs on the ground (This latter point was usually missed). The number of pilots and trained men on the ground will depend on the number of machines used. The keeping of machines in repair can only be carried out by men trained to such work and each machine should have trained men with it. Most firms which supply aeroplanes would allow men to do some training at their works. ...'

Captain Burke, who was one of the founder members of the Air Battalion and a trained balloonist, in addition to being a very efficient aeroplane pilot, was also one of the first to bring official attention to the importance of the trained mechanic to an efficient air arm. He also recommended that for every two machines the crews should consist of two pilots, two mechanics, one sailmaker, one carpenter and two trained riggers. He finally proposed that a flight of aeroplanes should all be of one type with the same type of engine. In view of

*Author's italics.

24

the diversity of types that were coming into the Air Battalion this was another far-seeing approach.

Before the contribution by the Royal Engineers to the air arm is finally concluded, some information on these dedicated men would not go amiss. The sappers were recruited from the artificer and handiwork trades and were considered skilled enough not to require basic technical tuition. However, some specialist individual training was given, particularly to young recruits. The sapper was responsible for all the mechanical and electrical work of the army, including the new aviation branch when it was accepted by the R.E.'s in 1878, but excluding the artillery and armament fields.

For the new air branch reliance was placed on the basic trades, the necessary knowledge gained being developed into new trades geared to the new technology. By 1912 the R.E. trades now included several aviation trades and the trade classification had been stabilised. The rates of pay of the Air Battalion in 1912 was commensurate with the rank and technical ability of the individual and it also depended on the group, mounted or unmounted, to which he was attached.

A major technical crisis in 1912, when structural faults in a number of monoplanes resulted in a few fatal accidents, was the occasion for a detailed report by the Department Committee on the accidents, from which came an official understanding of the work of the air mechanics. This is printed in full to show the Committee's praise and their emphasis on the need for a large number of trained mechanics.

'... 53. The Committee felt also that the lives of those who fly aeroplanes depend to an important degree on the skilful and conscientious manner in which the mechanics of the Royal Flying Corps carry out their work of examination and adjustment of the various parts of an aeroplane, and they wish to bring to the notice of the Lords Commissioners of the Admiralty and the Army Council the importance of ensuring that as large a number as possible of the mechanics of the Royal Flying Corps are adequately trained without delay to perform their duties in an efficient manner.

The whole RFC on parade, possibly at Netheravon, about June, 1914 comprising No. 1, 2 & 3 Squadrons. IWM.

'The Committee realise that the organisation of the Royal Flying Corps, when matured, will render possible the training of the requisite numbers, but they suggest that during the present stage of its development, to supplement the training establishment of the Royal Flying Corps, two or three skilled mechanics for each squadron should be specially engaged for a time to act as instructors and to set a standard of technical workmanship, while advantage should be taken of the facilities afforded by private firms, both at home and abroad, for teaching men in their workshops. . .'

In the last case little confidence was felt in the ability of the firms to impart sufficient technical knowledge to enable trainees to attain the high standards which the R.F.C. demanded. Mr. O'Gorman, the Superintendent, Royal Aircraft Factory, didn't think so, either, and on being approached by the Director of Fortifications and Works to help in a stop-gap scheme to attract highly skilled civilian tradesmen into the R.F.C. his proposals were realistic, if slightly unorthodox.

He virtually ignored the aircraft firms as sources of supply of skilled men and concentrated instead on the established engineering and shipbuilding industries, where engineering was based on sound principles. Mr. O'Gorman had little time for the standards of the embryonic aircraft industry. He sent out his own foremen to the Midlands, where the more suitable men were employed, to attract half a dozen men at a time. The intriguing question as to how these men were attracted, and by what, is unfortunately left unanswered.

Having obtained the men he then proposed they would be employed at the Royal Aircraft Factory (R.A.F.) for about four months to be taught the basics of aircraft maintenance, including erection, servicing and stripping aviation engines and fitting them. His object was to rate their capabilities and weed out the unsuitable types of tradesmen, from a service point of view. He suggested they be offered a better-than-average rate of pay and be given conditions more in keeping with their para-military status.

On May 13th, 1912, a major reorganisation of the air arm had taken place, with the formation of the Royal Flying Corps from the Air Battalion. The last link of the Royal Engineers with military aviation was finally broken. From now on the R.F.C. was on its own as a military service, although the decision to have military and naval wings within its structure brought the first squabbles between the Army and Navy chiefs as to whom should have control over this revolutionary air arm.

Requirements for the training of mechanics were more realistically appraised. The R.F.C., on the day after its formation, asked for tradesmen, both skilled and semi-skilled, priority being given to:

Men who had served as apprentices, or improvers, in general mechanical engineering and had also served in a petrol motor engineering works, including engine test work, or as an engine mechanic. They were required to have a knowledge of general motor engineering, the principles of magneto and coil ignition and be able to make intelligible sketches of machinery details and rough calculations.

These men were to be the technical cream of the expansion and on selection by the O.C. Military Wing could be instantly promoted to sergeant to fill existing vacancies. They would be on probation for one year and if unsuitable be liable for discharge.

A second class of men were required to pass a trade test, and if successful were graded as 1st Class Air Mechanics from the date they completed their basic training. They were eligible for promotion. A third class of men were needed who could be recruited into semi-skilled trades such as machinist, chauffeur, wireman, plumber's mate and motor fitter.

The physical standards were not clearly defined, except for a detailed requirement of chest measurement, and expansion related to height and an age group of 18 to 30. Height was at a minimum of 5ft 2in (158cm) and the average chest expansion for the grading of height was 2in (50mm). The average physique of men at the turn of the 20th century was well below today's average. Consquently the standards had to be made to suit.

The terms of service were for four years with the Colours and four years in the Reserve. Men of other arms of the services who elected to transfer to the R.F.C. had to have their service adjusted so that they would also complete four years with the R.F.C. plus the four years reserve.

These transfer men were on probation for six months. Senior N.C.O.'s (Sergeants and above) who transferred had to agree that they would accept the minimum rank of Sergeant. For other ranks it was conditional that all transfers had to accept the rank of private from leaving their regiment or corps.

They were liable to be employed either for Naval or Military purpose as required.

The class of recruit who was accepted were men of above average intelligence, with a certain amount of education equivalent to the standard of a 3rd class school certificate.

The rates of pay for the four ranks of the R.F.C. of 1912 (there was no corporal) were:

Rank	Daily Pay	Messing	Quarters	Rations
Warrant Officer	9s 0d (45p)	3d (1p)	1s 11d (10p)	6d (2½p)
Sergeant	6s 0d (30p)	3d (1p)	9d (4p)	6d (2½p)
1st Class Air Mechanic	4s 0d (20p)	3d (1p)	9d (4p)	6d (2½p)
2nd Class Air Mechanic	2s 0d (10p)	3d (1p)	9d (4p)	6d (2½p)

The urgent need for expanding the R.F.C. decreed that little time, or money, could be set aside to train new recruits, hence the emphasis on skilled trades; at least the background of basic knowledge was established. It was to be several years before the R.F.C. was committed to technical training schools, when the voracious appetite of the war machine finally required a greater output of trained men than the traditional system could supply.

* * * * *

The establishment for each aeroplane squadron was for 12 aircraft. The first two squadrons formed in the R.F.C. were No. 1 formed from No. 1 (Airship) company, and No. 3 from No. 2 company of the old Air Battalion. No. 1 Airship and Kite squadron had dirigibles Beta, Gamma, Delta, Zeta (the Clement-Bayard) and the Elta on charge. The squadron also had man-lifting kites and free balloons and carried on as an airship squadron until 1st January, 1914, when the airships were handed over to the Naval Wing of the R.F.C.

If the daily routine work reports are any indication, 5.30 a.m. was the witching hour for No. 1 squadron ground crews. This appeared to be the standard time to commence flying the airships to utilise the calm dawn air.

In early 1913, No. 3 squadron devised a rota which enabled skilled mechanics to gain wide and varied experience of the aircraft and engines on the unit. The system was that selected men were sent into workshops from the flight where, under skilled supervision, they learned the more exacting repair work. Conversely, skilled workshop personnel were sent out into the flights for a tour of duty. Also, when an engine came into workshops for major overhaul or repair, the mechanic in charge of the engine came with it and carried out the work under supervision.

This method of training was put out to other squadrons for information and use, if suitable. No. 1 found it to be impracticable, on the basis that the squadron had a large variety of airship engines. Their method was somewhat similar in that when an engine, or lorry, was due for major work which required the services of workshop, the mechanic responsible for the engine or lorry came into the shops with it. They did the work assisted by the workshop staff.

The creation of the Royal Flying Corps, the first major British technical service of the 20th century, attracted many young men, products of Britain's highly organised industrial background and enthusiastically drawn by the magic of flight. Such was the response the R.F.C. was able to hand pick only the best, and this set the standards by which the new service was able to expand without too much difficulty, or at least without breaking down, when the testing time of war finally came.

Recruiting for the Naval Wing of the R.F.C. was slightly different. The Wing had more ranks and the system was geared to Naval procedure and requirements. The Naval Wing required men from the following trades; it made no attempt to group these trades in order of skills but the tradesmen had to have experience in:

General upkeep, construction and repair of aircraft, trueing up, etc. Fitting, turning. Cycle mechanics. Motor driving. Carpenter's work, joinery, cabinet making etc. Boat building. Fabric work on airships or aeroplanes. Care and maintenance and repair of petrol engines, i.e. men who have served in petrol engine works. Coppersmith's work. Electrician's work.

As with the Military Wing, experienced civilians could enlist direct as Chief Petty Officer Mechanic or Petty Officer Mechanic, but they were only to be allowed to serve a maximum of 8 years, plus four in the Reserve.

Physical standards were basically similar to the Military Wing, but with nearly twice the number of ranks the pay was more varied and the administration was more complicated. In the Military Wing all the tradesmen were grouped into just four ranks; the Naval Wing proposed basic ranks were twice as many and were:

Chief Petty Officer Mechanic, 1st and 2nd and 3rd grade
Petty Officer Mechanic
Leading Mechanic
Air Mechanic, 1st and 2nd grades.

These ranks were graded into three main trade groups, General, Engine and Artisan Branches. The men were able to transfer between groups if they had the necessary qualifications.

Men were allowed to return to the Navy after their R.F.C. service had expired and arrangements were made that any promotion they were due would not be jeopardised. They could also be dismissed if their character or technical ability warranted it.

These proposals eventually crystallised into a more substantive and comprehensive recruiting scheme which was published. Syllabuses were given and included method of teaching with a typical programme for the three month's instruction. At the Naval Depot most of the syllabus was devoted to basic recruit training. Early morning was given to the pleasures of physical training (P.T.). The remainder of the day was devoted to drill, pistol practice, lectures and technical instruction. On completion of six weeks at the Depot the men were posted to one of two units:

The Isle of Grain Air Station, for technical tradesmen
The Airship Training Station, for those being trained for this type of work.

Men invalided for injuries received in the course of service were awarded pensions as laid down by the Naval Regulations, which were from 6d (2½p) to 2s (10p) according to the severity of the wound or injury. In the event of death occuring within seven years as a result of an injury, the widow received pensions in the same way as those of the R.F.C., which varied from 5s (25p) to 9s (45p) per week and children from 1s 6d (7p) to 2s (10p) per week

* * * * *

June 1914 was a minor milestone in the technical progress of the R.F.C. In that month, the entire Military Wing was assembled at Netheravon for a month's combined training. Every aspect of operational and training requirement was carried out as near as possible to actual conditions. By means of lectures, meetings, discussions and conferences, the various problems involved in a growing military air service were thrashed out and co-ordinated. Flying and technical training received equal emphasis. A request for suggestions had been previously circulated throughout the service and carefully compiled technical lectures became part of the Netheravon Camp syllabus.

Observation from the air, the prime function of aircraft as then visualised, was pursued with great determination. The logical developments for military aircraft were given a thorough trial. Arming of aeroplanes with rifles and machine guns, bombs and the dropping of them, air photography and wireless telegraphy were all treated, and modified as necessary.

The ground crews, in addition to their usual servicing and maintenance work, carried out exercises in aeroplane handling, dismantling and stowage in lorries of the same aeroplanes and their transportation across country in convoy by day and night.

They call us "THE EYES OF THE ARMY"
For we scout for the foe far and wide,
And with all information worth having
We keep the powers fully supplied –
There are Corps who bear much longer records
For brave deeds, yet History will find
That in the great fight
for the cause of the right,
OUR AIRMEN were not FAR BEHIND.

FROM ONE OF THE
R.F.C.

Chapter 3
Training the Mechanics

At the outbreak of war the Royal Flying Corps and the Royal Naval Air Service were unprepared for the rapid rate of growth of their embryonic service and the large numbers of highly qualified tradesmen that would be required. The miniscule air arms were still operating to a slightly pressurised peace time routine, and in the general fervour of 'the war would be over by Christmas', were not extending their efforts too much to prepare for a long war by a rapid recruiting of qualified men.

As a result, many thousands of skilled men, impatient with the slow recruiting process of the air services, and sublimely anxious to get into the fighting before it ended, turned to the Army. The air arms lost forever the services of a great number of the types of men they were to need so desperately. But the recruiting authorities were still able to pick the best despite the increasing defection to the Army, and to get sufficiently skilled men who required only the minimum of training on the 'stick and string' types in operation in 1914.

Training of air mechanics up to the end of 1914 was to the syllabuses laid down on the formation of the R.F.C. The skilled tradesmen enlisted were given a rigorous trade test which, if successful, was followed by recruit training at Farnborough and Eastchurch respectively. Further technical training necessary to understand the peculiarities of aeronautical engineering was also provided.

An RFC workshop lorry showing grinder, drill, lathe and forge. The lorry was a Crossley and in general use. IWM.

Like the R.F.C. the Royal Naval Air Service relied on first recruits to be skilled men, needing the minimum of training. These were given basic training at Farnborough, with special emphasis placed on a course modified to help them in their future calling. On completion of the course the ex-trainees were posted either to an air station or a ship on R.N.A.S. duties.

Some time elapsed before a regular routine for training the mechanics was established. Comprehensive technical training, as with the R.F.C., was a low priority in the months immediately following the outbreak of war.

It was decided by the R.N.A.S. that from 1st September 1914 recruits would have a three months course, the first six weeks at the Naval Depot at Sheerness. After this first period seaplane classes trained at the Naval Flying School at Eastchurch or the Isle of Grain air station for practical instruction. The syllabus was based on regular two week periods. The first three periods were devoted to physical drill, technical instruction or lectures and pistol practice.

1915 saw the realisation that recruiting and training would need to be stepped up. The aeroplane was an important factor. The old system, of sending some skilled men direct to squadrons to learn their new skills or by an 'on the job' scheme with reserve squadrons, needed drastic revision. Trades in current demand had increased to the complexity required to service the aeroplanes of 1914-1915:

RFC air mechanic trainees assembling rotary aero engines during training at Reading in 1917.
IWM.

Fitters	Turners	Wireless mechanics
Riggers (Aeroplane)	Pattern makers	Photographers
Carpenters	Blacksmiths	Sailmakers
Joiners	Coppersmiths	Tinsmiths
Woodworking	Electricians	Acetylene workers
machinists	Instrument makers	Sheet metal workers
Armourers		

'Back-up' trades required to give essential support to the ground crews were:

Motor car drivers	Trimmers	Upholsterers
Motor cyclists	Tailors (for Sailmakers)	(for Sailmakers)
Shorthand typists	Clerks	

While the great majority of the aeroplane trades could be employed for lighter-than-air craft, these craft also demanded their own specialists of:

Balloon operators	Rigger (Airship)	Winchmen

The recruits for the expanding air force signed on for four years plus four years reserve, or for 'hostilities only'. After acceptance they moved to South Farnborough for their trade tests. If successful, they stayed at the depot for four weeks recruit training. After completion any extra training which could not be carried out on the depot, was done at the Aircraft Park.

One priority of training for both air services was to produce men who were self-reliant and adaptable, who could work efficiently on their own without supervision. It was, and still is, an excellent policy and, subject to an unavoidable lowering of standards that was inevitable during two long World wars, has been the reason why Britain's air services tradesmen have been considered the best in their field.

One of the early pioneers who did a riggers course at Farnborough in 1914-1915 was Air Mechanic Robert Davidson who was very well qualified at that time, an apprentice marine engineer, student of mechanical engineering in his fourth year and a holder of today's equivalent O.N.C. He had eight days recruit training at Farnborough and was then arbitrarily selected for training as a rigger at the Aircraft Park just across from the recruit school. Each entry comprised 15 trainees and they were taught the basic theory of flight and stabilities, with practical work on how to splice control wires and make piano wire loops for wing bracings, repairs to ribs and struts and to holes and tears in canvas coverings. On the aerodrome the men were taught how to erect and true one of the BE2C, Henri Farman or Bleriot training aircraft, using instruments to measure angles of incidence and dihedral, and how to dismantle and load the aeroplane onto a lorry for transporting across country. This last was a vital part of their training, for it was the task of the rigger to salvage aircraft for the valuable engines and instruments that were always in short supply. A volunteer was selected from the class to go for a test flight, surely an incentive to do a good job.

Because of an acute shortage of instrument trades riggers were also required to understand and service the instruments in current use; aneroid altimeter, airspeed indicator and compass.

Like the riggers, the fitters were taken, step by step, through their syllabus, commencing with the theory of engines; they were given a sound knowledge of components, carburetters, magnetos and water pumps. Their training aids consisted of elderly engines in various states of assembly and a collection of components. Few of these were sectioned and practical training was in the dismantling, cleaning, inspection and rectification, re-assembly and adjustment.

Civilian engine mechanics were experienced only on the car engines of the day. The current in-line engines were based on these and transition from car to aircraft engines was comparatively simple. The R.F.C. course emphasised better procedures, higher safety standards and up-to-date theory and techniques. Fitters stripped the different types, Gnome rotaries, Renault stationary water-cooled, old Anzani and Green engines and the first Royal Aircraft Factory (R.A.F.) engine, which was based on the Renault. After assembly the engines were tuned by valve timing, ignition timing and carburation, the magneto settings, and finally given a test run.

It was emphasised that the work had to be right. There was no excuse for the attitude 'that will do' which was accepted as a criminal outlook and punished as such. Too many aviators were depending for their lives on engines, which even in peak condition were never reliable, without compounding the risks by careless workmanship. This attitude remained the keynote of all training and aircrew were seldom let down, literally, as a result of poor maintenance.

In addition the fitter was given a fuller understanding of his craft in the basic side by being taught how to remetal bearings, bed-in crankshafts, fit and balance connecting rods and align cylinders. He was also taught how to maintain his own specialist instruments, such as they were, in the same way as the riggers.

*　*　*　*　*

Photographers, instrument fitters and armourers of the so-called ancillary trades, because their work was closely involved and complementary to the fitter and rigger, were also taught at Farnborough, together with allied trades, the turners, blacksmiths, tinsmiths and welders. As it was current policy to repair aircraft in the field as much as possible—this was before the great Aircraft Repair Depots—the workshop trades were also taught, after their basic syllabus had been fulfilled, how to operate with, and from, the workshop lorries.

These vehicles were comprehensively equipped, containing lathes, fixed and portable drills, emery wheel, tool grinder, forge and anvil and lighting, all powered from a petrol engine driven dynamo. The lorry had its own charging board and an electrician was a necessary member of the crew.

The technical knowledge acquired at Farnborough was used practically to produce serviceable aircraft components and fittings. When one considers that Farnborough was the only large R.F.C. training school and repair and maintenance unit in 1915 it seemed only logical to help produce such fittings, and as the school was going to compete with the civilian aircraft industry, its policy becomes clearer.

The expanding R.N.A.S, decided it also needed more training establishments. Cranwell, in Lincoln, had become an airship and aeroplane centre and this camp was developed for technical training. But an urgent demand was raised for a large reception centre for all arms and branches of the Navy in which some elementary training could also be carried out, and large enough to accommodate any forseen expansion in the future.

The choice fell, appropriately enough, on the Victorian showplace of Crystal Palace, in South London, built to display exhibitions of technology as advanced in its day as any in the world.

A.M. Clarke, G. wanted to be a rigger and had taught himself wire splicing before he went for his interview. When asked what work he did he replied that he was a wire splicer, producing an example to prove it. On the strength of that he was classified as Acting 1st Class carpenter rigger. At Crystal Palace he contracted German measles; no service training school or camp seemed immune from its quota of infectious diseases. He was examined by a doctor and put into the Sick Bay with several others.

The victims were sent to Joyce Green where they spent three weeks convalescing before being discharged. Their favourite nurse kissed them all when they left. Shortly after she went down with measles.

The tremendous success of the aeroplane in helping the army and navy in the opening campaigns of the war, forced the final acceptance that this new weapon was as vital as the artillery or submarine. The advent of trench warfare stabilised aerodromes on a semi-permanent basis. The R.F.C. and R.N.A.S. demanded more and different types of aircraft which necessitated a rapid expansion of the aircraft industry.

The natural result of the increased aircraft output was for more trained manpower to service and maintain them. In 1915, although the principle of selecting civilian skilled and semi-skilled trades was still strictly adhered to, the standards of entry were lowered. Those who came to enlist, prepared for a stiff technical examination, were often surprised at the almost ludicrous ease with which many of them passed.

Inconsistency was a rule during the first two years of the war, incurred necessarily by the need to get mechanics out to the flying units. Until the long overdue training schemes were standardised in 1916-17 the R.F.C. tried various methods to increase the intake of technical men, including the lowering of technical standards. One of these methods was a transfer scheme, to bring back into the R.F.C. those highly skilled men who had joined the army regardless of how important their specialist knowledge would be to the country. The scheme was only partially successful, but those who did respond were gratefully welcomed.

At the Regent Street Polytechnic, special days were set aside to enlist first class tradesmen. Their qualifications would be such that further technical training was considered unnecessary, and these men were invariably posted directly overseas on completion of their recruit training. The wisdom of sending men, skilled in engineering trades but untrained and ignorant of the basic requirements of aircraft operation and maintenance, straight to units is open to debate. It is, however, a tribute to these men that they learned quickly in the units and were soon skilled in their service trade.

Testing was also done at Farnborough from where the qualified tradesmen were mustered into a different trade from their own civilian skill. Air Mechanic W. J. Nicholson was both a transfer from the army and subject to the willy-nilly approach to trade requirements. Nicholson, who had previously seen action at the Somme (and had been hospitalised as a result) volunteered to join the R.F.C. in response to a call for machinists and blacksmith's strikers. He said, '. . . the test for strikers was to hit a post several times, into the ground. The test for machinists, for which I applied, was to turn a pin 0·625 in diameter on a lathe, using a micrometer. . . I passed . . . They were full up with machinists.

... Did any of us know anything about petrol motors? I told the Sergeant I had a motor cycle and did my own repairs. I was in. . .'

Volunteers who passed their trade test were given the certificate which was necessary when applying to enlist. The results from the Regent Street centre were successful enough to set up similar centres around the U.K. However, it appears that sometimes the apparent quantity was considered better than the quality.

At Farnborough one practical test survived to become a hardy annual, almost to the present day. This was the filing and fitting exercise, for which the candidates had to file two pieces of rough mild steel to fit as per blueprint dimension, usually a square piece within a square hole.

An illustration of the uncertainty of trade selection with its fluctuating demands is well shown in the case of Air Mechanic T. H. Arnold. He joined the R.F.C. as an electrician in January 1916 and spent three months at the Curragh before being posted back to Farnborough, and then to 25 Reserve Squadron at Thetford, where for nine months he had no work in his trade. So he was remustered to engine fitter. Some months later he was posted back to Farnborough again where he was further remustered, this time to armourer! He then went to France.

Air Mechanic Cornish was attracted to the R.F.C. and decided to join that service instead of the infantry in which his two brothers were serving. He joined as a sailmaker and went to Duke of York's H.Q. in London for his test. He said ... 'The different testers were in lorries, mine stretched a piece of fabric across a bucket, he then cut a slit in it and told me to sew it up, well I was able to use a straight needle as I had been working at a tailor's shop. It got me guessing, though. Anyway, I pulled a needle from under my lapel, threaded it, waxed it and started to twist it. The examiner said, 'You pass'. It was a little bit of bluff on my part. Weeks afterwards I found out what a curved upholsterer's needle was, which was the proper type to use'. The success of his bluff was due to the waxing of the thread.

Air Mechanic A. W. Gray, while under training with the Infantry, contracted an ear infection which prevented him from going overseas. He was given the option of working on the land or passing a trade test for a technical unit. Some choice! Gray passed a test for turning which required him to make a $\frac{1}{2}$in. Whitworth male and female thread. As a result he was detailed to join the Royal Engineers Railway Operational Dept. Not wanting to be a 'Casey Jones' either, he goes on '... As the representatives of all the technical corps had a separate office and being desirous of joining the R.F.C. I secured an interview with the officer representing them, who told me that I could not join for the duration of the war, but only on a time serving basis—4 years with the colours and 4 years on Reserve. I agreed to do this and was sent to Farnborough North Camp'.

At Farnborough he was asked again by a clerk if he wanted to join for the Duration or 4 + 4 years. He said Duration! He had to sit a similar lathe test but his obvious familarity with the machine excused him the test. Gray had been employed by a firm of experimental engineers on work for the R.A.F.

Recruit drill was held at Farnborough North Camp, on Queens Parade ground, near Malplaquet Lines. The R.F.C.'s pace of 120 per minute was set by synchronised metronomes with lines of drummers to give the necessary audible beat to the squads of dusty, sweating men. Swagger canes, a distinctive feature of R.F.C. other ranks impedimentia, were always carried. Training was on the R.F.C. pattern, with its emphasis on strong discipline, 'learning how to walk proper', marching, saluting, guards duties, funeral drill (essential), rifle and bayonet drill and pistol practice and swagger cane drill. A.M. Hitchins found the comfortable 'maternity' jacket of the uniform tended to be rather warm under these conditions.

Lectures were given on esprit-de-corps, personal cleanliness and hygiene. Personal standards were high, all recruits having to report to a police tent for inspection before walking out. All this, coupled with uniforms supposedly based on the French Chasseurs design and tailored to the individual and one begins to understand the reputation for smartness of the R.F.C.

On 5th November 1915 the War Office decided that men destined for squadrons would be trained on the Reserve Aeroplane squadrons, and men destined as specialists would be trained on the Reserve Aircraft Parks. This was a good scheme and functioned well. Many of the squadron mechanics who missed out on Regent Street Polytechnic had their initial training on a Reserve squadron. In May, 1915, there were five of these units, by January 1916 there were 18 and by November, in the great enlistment year of 1917, there were 68 Training squadrons, as they had been renamed.

As a means of dispersal of training centres and in an effort to influence the Irish of the importance of the war on their own survival, a school of training recruits, was set up at the Curragh, near Dublin. The scheme was not a great success although persevered with. Initial conditions were bad, as might be expected in a period of ebb tide in the country's war effort, and in a country which was partially hostile to the British troops and who resented the use of Irish soil for military bases.

Air Mechanic Arnold was among a group of recruits posted to the Curragh in early 1916. They marched across London in their brand new hobnails then travelled all night without rations to Holyhead, nor did they receive any food until they reached the Curragh.

Everything was in short supply, one basin of tea sufficed for 10 men,' ... passing it to each other, watching where the others had touched the basin . .'. This little ceremony alone made Arnold, in his later life, keep a cup for his own personal use. Recruit training lasted three months, after which the recruits returned to Farnborough. Because of the crowded conditions disease inevitably broke out at the Irish camp; cases of Spinal Meningitis occurred in Hare Park, Rath and French Furze Camp, and a number of men were moved into Kildare Barracks.

When the men arrived at the Curragh they were issued with a palliasse which was filled with (allegedly) new straw, 24lb per man. After a period of time the straw was replaced. It is quite possible that this old straw might have had some effect on the infection rate.

Recruiting and training for the R.F.C. had presented no major problems until mid-1916, when Sir Douglas Haig requested a further expansion of the R.F.C. to 56 squadrons by the spring of 1917.

Because of this shortage of skilled men and the slowness in finding and training new recruits, the projected expansion itself was slowed down and a provisional scheme was put into operation. This expansion demand, plus the pressure from the operational theatres for more mechanics to man the already forming squadrons, finally forced the issue and it was decreed that a major technical training programme be instituted. Recruits would have to be completely trained from scratch as tradesmen.

The long term effect was good, because the men were trained to R.F.C. methods and standards without being influenced by their civilian background. Course syllabuses were laid down covering the entire range of the trades and the efficiency of the air service benefited enormously as a result.

Before this was realised the provisional scheme had been introduced whereby a form of local training was originated by utilising the technical resources of colleges, polytechnics, technical schools and some universities. Letters outlining the scheme were sent to these authorities, together with a questionnaire asking for details, teachers and equipment and an estimate of how many men could be recruited and trained locally. For every man accepted and trained for air mechanic standard the school authorities received 1/- (5p). This award included the cost of recruiting and training. As the scheme got under way and the flow of trained men began, so the award was cut to 9d (4p). Shoestring economics indeed.

The courses were of 8 weeks duration and the trades taught were Fitters and Turners, Acetylene Welders, Coppersmiths, Blacksmiths and Electricians and Magneto Repairers, Woodworkers (Carpentry and Joinery) and Engine Assemblers.

After nearly two months at Farnborough, Air Mechanic Gray, with others, was posted to the Woolwich Polytechnic centre and the party were housed in nearby R.A.S.C. barracks, where they were elevated to the luxury of an iron bed with straw stuffed palliasses. Each barrack room held about 30 men.

At the centre the course comprised machining, working to fine limits, bench fitting, making templates, and a short syllabus of lathe work. Instructors were civilians. Disciplinary progress was taken care of every Saturday morning on a small parade ground.

The C.W.S. Jam Factory at Coley Park, Reading, was taken over on 21st July 1916, to train 500 fitters and riggers in addition to 300 officers. Reading had been previously known as No. 1 School of Instruction, and had been formed on 1st December 1915.

The course initially lasted fiv weeks to teach semi-skilled fitters and riggers a general knowledge of the trade with a specialised knowledge of one engine or aeroplane. The 'school trained' (S.T.) men, as they were known, were sent to squadrons to supplement the skilled men, and units were required to report on their technical efficiency to prove this method of training. The courses were later extended to eight weeks and output was approximately 125 fitters and riggers per week, or the planned output of 1,000 men every two months.

In 1917 a scarcity of fitters brought a revision of the training scheme. The Fitter (learner) as he would be known after his eight week course at Reading, went on to Edinburgh for a further eight weeks at the Scottish school or to the Central Flying School. He would then be classed as a fully trained Fitter Engine and be issued—officialdom's phrase — to units as such. It seemed rather contradictory to double the training period during a time of great scarcity.

The fitters had their engine instruction divided into three broad groups: rotary, stationary air cooled and stationary water cooled. The aeroplanes were divided into pusher and tractor types. Training engines and airframes were unfit for flight and written off as such; there was a sufficient selection of types to give trainees a good grounding.

The engine mechanics bench work was done in small workshops equipped with belt driven machinery for the minor work of drilling and grinding. In other shops engines were

Trainee engine fitters testing a 120 hp Beardmore aero engine at Reading in 1917. Note primitive engine stand and W.O. pilot. It's just as well the photo is posed. IWM.

set up for complete overhaul techniques. Tuning and running of engines was carried on outside with the particular engine mounted on a stout wooden stand, and propeller drill was amalgamated into the starting procedure.

Sailmakers and carpenters were given ample space and equipment. Foot treadle operated sewing machines were kept hard at work sewing the fabric into the envelopes required for covering the major components. These were fitted by other classes — each took a turn — and carefully secured to rib and spar. Various methods of fabric repairs were taught.

Carpenters were taught in adjacent classrooms. Their work was more precise and exacting than that of the average rigger or mechanic, for they made aeroplane parts which had to meet the same specification as the original. With crash and battle damage to the all-wooden aeroplanes reaching tremendous proportions, theirs was a busy and vital trade. The majority of sailmakers and carpenters were destined for the Aircraft Parks and Depots, where their output was in reverse proportion to their small numbers. Each squadron had at least one resident sailmaker and carpenter.

To the men who received their technical training at Reading, this famous First World War school had mixed memories. The jam factory had never produced jam; it was a newly completed building which the Army had commandeered. A variety of engines and aeroplanes currently in service, and categorised, were positioned in the halls.

On completion of the course each fitter was given an instruction record which showed classes attended and the types of engines taught. A. M. Nicholson recorded that he received preliminary instruction on the Renault and R.A.F. engines. In addition he was given a few days on Beardmore engine assembly, basic blacksmithing, valve grinding, propeller swinging and a run through on the R.A.F. magneto and carburetter. He passed out as Air Mechanic 2nd class engine fitter.

* * * * *

A prolific recorder of his R.F.C. days, A. M. Hague, was posted to Reading for his rigger's course and found the ex-jam factory full to overflowing with men and machines; training aircraft included BE 2c, Avro 504, FB5, etc. Here Hague and his contemporaries learned to dismantle and erect different machines; in addition to their rigging instruction Hague's course were given brief instruction in theory and practical work on Monosoupape, Gnome and Green engines. Swinging props, construction of plugs and theory of flight were all included.

On the last subject he found the views of different instructors somewhat amusing, if also confusing. '... On going to Instructor Smith, he might say, "You're from Instructor Jones. Well, forget what he told you; he said one third of the lift came from the camber on top of the plane, didn't he? Well, I have proved it does not. I have worked on an aerodrome and have brushed dust off the top planes after flying; dust would not be there if there had been lift on top ...'. A somewhat interesting deduction which the aerodynamicists of the day must have overlooked!

A few of his course were selected to take a manufacturers course at the Bleriot Factory at Addlestone, then making a secret fighter. The men were given 18/- (90p) per week for their digs, but found no one wishing to take them, until the local police solved the problem. At the factory they found they were not welcome either, being regarded as nuisances who had to be tolerated, who just wanted to fool around with the girls. Previous servicemen must have set a doubtful example! Hours of work were 6 a.m. to 5.30 p.m. and they clocked in. The secret aeroplane was a SPAD7.

Instruction was informality itself, the air mechanics walking around the factory watching actual operations and asking questions and taking notes. Hague found the foremen and chargehands most co-operative and amassed considerable information. When his notebook was examined by the manager at the end of the two weeks course Hague was heartily congratulated. His industrious application might also have changed the manager's opinion of their potential girl chasing activities.

Hague was watching a fitter assembling an undercarriage when the fitter asked him would he like to have a go? Hague assented and fitted the bolts, washers and nuts in the approved fashion, cut the superfluous amount off the bolts and rivetted the cut ends to mushroom shape. The work was examined by an A.I.D. (Aeronautical Inspection Directorate) Inspector, who asked Hague did he think he had done a good job? Hague thought he had, despite not being a metal worker. He was deflated. The A.I.D. man told

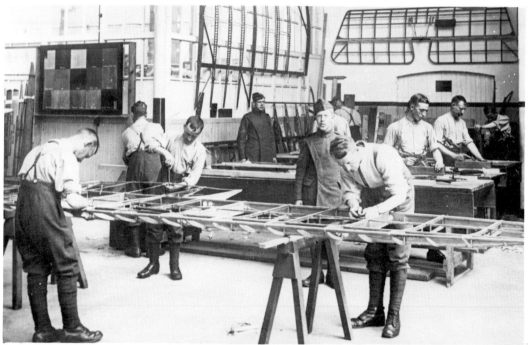

Carpenters under training at Reading preparing planes before the fabric is fitted, about 1917. IWM.

him he had tapped the bolts too much and had probably crystallised them.

This was interesting in view of the general practice of the day in removing apparently serviceable bolts and nuts and other components from crashed aircraft and putting them back into stores for re-use. Knowledge of metal fatigue was limited.

* * * * *

The food at Reading could be nauseating: one succulent breakfast was porridge on which would be placed a soused mackerel or herring. Someone must have liked it. Tea was also rather puzzling in its gastronomic approach, two thick half slices of bread, sufficient Tickler's jam for one slice and sufficient dripping for the other piece. Gray knew men who would scrape the dripping on to both pieces and put the jam on top. Ambrosia? It did seem inconsistent to give men of the fighting services such food with its poor calorific value and still expect them to expend so much physical energy.

By 1917 food had improved slightly, despite the shortages. Gray describes a typical R.F.C. menu of that time. Breakfast varied, watery porridge followed by bully beef (for breakfast) or occasionally fried bacon and bread, or boiled bacon and bread and jam. Dinner still consisted mainly of the old standby, bully beef stew with unpeeled potatoes; root vegetables were cleaned by scrubbing with a bass broom in a bath of water; or cold boiled bacon. Rice pudding, when served, was made in a portable boiler — or field kitchen — in the ratio of two pints of condensed milk to about six gallons of water, quantity of rice unknown. Bread was rationed to one thick slice per man per day.

Trainees were issued with a booklet, 'Royal Flying Corps Technical Notes, 1916', which was an excellent and revolutionary production for its day: it illustrated and described a variety of engines and aircraft, the latter subject directed mainly at rigging. Wireless and photography were also briefly described. The fact that the book had been produced and distributed was a great advance in technical training. As a supplement to the courses it was a valuable piece of literature and pointed the way to the standards that were being aimed at. It could be considered the first technical training manual.

In February 1917, the Technical Training Schools were reorganised. The whole came under Air Organisation Directorate Department (A.O.D.D.). The Netheravon and Edinburgh Schools were disbanded and their staff, recruits and equipment were absorbed by Reading. The new Schools of Technical Training (men), came directly under Director of Air Organisation (D.A.O.), the School of Scottish Fitters passing out of the control of the Training Brigade. The School of Preliminary Training Polytechnic, remained as before the change.

With the formation of new establishments or reorganisation of existing ones the combing out process went into reverse to see if fit and surplus men could be shaken out for service in the war theatres. Everything possible was done to equate the rapacious demands of the front for infantry, with the requirements for tradesmen to operate aircraft for the benefit of those same infantry. It perhaps explains why men were classified, graded and numbered, rather than treated as humans, it made it so much easier to shuffle them around.

To supply this demand as cheaply as possible the civilian authorities substituted women in men's jobs, and progressively lowered the reserve occupation standards.

*   *   *   *   *

Letters from veterans of the R.N.A.S. give a good insight into the conditions of disciplinary and technical training. Air Mechanic C. Jackson joined in July 1917 at Birmingham and went to Crystal Palace for a three weeks course. He found the food was good, unusual in being supplied by an outside caterer, J. Lyons. The men lived well, having a cup of hot cocoa and a biscuit on rising. After half an hour of gym exercises, breakfast was from 7.30 to 8 a.m.; recruit training started at 9 a.m.

Air Mechanic H. A. Clarke enlisted as a boy mechanic of $17\frac{1}{2}$ in November 1917, for a 12 year engagement. At Crystal Palace after the normal swearing-in, vaccinations and inoculations, he was issued with kit, which included hammock, deep sea kit bag, ditty box, oilskin coat and three white blankets.

Through the young eyes of Air Mechanic H. Vale, the whole place seemed a confusion of uniforms and warlike disorder as he enquired to enlist for the R.N.A.S. in 1917. To add to his confusion he was subject to standing jokes by the cheerful P.O.'s on what vacancies were available; 'Stokers for airship duties (very few vacancies), Fog locker attendant and Crow's nest cleaners (plenty of vacancies)'.

Vale was attested at the Palace and within a few days was called up for medical, kit, etc, in that section of the building known as the School of Arts. On his first night a Zeppelin chose to bomb London and because of the danger from the thousands of glass panes, all personnel had to disperse in the grounds. A memorable beginning. When he was interviewed by an Engineer Commander R.N. for a trade, he had no idea what to choose, having been previously employed in clerical duties. When the Commander suggested oxy-acetylene welding, Vale agreed without any idea of what the trade was or what it involved.

From Crystal Palace recruits were normally sent to one of the R.N. Depots or Barracks for their disciplinary training. Most of these depots were close to the sea. One such typical place which gave many ex-R.N.A.S. mechanics memories to store for the future was Fort Tregantle. Others were Fort Withens, Codford Camp and Blandford Camp.

Fort Tregantle was a truly typical Naval Barracks perched on wind swept cliffs on the coast at Whitesands Bay. Vale gives his graphic description of the place. '. . Our first view of the Fort gave us a shock ... Our sleeping quarters were huts sited in exposed positions on top of the cliffs and the mess deck was the lowest floor of the building. The ablutions were a row of water taps above a long wooden trough out in the open air, where we washed in icy cold water and used a cut-throat razor, Navy issue. After breakfast we paraded on the main parade ground where the Admiral read the morning prayer each day. We spent the next six weeks there continually marching, saluting and forming fours, only occasionally standing-at-ease.

'From our first day at the Fort we began to be taught to refer to everything in Naval terms, thus, the Admiral's quarter became the quarterdeck to be saluted every time one passed it, the parade ground became the Main Deck, and left and right became Port and Starboard. Our uniform at that time was of navy blue 'square rig' style, with peaked hat, breeches and puttees for working and slacks for 'going ashore' or going on leave, but as we were not blessed with either of these privileges during our stay we mostly lived in what the Navy termed 'Rig of the day, No. 2'.

Air Mechanic Sutton had a typical service introduction to Fort Tregantle for when his party arrived at the nearest railway station they found no transport for them and had to hike to the Depot carrying all their kit. They reached the place at 2 a.m. and after a meal were up again at 6 a.m. but Sutton said the lads were all in good spirits.

Fort Witheroe, in Devon, was a Depot used to accept part of the great overflow of recruits in 1917 and to it went Air Mechanic J. R. Rider, who joined as an apprentice instrument maker at Liverpool in February 1918. Conditions appear to have been much as Fort Tregantle with a similar Naval routine.

Rider gives us details of a constructive form of punishment inflicted on the boys. The example he quoted to illustrate this arose from the discovery of a spent match under one of the beds. Smoking being a heinous offence and no one owning up, all the occupants of the hut were made to descend the 100 steps or so cut in the nearby cliff — Witheroe was similarly sited as Tregantle — collect a boulder and carry it back up the cliff. The reason became apparent for this pre-planned punishment, for new camp roads which were being made required stone ballast.

Halton Camp was first used as an overflow pool for recruits awaiting their turn for the courses at Reading. The object of authority was to form one central school at Halton for fitters, riggers and allied trades and to be the venue for boy training scheduled from 10th September 1917.

Air Mechanic Armitage was among the first batches sent to Halton. The camp was deep in mud. Conditions were chaotic. Overcrowded tented accommodation ensured a regular contribution to the isolation of wire-surrounded compounds which housed untouchables who had contracted infectious diseases such as scabies, meningitis, smallpox. All recruits were vaccinated and isolated and had to sit out the incubation period before they were allowed to move out of the compounds or be posted. It was six months before Armitage had a hot bath and that at the Union Jack Club.

There were over 500 applications in hand from boys wishing to join the R.F.C., so the service went ahead to recruit a second batch of 500 boys under the same terms of engagement, that is, after reaching the age of 18 to sign on for the standard terms of 4 years with the Colours and 4 years in the Reserve.

A further proposition was put forward to enlist another 2,000 boys, a 1,000 of these from Ireland. Training for the Irish boys would be in Ireland, using existing aerodromes as sites for schools as soon as facilities could be laid down. By this means it was hoped that more Irishmen could be induced to volunteer for the R.F.C. Enlistment age for the boys during the war was 16 to 17½ and they had to be medically classified Category A. Their pay was the normal rate for boys, that is 8d (3p) minimum a day. If they were still on this rate on reaching 18 they were classified A.M. 3rd Class but if, during their boy service their pay was increased to 1/2d (6p) or 1/8d (8p) a day, they were classified A.M. 2nd Class. Education and moral standards were required to be high, schooling to Standard 6. They were required to produce certificates as proof of good moral character and of birth or baptism, and have the written consent of their parents to join the R.F.C.

After all the necessary conditions had been met, a Special Recruiting Officer selected suitable lads and made arrangements for their final intake. There was quite a free flow of boys and the Ministry of Labour found many employed in non-productive jobs who would be available for recruiting.

The technical training was still not organised and eventually authority decided to distribute the boys in small parties around Cranwell. Boy Hardwick went into R.N.A.S. workshops and spent several weeks helping to manufacture new skids for the Avro training aircraft. The skids were of laminated ash and bent by steam supplied from an old donkey engine boiler. He was also employed in haymaking on the aerodrome.

Eventually training began, the syllabus following the standard pattern, with the boys having to take copious notes which were later checked out by their instructors, a method which persisted until after the Second World War when it was replaced by more efficient training aids.

*　*　*　*　*

Codford Camp, in Wiltshire, was another of the overflow centres for Crystal Palace. To this camp direct from Leeds, where he had enlisted in March 1918, came Air mechanic W. K. Turner. After the R.A.F. came into being, batches of recruits were posted alternatively to ex-R.F.C. and ex-R.N.A.S. stations. Turner went also to Blandford.

In accounts given by Turner of his life in the R.A.F. he has the added advantage of quoting from original letters. It is quite possible that accounts given by some of the veterans can be dimmed or slightly distorted by a memory gone rusty over the years.

Another major recruiting and reception centre was Blandford Camp, Dorset, originally established by the R.N.A.S. for training purposes, and enlarged on the formation of the Royal Air Force when it became a Reserve Depot and Records Office of the R.A.F. About Blandford, Turner had this to say. He is quoting from a letter written 21st March, 1918. '. . Breakfast today at 6.30 was alright—porridge, kippers, tea, bread and margarine — as much as we could stuff. . .' Turner says the quality of the meals did not last'. . .as the U-boats made more inroads in our shipping, and for a week or two in the late summer we had no bread at all, only ships biscuits, absolutely uneatable — and I had just had three teeth extracted. However, when the war ended both the quantity and quality of the food was very satisfactory. . .'

In the R.N.A.S. he was an Air Mechanic 2nd Class (E) and when he came under the R.A.F. his equivalent rank was Air Mechanic 3rd Class Fitter General.

* * * * *

Young Vale, who had given a graphic description of Fort Tregantle, describes equally well his time at Letchworth, training as an oxy-acetylene welder. Letchworth was not a school in the strictest sense as was Reading or Cranwell.

'The welding classes were held in a separate shed outside the building. Oxygen and acetylene were piped all along the benches, oxygen from a battery of cylinders outside, while the acetylene was produced by a large INCANTO water-to-carbide generator in an outhouse. There was a separate hydraulic back-pressure unit at each working bench as a safeguard against fire. The welding training consisted of classroom work making detailed drawings of welding blowpipes, oxygen regulators, gas-producing plants, etc., the study of metals and a very comprehensive amount of other theoretical work, which occupied about half the training time.

'The practical work consisted of a repetition of welding test-pieces of various metals and alloys, brazing, silver-soldering and oxy-acetylene metal cutting. As pupils became proficient they had a trade test and after passing the test were put on productive work such as the manufacture of various welded strut fittings, tailskid fittings, copper pipes for petrol systems, etc., all of which were inspected and then sent to a Stores Depot as spares. The training period for welders was six months, after which they were posted to units where their trade was required.

'After the final passing-out tests we were given seven days leave, and railway passes to enable us to report to whichever units we were posted to.'

* * * * *

Towards the end of 1917 Government authority was given to the event which both air services had been expecting, when Parliament passed the Air Force (Constitution) Act 1917, which made provision for the transfer or attachment of officers and men of the R.F.C. and R.N.A.S. to the proposed new Air Force.

An overriding clause stated that 'All warrant officers, chief petty officers, petty officers, air mechanics, aircraft men and other ratings who, on the date prescribed by the Order in Council belong to or are attached to the R.N.A.S. and all warrant officers, non-commissioned officers, men and boys who, on the same date, belong to or are attached to the R.F.C., will be transferred to the Air Force, with effect from the date to be fixed by the Order of the Air Council. Royal Fleet Reserve ratings will be attached only'.

That date, 1st April 1918, saw the end of an era and the beginning of a struggle by the new independent air force to retain its identity against the established two other services. Many years were to elapse before it was finally accepted by those same services.

* * * * *

Cranwell from a trainees view in 1917-18, is well described by two ex-mechanics, Mansfield and H. A. Clark.

Cranwell seems to have been a good camp. According to Mansfield he '...could not praise it too highly. We were accommodated in a brick hut in comfortable conditions. Discipline was fairly strict, but not irksome. We were allowed a long weekend leave every six weeks and a short weekend every two weeks. . . Night leaves were given on certain days when we could travel to Sleaford. . .' His best compliment was to say that he didn't know how well off he was until he was drafted to H.M.S. Campania.

Mansfield was there during five months in 1917. His course went through the six weeks of rigorous Naval drill and physical effort before being posted to the workshops for their technical work. He took a test, fitting a bearing, which successfully upgraded him to 1st Class A.M. at the end of the course. Mansfield also had to overhaul a Gnome rotary which on completion had to run at 1750 rev/min.

Clarke arrived after Mansfield had left. As a boy fitter his course of nine months included filing rough castings of set spanners to finished sizes (production method again), scraping and filing connecting rod and main crankshaft bearings and fitting. Practical work further included oil cooling and ignition systems, carburetters, stripping and reassembling Rolls-Royce, Sunbeam Arab and Le Rhone 80 h.p. rotary engines, and fitting them into Handley Page, D.H.6 and Sopwith Camel and Avro 504K respectively.

With future sea service constantly in mind, the boys were taught to swim at least two lengths of the bath in a canvas suit. Entertainment was mainly by that most popular of service fun, irregular local talent camp concerts, with the added treats of one night a week outside the camp and the week-end passes. Where a cinema was available the lads gazed fascinated at the flickering 'rain-swept' screen or shouted ribald comments at the actors. All good fun.

The training of R.F.C. riggers and fitters has necessarily been described in some depth, for the reason that these two trades were by far the greatest in numbers and most universally required with their affiliated trades to service and maintain all types of the aircraft in use. Workshop trades were ready in Squadron, Aircraft or Depot workshops to repair, renew or service aircraft as required. Other trades depended on the duties of the aircraft, whether artillery observation, reconnaissance, fighter or bomber, or on maritime duties and, as the war progressed, these trades were required in ever increasing numbers.

*   *   *   *   *

The first School of Wireless was established at Brooklands Aerodrome on 15th November 1915 and five days later was formed with a Headquarters, a Flight of four aeroplanes, and Experimental and Instrument sections.

Brooklands dealt increasingly with the tactical and practical use of wireless by aircrew and artillery, being named successively Wireless and Observers School, Artillery and Infantry Co-operation School and Royal Air Force and Army Co-operation School.

Training of wireless operators finally became possible in greater numbers when a School for Wireless Operators was formed at South Farnborough at the end of 1916. Output of trained operators reached a total of 600 in 1917, which the following year was intended to reach 1,050. Educational standards were pitched at a more realistic level.

Two other schools were instituted, No. 1 at Flowerdown, near Winchester and No. 2 at Penshurst. At all three schools the mechanics were taught procedures of operating, servicing and maintenance of the old bulky sets then in use.

Air Mechanic A. W. Drinkwater, who joined in 1916 had to pass an education test at Regent Street. After his recruit training at Farnborough he went to its wireless school for a four months course. Tests were carried out when the class was ready for examination and passing out. It consisted of sending and receiving three standard test messages, i.e. 78 letter messages. More marks were given for reading under difficult conditions than for sending. Tests and practice on the buzzer for operators left much to be desired. The rate of sending for tests was 20 words per minute (five letter words).

Operators also had to have practice in lamp signalling, but it was estimated that a man who could operate well on a tapping key at 20 words a minute would be able to operate a lamp at similar speed.

Like the wireless sets the use of the aerial camera was another of the great developments in military communications. Its asset was so great to the battle planners that almost every artillery observation and bomber aircraft was eventually to carry a camera. The increasing demand for photographic information and recording developed into a request for the formation of a suitable school and in January 1915, the first photographic section was formed.

From this small acorn grew the School of Photography in December 1916 at South Farnborough. In January 1917 it became a separate unit of the Administration Wing, came under the Training Brigade in April 1917, and in October of that year moved to Farnborough where it remained for many years.

As photographers were originally enlisted as such, there was no basic trade knowledge or theory given. They were introduced only to the equipment they would be using and the methods of operation adopted by the R.F.C. As Air Mechanic Massine wrote '... Cameras were box type with 5in x 4in glass plate magazines, a full one on the top and an empty one to receive the exposed plates fitted below. Plates were developed in racks, printed through horizontal enlargers, the prints dried by soaking in methylated spirits, blotted off and the print passed through a flame for quick drying. ...'

Just as aircraft tenders were developed for use with aeroplanes and workshop lorries for repair work in the field, so mobile darkrooms were eventually developed. But that was to be later when aerial photography came into its own. In 1915 the art was still in its infancy and use was made of huts, hangars and tents.

As a result of collaboration between Lt. Moore-Brabazon and the Thornton-Pickard Manufacturing Company, the beginning of 1915 saw the introduction of the first camera specially designed for use from air to ground, the Type A.

This was the camera on which the first trainees were taught, together with an adaption of this camera using the Mackenzie-Wishart slide. The syllabus included manipulation of types of cameras in use and changing box magazines; method of altering width of shutter slip and winding and release of shutter tension; taking photographs and analysing them, particularly with reference to artillery work. The theoretical aspect of photography in all its known phases was also taught. But with the vital needs of fighting in mind, when it was so necessary to get photographs into the hands of the general staff quickly, greater emphasis was placed on fast developing and printing — and fast transport of the prints to those who needed them. This naturally meant knowing how to ride a bike, until motor cyclists took over.

*   *   *   *   *

On 1st January 1917 the vast sprawling acreage of Farnborough, already incorporating an aircraft production factory, recruit school, wireless and photographic schools, now added the School of Armourers to its complex.

Each course of 1,100 men was of four weeks and no man was removed from the course, or posted, until he had either completed the course or been proved unsatisfactory. The dangers inherent in their tools of trade were too real to allow doubt in the competency of the man manipulating the erratic bombs of the day.

The R.N.A.S. used its long-existing naval armament training school at Eastchurch to train its ratings in aircraft armaments and instituted an eight week course, which covered specialist arms and a syllabus very similar to the one in use at the Farnborough school.

Towards the end of the Farnborough course some men were posted to units as assistant armourers, and those with suitable qualifications and aptitude sent to Hythe for further training as Gunner Observer aircrew.

Electrical trades were given basic theory of electricity biassed towards aircraft and equipment. Their numbers at this time, and for many years after, were few as the aeroplanes and airships had very little electrical equipment, except that necessary for wireless operation. The normal establishment of aeroplane electricians on squadrons was one per flight, with several ground electricians on strength in workshops.

Training aids at Farnborough were minimal and the electrical trainees followed similar procedure with the rest of the trades, combining their practical work with production, filling and testing batteries, wiring equipment, checking and reconditioning.

After the formation of the Preliminary School of Technical Training, numbers of electrician trainees were sent to Regent Street for their basic training, there to be taught shunt motors, 3 wire balancer, accumulator charging, arc lamps, motors and cone wound generators, and operation of switch board panels. There was virtually no specialised aircraft electrics.

The school at Cranwell devoted a section to the teaching of electrics to R.N.A.S. ratings, who were given a six months course.

Instrument Repairers were in a somewhat different category to the electricians in that the trade was limited in numbers. Air Mechanic F. Barrett, who was trained at Farnborough in 1915, had to dismantle and reassemble an altimeter for his trade test. There was no comprehensive syllabus; all instrument trades were highly skilled men and would have been taught during their apprenticeship such instruments as were used in aircraft had this been applicable to their apprenticed firm. If not, Farnborough gave them a course.

* * * * *

The static form of warfare required a great need of kite balloon sections for artillery observation. The War Office prior to 1915 transferred men to the R.N.A.S. for balloon work, but took over responsibility for all kite balloons in France in the autumn of 1915. The Admiralty continued to supply equipment until July 1916, when the War Office finally took over all land based sections.

A Kite Balloon Training Depot was laid down in March 1915 with H.Q. at Roehampton to train officers and men of both air services. it remained the only school, until the increasing demand for more sections by the Army — a measure of the balloon's success—enforced the opening of two more schools in July 1916. Among the early balloon men who trained at Roehampton, on the polo ground, were many London policemen and General Post Office tradesmen.

Training the men at Roehampton took some time to get off the mark with an organised syllabus, according to the experience of a few of the old balloon men. Air Mechanics E. S. Ambler and A. C. H. Chiverton both joined in 1916. Chiverton was sent to Farnborough, where he did his recruit training and was posted direct to a balloon section without any training whatsoever.

Ambler, on the other hand, was at least posted to Roehampton after his recruit training. But he did no technical training there, rather he was used for fatigues, spending his time in maintaining portable boilers, before he had a spell in hospital. From the hospital he was posted to 44 Kite Balloon section, just forming.

The section moved up to Rolleston Camp on Salisbury Plain for its 'working-up' period, training in very rough conditions. Lessons were of the 'on-the-job' variety, knot-making, parachute packing, balloon handling, launching and retrieving with drills and route marches. Ambler was not strictly a tradesman, neither was Chiverton, but both were essential members of the balloon handling party.

At Roehampton the technical training was intensive. The majority of balloon mechanics were non-specialist in that they were mainly handling crews. The course syllabus, however, thoroughly taught them and the specialist riggers all that they required to know. In action the loss of balloon observer or balloon was too easily achieved by the normal hazards of shrapnel and bullet, without adding further to the vulnerability by an inefficient ground party.

Training ex-civilians how to fill, walk, launch and retrieve balloons and how to handle the multifarious ropes and guys was often a distinctly hazardous affair. The process of teaching raw, non-technical rookies to realise the dangers inherent in filling a balloon with a highly inflammable gas could be dangerous. Both inevitably resulted in some casualties.

Those who were truly non-technical often suffered from their own non-appreciation of the dangers involved. Too unthinking to avoid a whipping rope, or thoughtless over the consequences of flame near a gas cylinder, some men were lifted into the air entangled by rope or severely injured by a bursting gas tube.

Launching a balloon required 53 men distributed as follows:

8 men on picketing lines	15 men on three bow lines	3 men on stern guy
23 men on ground rigging	4 men on mid guy	

* * * * *

In the early days an instructor often faltered under the pressure of the rapidly growing service to get men out of the schools as quickly as possible. He was not helped by the lack of knowledge, the frequent change of theory and practice, and the shortage of equipment. But he persevered.

Recognising his importance, authority quickly became selective in his choice. They wanted men of infinite patience who were experts in their field, who were articulate and imparted their own confidence to their classes. In general they succeeded. The recognisable qualities of an R.F.C. or R.N.A.S. tradesman, his reliance, his ability to work quickly, efficiently and safely under stress and often without supervision did not just happen. The qualities were imparted by sound instruction from the parade ground to the technical school.

The standards of technical training throughout the flying services had progressively risen, to keep pace with the advances made in aeronautical design and the modern aircraft introduced so frequently into service. To ensure the trainee mechanics received the best instruction, the Directorate of Training tackled the problem at its source, the Instructor. Special courses were laid down for them which required a very high standard of knowledge and pass rate. The consequent high quality of work from the average air mechanic during this bleak war was the unpublished reward of these men.

48

Chapter 4
In Action

When war was declared the R.F.C. had only four operational squadrons, No's. 2, 3, 4 and 5, mobilised and ready for service. Two other squadrons, No's. 6 and 7, operating on a part reserve, part training basis, were both stationed at Farnborough. The four mobilised squadrons flew to France during early August with, as was the custom, a number of air mechanics flying in the aircraft. The remainder of the squadron personnel support parties, together with the Aircraft Park from Farnborough, followed by road, sea and rail to Amiens where the four squadrons were concentrated.

Almost immediately the whole force moved from Amiens to Mauberge, on 17th August, the ground party receiving tokens of entente cordiale from the French people on the way. The total R.F.C. strength to arrive in France was 105 officers, 755 N.C.O.'s and men, 63 aeroplanes and 96 motor transport.

The squadrons suffered their first casualties before going into action. A pilot of 3 Squadron, with Air Mechanic Barlow as passenger, crashed in the U.K. on take-off for France and a B.E.4 with Air Mechanic Parfitt as passenger, crashed on take-off at Amiens. All were killed. It was the beginning of a costly and lengthening list.

From Mauberge the squadrons carried out the first air operations of the war, reconnoitering the advancing German forces. Very soon after their arrival, because British troops and others assumed all aeroplanes were the enemy and fired on them, it was decided to make identification of R.F.C. aeroplanes easier and large Union Jacks were painted under the wings. Unfortunately, at height, the red crossed bars of the 'Jack' were confused with the German crosses and the aeroplanes continued to be fired on. Eventually, after some damage to the aircraft and near escapes for the crews, the roundels of the French Air Force was adopted, with the colours reversed. This became the standard British marking.

The stay at Mauberge was shortlived for, as a result of accurate observation reports of the enemy by the squadrons aircrew, and acted upon by the Army, the retreat from Mons was begun. The four squadrons stayed together as far as possible, sharing the rough fields on which they stopped temporarily en route for Paris. The pilots, conditions permitting, carried air mechanics with them as insurance should they be forced to land with mechanical failure, an ever-present fear in those days.

To men like Air Mechanics H. Knight and Broadhurst, both of 5 squadron, the names of Le Cateau, St. Quentin, Le Fere, Compaigne, Senlis, Juilly, Serris, Pegarches and Melun, exotic to English ears, evoked memories as the settings for short periods of high danger, long hours of hard work, utter tiredness, but no boredom or lack of enthusiasm in what they believed. At Le Cateau, because a Henri Farman refused to start it was burned, probably the first example of a 'scorched earth' policy carried out by a flying service.

RAF mechanics removing a rotary engine from a crashed aircraft at the Aircraft Repair Depot at Flang du Fliers 12 July 1918. IWM.

While the aircrew were comparatively detached from the war at this stage, the squadron support parties, having to move by road, saw the war and the suffering of the refugees from close quarters. The convoys lived off the country, for supplies of rations were extremely unreliable and their quantity and content uncertain. During this famous retreat the mechanics were putting into practical effect the theory of squadron mobility and pre-war exercises. They were harried from dawn to dusk and were forced to make use of all they had been taught in aeroplane dismantling and convoy work; their very lives depended on it.

Air Mechanics George Alderton and Gillings were soon in the thick of the retreat. Alderton had joined the R.F.C. in 1912 — one of the originals — and had served in Limerick before sailing for France as an engine mechanic with No. 2 Squadron. Gillings had flown on a reconnoitering flight and had been shot in the stomach. On landing, Alderton told Gillings he should go to the First Aid Station, but Gillings refused, preferring to take his chance with his friend who was driving a lorry in the retreat. So the two of them set off making their way to Paris by a roundabout route dictated by the advancing German troops. They made safety.

One of Alderton's more gratifying memories is when he helped to load a 100lb bomb on to Lt. Rhodes-Moorhouse's B.E.2c for that pilot to deliver to Coutrai. Unfortunately, Rhodes-Moorhouse received mortal wounds in the operation but was subsequently awarded the Victoria Cross.

The high temperature of that summer affected the engines, reducing their already low power. To keep them at their peak output the mechanics were continually cleaning plugs, resetting magnetos and cleaning and scraping the valves with their small issue kits of tools, often until late at night or into the early hours. Aeroplanes were picketed out and the mechanics slept in the cockpits, or under the wings, or on some occasions, inside a dry barn. After the retreat, sleeping out was still practised even into the winter, but tents and hangars were pressed into use until eventually more permanent accommodation was used.

The men lived rough, nearly as rough as the fighting troops during that mobile period of the war, and whilst not exposed to the dangers these magnificent Old Contemptibles were facing from the enemy assaults, the ground crews expended much energy for the common good in keeping their flimsy charges airborne. The aircraft of 2 and 4 squadron (BE2), 3 (Bleriot and Henri Farman), 5 (Avro and BE8) had not been designed for the rugged conditions to which they had been subjected and suffered terribly. Repairs had to be improvised in the cover of farm buildings, in the lee of trees but mostly out in the open fields, in all weathers.

Aircraft deterioration caused by exposure was mitigated by the fairly dry summer but there were many servicing problems that had to be resolved. Bringing up fuel, oils, greases

RAF mechanics at work repairing crashed and damaged aircraft at the Aircraft Repair Depot at Flang du Fliers 12 July 1918. IWM.

and spares, to aerodromes by roads that were becoming increasingly blocked by troops and refugees, only to find the aeroplanes had left was one of the major supply headaches. Often the ground crews received just a few hours notice to pack up and go. With the very real danger of being cut off, packing the aeroplane tenders and workshop lorries and dismantling the mobile hangars where erected, was developed to a fine art. As was getting the aircraft away. The possibility of capture was a great incentive.

At Juilly a number of mechanics were detailed to defend a sunken road against the enemy until 3 Squadron got away. Their army type training stood them in good stead. A breakdown party, sent to collect a force-landed Bleriot was nearly encircled by Uhlan cavalry. At Chantilly the R.F.C. used petrol bombs—probably the first time by any air force and a forerunner of the infamous napalm bomb — by filling finned canisters each with a gallon of petrol which ignited by impact. The bomb was designed to be used against the enemy's aeroplane hangars.

The Battle of the Marne was followed by the equally critical Battles of the Aisne and Ypres and marked the end of the first phase of the war. It ended also the mobility of troops and squadrons, which had been a feature of the campaign. From now on trench warfare came into being and stabilised the positions of friend and foe.

Man appears to be at his technological best when designing weapons and equipment for use in war. This war was to strengthen this view dramatically. The development of the aircraft and its associated auxiliaries provide a striking example.

The early W.T. sets were extremely heavy and bulky, weighing around 75lbs each and so large that when installed there was no room for the air observer. Ground wireless operators were only able to receive from these sets, which made communication difficult. Eventually, after much development the lighter Stirling set was issued in late 1915.

Air Mechanic Swain (second from left) with an Armstrong Whitworth RE8 of 16 Squadron. France 1918. P.S. Swain.

The first stage of the growth of wireless communication in the R.F.C. ended when a wireless aeroplane was detached to each squadron from No. 4 Squadron. The second stage began when 9 Squadron was split into two flights, one flight per wing, with its H.Q. handling all the W.T. equipment. The purpose of the squadron was to supply W.T. equipped aeroplanes as required by army corps.

As the importance of their work was realised and the demand for their services became greater, the H.Q. personnel and the flights were strengthened. The rapid development that took place was such that wireless flights were incorporated into every squadron where wireless was needed. By April 1915 the system was working so smoothly that 9 Squadron was disbanded and the personnel, were posted to the Aircraft Park. Six of the air mechanics went back to England and, under the command of Capt. H. C. T. Dowding, later Air Chief Marshal of Battle of Britain fame, reformed 9 Squadron, which became the R.F.C. Wireless School.

Running parallel with wireless expansion was the development of air photography, which like the wireless service had been tested before the war to the limit of its potential.

The first aerial cameras were hand-held of the folding type, usually the personal property of the pilot or observer. There was no photographic section on the squadrons. The first successful air camera, the 'A' type, was produced by the Thornton-Pickard Manufacturing Company, in conjunction with Lts. Moore-Brabazon and Campbell. It was a box camera with a recessed lens and used 5 x 4 Mackenzie-Wishart plates.

For squadron and H.Q. use, a mobile darkroom was eventually designed based on the same chassis as the workshop lorries. Communication between darkroom and aeroplane was usually by a messenger mounted on a bicycle. The darkroom had to be near a source of clean water and if this was not available from an urban supply the unit would endeavour to find a clear water stream.

With the advent of specialised photography came the ground photographic trades to service the cameras, develop the plates and produce the thousands of prints that were needed. These mechanics had a job that required speed of operation and steadiness of hand and judgement in much the same way as other trades. Vital photographs that had probably been taken at high cost in lives were being demanded and the photographers could not afford bad workmanship.

*　*　*　*　*

The progress of a most important arm of military aviation, bombing, had been carried out in desultory fashion. It too, had been subject to pre-war experimenting, and in a 'Heath Robinson' manner during the hectic days of the retreat. Racks had been fitted on the outside of the fuselage to carry hand grenades. When a more realistic approach was adopted and the aircraft were fitted with bomb racks, the incidence of risk was still very high. The early bombs had no safety fuses and 'hang-ups' of bombs were common. Defusing and getting these 'hung-up' bombs off the racks after the aircraft had landed was a job only for the skilled and dedicated.

The only British bombs available at the beginning of the war were the Hales 20lb (9kg) and 100lb (45kg). Before these could be produced in sufficient numbers the squadrons were issued with 10lb (4.5kg) shrapnel bombs, painted red and fitted with stabilising parachutes; these were thrown overboard by hand. Another temporary stopgap was the issue of converted French shells, called Melinite bombs; they weighed 26lb (11.8kg), were detonated by a nose striker and were extremely sensitive and dangerous. With these the armourers began to face the perils of their trade. Enterprising air and ground crew tied the bombs on to the upper longerons with string, cutting the string and pushing the bombs off when over the target.

An example of the hazards unavoidable with the job is given in the case of a disaster in 3 Squadron. One of their Morane aeroplanes was bombing up with Melinite bombs, which had only a lead shearing pin, when one of the bombs dropped and exploded, killing 12 men and wounding four others. The aeroplane was totally destroyed. The Melinite bomb was finally condemned as unsafe.

To carry a machine gun as a weapon of offence and defence had been in the forefront of the military mind as soon as the aeroplane was considered a success. Experiments had been made, but the problem of firing forward through the propeller had not been solved. Some aeroplanes had been specially built to overcome this problem by placing the engine to the rear and have a free-firing machine gun on a forward pivot in the cockpit in the nacelle. The Vickers Gun Bus (FB9) the FE8 and the DH2 are examples.

The advent in 1915 of Fokkers' and later, Constantinesco, interrupter gear to allow machine guns to fire through the propeller arc was the go ahead for the design of the biplane fighting aeroplane as we know it. The armourers trade, previously occupied in bomb armament now included gun armourers. To the latter went maintenance of the Vickers and Lewis guns, loading of the belts and pans (although in this operation many gunners preferred to load their own), the interrupter gear and its sychronisation.

* * * * *

The first wartime winter brought the additional problems of cold weather maintenance. Intense cold, snow and frost turned comparatively simple tasks into long drawn out jobs hampered by freezing metal and hands. Radiators of the water cooled engines froze and had to be carefully thawed. The castor oil of the rotary engines degenerated into a gum that refused to pass through passages and clearances; it, too, had to be heated before use. Greases hardened, dope and varnish thickened. The only form of heating available was by coke braziers, a considerable fire hazard if brought into a closed hangar.

At altitude machine guns refused to fire, or misfired, from the effects of the freezing oil. Bombs hung up as a result of frozen mechanisms. The air crews suffered too in the open, unprotected cockpits! Jobs were extended by the bitterly cold conditions, often to a full day. The cold weather made the already poor surfaces of the makeshift aerodromes rock hard, which played havoc with the fragile undercarriages. The only reason there was less structural damage from this cause — discounting poor landings by the pilots — was that the aeroplanes themselves were so lightly loaded, and flying in general was curtailed.

Technology of cold weather servicing in active service conditions was in its infancy, and many years passed before answers to this problem were reached.

The R.F.C. of 1915 was a fairly simple organisation. It consisted of a main Headquarters responsible to a number of Wings. Each Wing had a number of squadrons, depending on the duty of the Wing. From each squadron, controlled by squadron H.Q., there were usually three flights, each generally consisting of four to six aeroplanes. Each flight was self-contained and able to be detached for several days at a time. A lesson from the mobile days.

The system of maintenance in use was considerably less complex than today and serviceability was based on 50% of aeroplanes held on charge.

All supplies of fuel, oil and spares were sent from the U.K. by road, sea and rail to the main supply depots. From these depots the supplies were delivered to aircraft depots, and daily to the flying units in the quantities required for the squadrons. Petrol and oil was held on a weight basis of 1 ton per squadron.

Reserves held by the squadron were:

Petrol — sufficient for five hours flying for each squadron aircraft, plus 100 gallons.

Oil — sufficient for seven and a half hours for each squadron of aircraft.

A reserve of 500 gallons of aviation fuel was held by the Army Service Corps at the railhead nearest to the R.F.C. Wing.

Spares were demanded by Flights through their own squadron H.Q. who in turn indented on their Aircraft Park.

The method adopted for repairs to aircraft was based on a three echelon system. This system was used throughout the war and became the basis, after development and modification necessitated by progress, of the system used by the R.A.F. until the introduction of Planned Servicing.

The echelons were utilised as follows:

1st   Flight servicing and maintenance only, together with minor repairs.

2nd   Full squadron facilities, such as the workshops, for more extensive repairs. This echelon was responsible for the supply of fuel and spares to the Flights.

3rd   Major repairs carried out by Aircraft Depots. This echelon supplied spare aeroplanes and engines and material and spare parts.

In addition to the facilities offered by the echelons the aeroplanes each carried a few tools, including a repair kit for replacing spark plugs or repairing broken petrol or oil pipes; engine, propeller and fuselage covers; and empty sandbags.

The terms of reference for Aircraft Parks were:

1   To maintain a percentage of spare aeroplanes for each squadron to whom it was responsible

2   To keep its repair workshops and power plants ready in working order for any repair work called for

3   To hold a proportion of spares, equipment and material for the aeroplanes and motor transport.

Other functions were:

1   To supply aeroplanes, engines, aeronautical material and technical stores to Wings.

2   To hold, and maintain in efficient condition, the reserve aeronautical material (including aeroplanes) for the Wings.

3   To hold reserve transport vehicles for the units it served, in addition to its own.

4   To carry out such repairs to aircraft and mechanical transport that cannot be undertaken by squadrons, but which were not serious enough to be sent to the Royal Aircraft Factory, or the aircraft manufacturer.

An Aircraft Park had to be sited where good accommodation and electrical power were available and where possible, sited across the lines of communication at tactical/strategical points.

The movement of transport of the R.F.C. was usually carefully controlled in order to avoid interfering with any troop movements but at the same time ensuring that the fuel, spares, or stores reached its destination as soon as possible. The Army always had priority.

*   *   *   *   *

To salvage an aeroplane from a forced landing near the front line often entailed considerable danger to the ground crew. Against the normal existence of the front line soldier this was as nothing, but to the air mechanic on his first visit among the 'muck and bullets' it could be a paralysing experience. They always had generous and sympathetic help from the soldiers.

If the aeroplane was to be taken back to base it was usually dismantled on the site of the forced landing (by permission of the enemy) and all the parts put on the lorry; sometimes a trailer was required. The propeller was put into a box and all points of ingress to the machine of dust, mud, etc. were covered. Whether or not the fuselage was stowed on the lorry depended on the type of aircraft. Where possible the fuselage was towed on its undercarriage.

When an aerodrome site was decided upon, the surface of the ground was studied carefully to see if it could be improved. On soft, rough ground the ideal was to use a steam roller but this was a rare luxury. The usual means was to march a company of men across the ground to trample it. A suggested method for rough surfaces was with an iron roller weighted with pieces of timber.

Running concurrently with the development of the aeroplane was the need to protect it against the weather when operating in the field. Different types of mobile hangars were designed, built and tested by the Royal Engineers and Royal Aircraft Factory (R.A.F.) with varying success. A tee shaped hangar, the R5, accommodating one aeroplane only was used in the first months of the war. Ultimately, the French Bessoneau, which the R.F.C. adopted in 1915, proved to be the best for field use.

Those that the R.F.C. used were later developments of that type. Special hangar erection parties were trained in transportation of the hangars in convoys of lorries, and the rapid erection and dismantling of the hangars. In winter, when the canvas doors froze, they were cursed by all, but despite the primitive construction of canvas on wood frames, the Bessoneau hangar became one of the minor war-winning pieces of equipment. By 1916-17 they were being built in Britain.

* * * * *

The experiences of three young air mechanics on a 'typical' front line squadron gives a fairly adequate picture of the life of 'ack emmas', whose services were as essential to success as were those of the aviators themselves.

Air Mechanic R. Davidson joined 18 Squadron at Northolt, where it was equipped with Vickers FB5's. The squadron moved to Mousehold Heath, outside Norwich, for working-up exercises; at this point Air Mechanic F. Barrett, an Instrument Repairer, joined the squadron.

While at Norwich, Davidson, an engine fitter, was sent with a rigger from each flight to the Vickers works at Crayford, Kent, on a week's course on the FB5, or Gunbus, its manufacture and maintenance. After two months operating experience the squadron sailed for France in November 1915.

It was standard practice that mechanics flew with the aircraft when the squadron moved from one field to another, and Davidson was disappointed when the aeroplane in which he was due to fly was written off at the last moment and he had to endure the delights of troop travel on the French transport system, but the congenial company of his squadron friends and the enthusiasm and expectancy of active service made the journey worthwhile.

Each Flight was equipped to be self-supporting if detached. Its transport consisted of a workshop lorry, equipment lorry, two transport lorries, two Crossley tenders and a motor cyclist. The workshop lorries, on one of which Barrett was employed, were staffed with a selection of allied trades and Barrett was soon employed in fitting W.T. sets to the aircraft.

The squadron, deployed as a mobile unit, was often under fire from German long range guns and had to use its mobile expertise to move out of range. It could dismantle hangars and gear and be on the move within four hours, move 30 miles to a new site, erect the hangars and have the aeroplanes ready for dawn patrol the next morning.

After their first winter in France the squadron received the third member of the trio, Air Mechanic G. E. Ryall, who came fresh from Reading, ready to do battle with the 120 h.p. Beardmores which engined the FE2b's which had replaced the FB5's in April 1916.

Ryall found living was rough. The men slept where they could, out in the open, under lorries or, bone tired after working a stint around the clock, on the floor of the hangar on a ground sheet with two blankets. The natural functions vied with those of eating and sleeping. Latrines were usually long trenches with a pole slung along its length, about 18in (45cm) above. They required a certain prowess to use and were filled in after a week's use. Petrol tins were cut and scattered around the aerodrome for urinating, or were cut to make wash basins, or filled with earth to make shelter walls.

In a welter of wood and fabric .... These early aircraft were very easily damaged and this sight was common. Methven.

There were no servicing cycles as we know them today. Aircraft were checked after each flight and refuelled and reloaded with gun ammunition and bombs. Minor maintenance and repairs were carried out by working until they were done, all night if necessary. All fuel tanks were filled by hand from 2-gallon (9 litres) cans through large funnels fitted with chamois leather filters. There were no Forms 535 or 700 to record the servicing life of the aircraft; log books were unknown. With the average flying life of an operational aeroplane not much longer than the combat life of its aircrew, which was very short, the information recorded would have been very sparse indeed.

An example of the work of 18 Squadron mechanics is given by Davidson. A squadron FE2b was shot up and force landed 60 miles away near Peronne. Davidson flew with the C.O. Major (later A.V.M.) Reid to inspect and assess the damage, which consisted of both main spars of the top centre section, engine cylinders and oil tank shot through.

A new wing section, engine and oil tank were drawn from squadron stores and transported to the crash. The squadron had earlier established a procedure for replacing the 12ft (4m) long top centre section, without dismantling the mainplanes. '... This involved supporting the aeroplane with trestles under the front and rear of the nacelle, one under the tail and one under each wing tip. As the upper tail booms were fastened to each end of the rear spar of the top centre section, you will realise that when this wing section was removed the balance of the plane was very precarious until the new section was in position. Fitting the new engine was straightforward, except that, being short of manpower I had to borrow four German prisoners-of-war and, as a result of the language difficulties I thought (at one time) the engine was going to topple over, so we manhandled it into position. We finished the repairs in about $2\frac{1}{2}$ days and the plane flew back to the squadron. ...'

* * * * *

In the spring of 1917 a 'flu' epidemic' brought Ryall one of his hardest working periods. So many mechanics were laid low that Ryall and a rigger, the only remaining fit men of his Flight had the onerous task of maintaining six machines, including helping to load and fuse the bombs.

As may be guessed by now, the squadron tradesmen, although often inadequately trained, invariably became a dedicated team. Ryall echoes previous remarks about inadequate training, '... Personally, I had served 12 months of my engineering apprenticeship, so working with engines was not so strange, but some mechanics hadn't the faintest clue. Luckily, our engine Sergeant and Corporal both knew their jobs. ...' It wasn't only aircrew training that suffered from the pressures of war.

The autumn rains brought a taste of one of the more natural plights of the war in France — mud. Dirt roads became quagmires and aerodromes minor marshes. Mud has always been a major factor in military operations, a natural occurrence that could quite easily turn an operation into victory or defeat. The aeroplane was no exception to its adverse influence. To get airborne it had to run along ground which was bog-like in its consistency, affecting its struggle to get into the air. Some, landing on a particularly bad stretch, turned over, their narrow section tyres contributing to this misfortune.

Vehicles containing supplies were inescapably held by the embracing mud. Bombs, ammunition, fuel and other supplies had to be carried by mechanics squelching in the thick, viscous ooze. Ground operations were slowed. Morale was not improved by the

Loading relief supplies for dropping into besieged Kut in Mesopotamia in April 1916. IWM.

Servicing an RE8 at No. 3 Western Aircraft Repair Depot in France. IWM.

constant fight against the mud and the continual cleaning of man and machine. To those who experienced mud on operations it will always be one of their worse memories.

The living quarters would often be inches deep from the rain and the advantages of the puttees became apparent in these conditions, long before gumboots came into use. On a well drained aerodrome with good metalled approach roads the drumming of rain on hangar roof or living quarter was usually a sign of a relaxing of physical activity. Whilst to aircrew it usually meant an extra few well-deserved hours in bed, to the ground crew it was the opportunity to catch up with belated servicing and maintenance tasks, without the added burden of aerodrome activity. Always presupposing the aeroplanes were under cover.

The rains were followed by the intensely cold winter of 1917-18, and the problems of 1914 were still unresolved. Engine radiators froze, some even on the approach when the engine was throttled back, most after a night out in the open. As a precaution against this, radiators were usually drained at the end of flying. Coppersmiths earned their keep repairing the burst radiators and blanking off the most vulnerable parts of the radiators. Pilots were instructed to keep the revs up as high as possible on landing, but the problem was not solved until manually controllable shutters were fitted.

A top overhaul was given at 50 hours, or when the military situation allowed, when cylinders were removed and the valves reground. Plugs were changed after each flight with the R.A.F. engine and occasionally a cylinder was changed. Carburetters were adjusted to give optimum performance at a specified height. On one occasion Davidson adjusted the setting of a Rolls-Royce carburetter as the pilot wanted to fly higher than usual, '... Didn't really know what I did ...' The aircraft reached an altitude of 19,700 feet (6,350m), something of a record. 'No oxgyen. ... Never heard of it so naturally didn't miss it. ...'

One of Davidson's more physically distressing experiences occurred in the previous winter and arose from the drill necessary when starting Beardmore engines in extremely cold weather. It was the practice to hold both hands over the air intake during start up, probably to give a richer mixture. In the Second World War, mechanics used their caps. On this occasion his hands were soaked with petrol but before he could jump down off the bottom wing of the FE2b the Flight Commander ordered him into the front cockpit, saying he was going for a weather check.

As Davidson noted,'... I hopped into the front cockpit and we were soon into snow cloud at 1,000 ft. (330m),' "Fire a red light for a wash-out" shouted the Flight Commander, and I struggled to get a red cartridge into the Verey pistol. Finally I had to use both hands to pull the trigger and I was never so glad as I was at that time to get back on the ground again. It was no joke to be in an exposed cockpit of a pusher plane without flying clothes or goggles in freezing weather. . .' A taste of what the aircrew endured.

Of any exciting moment in the long grind of hard work, Ryall thought that picking up a crashed aircraft from behind the lines was the most stimulating. On a salvage trip usually four men would go out with rations for several days. Ryall was the chef also and created his gastronomic delights in the nearest dug-out or trench.

As is usual with most of the air mechanics, they recognised their places in the scheme of things where danger and hardship was concerned. Ryall was no exception. He wrote,'... We didn't do any work really, the lads in the trenches did most of it. There was nothing very heroic in this because obviously this could only happen in a quiet part of the line and only happened to me once. A mile or so behind the line was really dangerous because our lorry and trailer used to come right up (to the site) and we had to look out for shelling. . .'

Shellfire was not new to many of them. 18 Squadron's aerodrome was shelled by 15in (38cm) shells during the German March offensive, which caused quite a flap. No harm was done, although the earth thrown up by one shell burst went over Davidson's head while he was waiting to pull the chocks from an aeroplane. The pilot waited not for the order to go, but went, without a run-up or check if the aircraft was damaged. The aerodrome was also bombed.

Barrett was often dirty, full of lice because of lack of baths and clean clothes, but agreed that compared with the fighting troops he was lucky in his environment. This was forcibly brought home to him after being involved in a crash returning from a patrol as a gunner. He received only minor injuries but at the Dressing Station saw the wounded coming into the first aid hospital, He was profoundly affected.

*   *   *   *   *

Sharing 18 Squadron's aerodrome was a fighter squadron, No. 43, flying Camels. To this squadron had come Air Mechanic Gray, from England on his first posting. Gray had travelled with two friends, Guest and Gould, to No. 2 Aircraft Depot at Canadas, reaching it after a long involved journey from U.K. via Boulogne, Paris and St. Pol. On the journey they passed the time trying to converse in French. The train was filthy, no doors, seat upholstery stripped and the floor thick with the remains of army biscuits, bully beef tins and even rifle ammunition. The train was overcrowded. Speed was 5 m.p.h., occasionally shooting up to 25 m.p.h. Several stops were made, long enough to allow the troops to mash tea. The first night was spent in a rest camp and the next day in a small station before finally changing trains at 2 p.m.

The spirit of the squadron was good from the start, for when a slightly apprehensive Gray entered the canteen for the first time he was met by a large banner hung across one end, exhorting all in foot-high capitals to SMILE, DAMN YOU, SMILE. He was soon put at ease by the regulars and quickly made friends.

His first week was spent in H.Q. Flight workshops understanding the idiosyncrasies of the Clerget engine which powered the Camel, with the emphasis on running adjustments. He was then crewed with a rigger, one Davis, and detailed to an aeroplane of their own. Between them they kept it serviceable, assisting each other as the need arose.

Endurance of the Camel was about 3 hours and if the aeroplane had not returned after that period it was assumed to be either shot down or landed somewhere. Two patrols a day, of approximately $1\frac{1}{2}$—2 hours each, were usually flown by each aeroplane unless an attack was on. There was no night flying. Tactics were usually to have one Flight getting airborne as another returned in order to provide continuous cover on the squadron's sector of the front line.

After an aeroplane returned its pilot was asked about its performance. If the engine was still in tune or the rigging was still alright the aeroplane was refuelled, re-armed and any minor combat damage repaired. More serious damage meant the aeroplane was taken to the hangar for the workshop tradesmen to get to work and if the damage was beyond their facilities the aircraft was dismantled and sent to the nearest Aircraft Depot. Paperwork was minimal.

The interrupter gear was a constant source of trouble on these aircraft. Because of wear creating a time lag in the gear and the differing qualities of the cordite in the .303

Wrecked Fokker DVII's and a Junkers CLI that were found by the Army of Occupation. Note all-metal fuselage and cantilever wings of Junkers. G. Hawlett.

ammunition affecting the speed of the bullet, it was not uncommon for the round to pass through a blade instead of between them. Gray changed one prop. which had seven holes in one blade, four in the other.

Changing an engine as Air Mechanic Hitchins described it, could be very tricky. Quite often there would be no lifting tackle available and after removing the split pins and nuts of the attachment bolts, the engine was manually lifted on to baulks of timber and eased forward until it could be lifted down on to a trestle. Hitchins said it took 2-3 men to lift a Monosoupape, Gnome or Le Rhone out of an Avro, Pup or Camel.

The squadron moved to La Gorge, near Merville, close up to the front, bounded on one side by the La Bassee canal and on the other by the Merville-La Gorge road. The surface of the field was poor, with ridged furrows and was the cause of a number of accidents, aeroplanes overturning or smashed undercarriages. The bungee rubbers just could not cope. The damage done by these ground loops or nose overs was at worst a propeller and a complete top wing change, with possibly some interplane struts, and the fin and rudder. At best the propeller and rudder were the sufferers.

The attitude of the local people to the Allies who were smashing their country to pieces in defence of them was usually quite good. Gray remembers with gratitude a farmer/station master and his wife who gave shelter to those guarding Capt. Trollope's plane, which the pilot had force landed in fog. Every morning there was a large jug of coffee waiting for them on the brazier. Many of the British have this fond remembrance of little acts of kindness done to them during those dreadful days.

In the German March offensive of 1918 the squadron aerodrome was shelled and they had to move out after the British artillery retreated onto the aerodrome. The squadron took off for Roye aerodrome in the Champagne district and in the confusion as the ground staff was getting away, one of the food lorries was abandoned. After 36 hours without food the ground party set up canvas hangars on a landing ground at Haute Avesnes, the cook only able to make them a drink of tea. The aircraft had arrived before them.

From Haute Avesnes Gray had the grim experience of visiting Bourlou Wood in the front line to retrieve a force landed aircraft, which ended up nose first in a shell hole. This sector had recently seen some hard fighting and the debris of war, including as yet unburied bodies, lay everywhere. The plane was salvaged and placed on the lorry and trailer but by then it was dark, so the party spent the night in shell holes. An artillery bombardment ensured that they got very little sleep.

On the way back two of them stopped near a balloon site in time to be included in the target of a German aircraft attack on the balloon. They both dived for cover and a warning shouted at a nearby Labour Corps soldier went unheeded. He was shot in the leg. The balloon was on fire and the observer parachuted to safety after being the target for a brief burst from the German pilot as he veered away.

Gray had another salvage operation under shell fire at Delville Wood. It was here that he and a friend decided to have a walk around the area before returning; shortly after arriving back on the 'drome Gray began to feel ill. A Cpl. Ward, known as 'Dad' to the ground staff, dosed Gray with rum, but the next morning Gray was forced to report sick. First diagnosis was tonsilitis until the M.O. asked if Gray had been near the front line recently. On being told , yes, the trouble was immediately diagnosed. The area had been shelled with gas shells, the liquid of which evaporated on contact with the air. Gray was very lucky in that he only caught a whiff of it, but even so the treatment required 5-6 weeks in No. 6 General Hospital at Etaples and a further 3 weeks convalescence. The hospital was bombed on the night he left, with severe casualties.

*　　*　　*　　*　　*

On squadron or Flight, at least the mechanics knew they were taking an active part in the war. In spite of their onerous duties there were times when the war came closer, that they saw for themselves something of the dangers that their own flying personnel were daily facing.

The sight of a swaying aeroplane making direct for a landing alerted everyone; the ambulance and fire tender (so called) would begin to move towards the predicted landing area. All would anxiously watch the aeroplane's progress. An uneven, 'careless' landing usually told the worst. Sometimes the aeroplane would swing and collapse in a welter of wood, fabric and wire — engine coughing abrupty to a stop. Wounded aviators, friend or foe, would gently be lifted clear of the wreckage by roughened, solicitous hands and carried to the ambulance. Sometimes the worst happened when, having crash landed the aeroplane suddenly burst into flames. Little could be done with the fire fighting methods of the day against the flaring inferno of petrol, oil, wood and fabric, and the horrified men could only stand helplessly as the funeral pyre burned.

After the small crowd of helpers had dispersed, mechanics would be detailed to clear the wreckage. From the burnt remains the smell of charred flesh would linger for days. Not a pleasant experience.

Those on the front line squadrons were thrown on their own resources for what little entertainment they could muster. Not for them the smashing of glass, cutlery and furniture by which their officers relieved their tensions and which was indulgently called 'high jinks'. If they were to relieve their own tensions in a similar manner it would be charges all round for barrack damages! Despite the wartime unity of officer and man the social gap was still very wide.

Occasionally, very occasionally, a few cases of beer would come through on the ration lorry and that same evening some mechanics would have a richly deserved break from the monotonous canteen tea or local wine. Sometimes the evenings were good, when comradeship flowered, wine flowed and songs sung; other times, after a particularly bad day the drinking was done to forget.

Going on leave was an adventure in itself. The mechanic would often virtually have to find his own way to the port of embarkation. There were few organised parties as might be expected from a close knit regiment. The R.F.C. was too far scattered. The mechanics leave period at first commenced from the port of embarkation of the operational theatre, which led to many severe curtailments of leave when there were serious delays. This was later modified to the port of arrival in the U.K. In extremely lucky cases the mechanics might get an aircraft flying to the U.K.

In the Depots with their large manpower the mechanics suffered from the greater discipline instilled, the monotonous routine of work and more work and the drab life. But how essential was their work, although it was plain and unrelenting, often planned with the background of production targets to be attained.

In most of the Depots, there soon sprang up the Concert Party, a typical British institution which in the services, with their emphasis on isolation and the throwing together of diverse types, became almost a necessity in the winter months to help relieve the boredom of the life. In the latter respect the concert parties of large manufacturing firms and the prison camps, are a fair indication. In the prison camps it was often a saviour from the near insanity brought on by the long cheerless days of captivity.

*   *   *   *   *

Air Mechanic P. S. Swain, with his garage background hoped to be trained as an engine fitter, but was disappointed and was posted out to France immediately on completion of an M.T. drivers course. He joined 22 Squadron in March 1916.

During the trip across the Channel Swain was surprised at the number of men who could wash their faces in one half tub of water. As a lorry driver Swain had the comparative luxury of his lorry to sleep in and use. He was once sent to pick up a crashed aircraft lying near the German lines, but the enemy gunners had left very little. Crashed aircraft in No Mans Land became an automatic target for the opposing gunners. One wonders just how much was the cost in shells to destroy many fragile aircraft which usually were either wrecks already or non-recoverable.

Not long after joining the squadron Swain achieved his ambition and was transferred to the flights as an engine mechanic. Training was strictly 'on-the-job'. Even allowing for Swain's mechanical knowledge, the technicalities of a 160 h.p. Beardmore engine was still more intricate than a 20 h.p. lorry engine, even if the principles were the same. Swain accomplished the changeover, but there must have been men making a similar move who found themselves out of their depth to the detriment of the machine they were alloted and the aircrew who flew in it. Although the majority of skilled men were able to adapt themselves successfully, one wonders how many aircraft may have been lost as a result of this policy.

As Air Mechanic Simmonds so rightly says, '... As we were all picked men who had been passed as proficient, we were not supposed to want any training. A very foolish way of looking at things, seeing that not one of us had ever spliced a cable, a very important part of your work. . . It was only my own workshop ability that enabled me to carry on. . .'

Later in 1917 22 squadron re-equipped with Bristol Fighters, giving up its Army Co-operation role and the mechanics became acquainted with the early teething troubles of the aeroplane. Engine maintenance seemed to consist of cleaning magneto points and plugs and curing oil leaks. Swain had his only engine course, on the Sunbeam Arab, in England. The riggers learned that truing up was more critical on these high performance aircraft.

During the German March offensive, Swain was at Vert Galland and he recalls, '... When Fritz broke through to Amiens I didn't know there were so many Flying Corps personnel in France. They were passing by for days. It was a very near thing. ...' This offensive overran many advanced aerodromes and landing grounds, with disastrous results for some unlucky squadron personnel. Some were able to hurriedly pack up and go; some had to get out with only what they stood up in. Militarily, it was decidedly a very near thing.

Late in 1918 Air Mechanic Swain was posted to 16 Squadron, an artillery spotting unit flying RE8's and based on Mount St. Elsi. The German forces were on the retreat and 16 Squadron, moving behind the advancing Allied troops occupied a former German Air Force aerodrome at Auchel (Lozinghem), housing their aeroplanes in the German wooden hangars, which leaked like sieves. It was cold, there was no heating and the mechanics resorted to using a blow lamp as a means of keeping warm. But not in the hangars!

The aerodrome had been previously bombed in its enemy occupied capacity, evidence graphically supplied by the shrapnel holes adorning and ventilating the huts. The wings of the battle weary RE8's became waterlogged, because of the leaking hangars and before each flight the underwing fabric had to be opened up to drain the water away, and repatched.

*   *   *   *   *

While man's newest form of flight had been developing into a deadly addition to the armouries of the fighting nations, what progress had the oldest form of manned flight made? And how had its use affected the ground staff?

A lot of development work had gone into balloon operation and the bluff kite balloon in general use was a much improved aircraft from the original unstable and spherical balloon. The latter balloon's limitations of stability had been apparent long before it went into action and had been the subject of much study.

Despite this, No. 2 R.N.A.S. section, equipped with a spherical type, landed in France in October 1914 and went into action above the sand dunes, near Nieuport, in support of the

Dover patrol. This action was short lived, for within five minutes a hostile battery had got the balloon's range and forced it to withdraw. Nevertheless, that first five minutes in the air was partially successful, for the observer located the enemy guns and signalled their position to the Fleet and a Belgian battery. In this section was Air Mechanic Goodwillie, a driver, who was later posted to No. 2 Wing.

Long before this action proved the point the seed for the great expansion of this service had been sown. Far-sighted commanders had realised its potential and prepared accordingly. Drawings of a French kite balloon had been obtained and production commenced, in order to replace the rotund balloon which had rendered such honourable service over 37 years. The new kite balloon was the 'Drachen' type B. The R.N.A.S. went all out to get this advanced balloon into production, to use its superiority for the primary task of spotting for the Fleet and along the front line, where they became immediate targets and were often subjected to intense shell fire, mortar and machine gun attacks. In addition they came under attack by enemy fighter aircraft.

A section usually consisted of the balloon and its equipment, a small 'nurse' balloon which, in effect, was a gas storage container, screens, a motorised winch and a dump of gas cylinders. The personnel of a section included a large number of men who were the army equivalent of labourers to manhandle the balloon. The war establishment of a Cocquet (which replaced the Drachen), section in September 1916 including the Commanding Officer, was four officers, 92 N.C.O.'s and men which included the top heavy numbers of 14 drivers and 48 balloon handling party.

To back up the sections in technical requirements, such as repairing operational damage, winch maintenance or carrying out modifications, a few skilled tradesmen were held on the strength of squadron H.Q.

A Russian Sikorsky Ilya Murometz bomber – possibly used by the French, a rare aircraft but very reliable – on maintenance in the field. A. E. Evans.

Air Mechanic A. C. H. Chiverton of London answered a recruiting poster in April 1916, which called for men of a fair standard of height and weight to become balloon crews. His account gives a personal and representative view of life in the shadow of a balloon. He was sent to France just one month after posting to Farnborough without any balloon training whatsoever. It took him two days to reach 6 K.B. Section, his new unit, then at Rouen and manned by R.N.A.S. ratings, many of them ex-policemen, who were gradually withdrawn as the R.F.C. mechanics became more proficient.

Drill had been evolved from 'common sense' movements using Naval terminology. When the balloon was pulled down by the motor winch the ground crew held on to the guy ropes and elsewhere, attaching sandbags on the guy ropes as it settled on to its 'bed', which consisted of a huge ground sheet. Screwed eye pickets were fastened around the edge of the bed and a continuous rope passed through the eyes. On this rope were secured short lengths of rope with a toggle at one end which was passed through the balloon rigging and secured as the balloon settled.

The riggers, in addition to daily inspecting, renewing frayed ropes, were also responsible for the basket, its contents, maps, binoculars and all other equipment. They also stowed the parachute on the outside of the basket, although usually this was personally supervised by the observer. The riggers also supervised any topping up with gas that might be required and carried out checks on the valve.

When large amounts of gas were needed for topping up, the 'nurse' balloon was used; small amounts were taken from the gas cylinders. The cylinder dump, for safety reasons, was normally kept well away from the site and lugging these 2 cwt (96kg) tubes about in muddy conditions proved hard work.

Like all service units having something to protect, a guard system was in force and Chiverton says that part of the guard's duty was to maintain the balloon in trim on its bed, slackening off the ropes if it rained and tightening them as they dried out. Muddy conditions were often created by heavy artillery traffic and the balloon, servant to the guns, was often sited in the same muddy area. This old enemy of all ground troops presented its own particular problem. If a mechanic carrying a heavy gas cylinder put it down for a few minutes while he rested, it could easily vanish in the thick mud.

Chiverton's balloon was first sited opposite Vimy Ridge and was frequently attacked. Because of its location the section was issued with two Lewis and a belt fed Vickers machine gun and with these they helped to bring down a German fighter pilot at Heudecourt. Some consolation for having been shelled every day for three weeks by a German gun opposite them.

Balloon sections began to appear along the whole front in ever increasing numbers. Some sections, like some flying squadrons, seem fated to be star attractions to the enemy. Often they would be under shrapnel shell and air attack simultaneously. A short category of incidents in 6 Section's operational life bear example.

One balloon was lost when an aeroplane flew into its cable, killing both aircrew. The balloon observer who had parachuted clear was killed when, on an uncontrollable swing under his parachute, he struck a tree stump in No Mans Land. His body was recovered at night with a rope.

Another balloon was lost in flames at Equancourt to an enemy aircraft. The defensive machine gunners were away, having been detailed to set up gas cylinders in the dump. The observer was badly burnt and was saved only by the balloon rigging catching up in a tree. At Combles the balloon had to be 'ripped' to save it in a gale.

The gas cylinders for the section were sent up from their filling point by transport and dumped nearby. Sometimes a railhead was used as a dump, as at Maricourt. This railhead was hit during the Battle of the Somme, June 1916, and the cylinders exploded for two days. During that battle the section was at Senlis and in walking the balloon forward through a cornfield the balloon men saw the results of that inhuman massacre. Wounded were streaming back, all stages of dying, and dead, on every form of transport, farm carts, wagons, anything that could be pressed to the sorrowful task.

Being so close to the front line, scruples of nicety were soon discarded; it was a case of survival, although the comradeship was tremendous. Despite this, or because of it, Chiverton had no scruples in pulling a ground sheet off a guardsman sleeping in the pouring rain, running away and then using it to cover himself and his friends. Because they had to find shelter where they could, often in the company of rats, they considered the act justifiable. And from this distance in time who can judge them?

The roughness of living as with most front line troops, brought the inevitable lice. Men would sit on the latrines, cracking lice in the seams of their clothes. On one occasion a party was taken to a Brewery baths, but the vats were so thick with scum that Chiverton refused to strip.

During the warm weather there would be a de-lousing parade and men would remove their clothes and have them baked in a large boiler, including their boots. As the clothes were thrown out of the boilers in large heaps there would be a mad scramble as 30 naked men grabbed for clothes which in some cases were better than those they had previously worn!

Water was of course a necessity, and collecting it often hazardous. Water parties usually went in at early morning to collect from established points, which were often under fire. Chiverton described some systems, '... We took turns. A party of six with rope on a water cart dashed in, found no one else there, knelt down while filling, picked up the rope and went off hell for leather out of the area after being filled up ...' and '... At another water point we collected dirty water. A canvas frame was made on timber and filled with water. This was dipped in with canvas buckets which had been standing in horse urine in nearby horse lines! The buckets had a wash off when dipped. We stood by awaiting our turn while the Australians filled up. A R.A.M.C. man stood by, throwing handfuls of chloride of lime in it. It was in a state when we filled our water bottles. . .' Water became so scarce that on a number of days the balloon men had a shaving brush wash in the remains of their tea.

In the winter of 1916-17 the water point was often frozen, as at Marapas, where pickaxes had to used. The gas filling valves of the cylinders would freeze and the men were often called upon to urinate over the nozzles to unfreeze them. No one was exempt, for Chiverton was called upon to do his duty although he was standing by the machine gun.

No. 6 Kite Balloon Section had a sorry end. The whole section was killed, wounded or taken prisoner when the Germans broke through at Gazecourt. The Guards were sent in to retrieve the situation. The luckiest was Air Mechanic Chiverton who had been sent on a course just before.

*   *   *   *   *

Air Mechanic E. S. Ambler, from Lincolnshire, was also serving on the Somme front, with 44 Kite Balloon Section, between Arras and Bapaume. In common with most sections they had their share of heavy shelling and bombing, and quite often had to move from site to site to escape attention and probably at the polite request of nearby troops. Moves were usually made at dusk, walking the balloon where possible through ruins, over fields, across streams, over any other obstacle.

The balloon was comparatively stable and able to remain aloft for long periods, which enabled observers to give more accurate ranging for their gun's objective, and sight more lucrative tactical targets. Its own limitation were obvious. Inability to manoeuvre, cumbersome in operation, wasteful of manpower and a prime large target were disadvantages well known, but accepted as a price for its value.

To an observer, it could never be exhilarating to see an enemy aeroplane diving towards you and looking into the winking eye of its machine gun, knowing that explosive and incendiary bullet were burying themselves in the bag above your head. Knowing also that even should you get clear, there was still several added risks to face, of a playful enemy pilot using you for gunnery practice, the burning balloon above enveloping you in its fiery folds, or being injured on landing, either on your own territory or in No Mans Land. Balloon observing could have its problems.

But what of those on the balloon site below? How did they fare? The short answer is, just as badly in fact.

For the diving attacks of enemy aircraft ensured they would be in line with the firing. Also, they had to stick to their posts under attack, both to winch down the balloon in the emergency and to retaliate with their own guns. The fear of a blazing balloon dropping on a site was no less acute to the ground crew, with a 'nurse' balloon full of gas, and gas cylinders stacked around.

The shelling caused constant shifting, with a gypsy-like existence, from site to site. Once the enemy guns had got the range of a site there wasn't much point in staying!

Balloon sites were unpopular, for if they moved into what may have been previously a quiet sector, their arrival soon altered that. The troops were, not unnaturally, a little peevish, for they liked the quiet life as much as anyone. So the balloon sections became pariahs among their own people.

The balloon men, the vagabonds of the oldest air service, more than any other men of the R.F.C., had quite the roughest time, being on a par with the fighting troops in the squalor and danger they endured. At Passchendaele alone, when information sought by the observers was so vital, the enemy reprisals were so strong that, to help the crews get through their tasks they were issued with a daily tot of rum. A measure of the balloon men's association with front line activities is that a disproportionately large number of them were killed and wounded in action.

*   *   *   *   *

The stories of these few air mechanics express what in effect was typical of the majority. In fairness, their tales should be told.

The experiences described by the mechanics are small glimpses of the conditions these men endured. But this tough life generated a tremendous comradeship which grew into the esprit-de-corps which is the aura of harmonious efficiency noticeable in all elite units. This spirit is a man-made thing, springing up naturally wherever there is a commonness of purpose, a desire to pull together as a team. It is no new sensibility. It has existed since man began to understand that working together for a common cause could also generate the better instincts of comradeship in man or woman. It is not the prerogative of any race or religion. It is one of the better qualities of man, unfortunately more often born in adversity with its inevitable byproduct of suffering.

Examples of the effects of purpose and fellowship in bringing out the best in man, even when he is at his animalistic low, are many. Never more so than from the occupants of the trenches in the First World War. Here, in the appalling conditions to which they had been subjected by their Generals, and with the exceptions of a few psycopaths, the spirit glowed, unquenchable.

The R.N.A.S. ratings operated balloons in much the same arduous way as their R.F.C. comrades, although perhaps without the same degree of danger to which those latter gallant men were subjected. As their way of life was totally influenced by the Navy, all the work done was directed towards Fleet efficiency. As the Fleet spent most of its time at sea, then that was where the balloons were to be found.

In the comparative security and good conditions of a vessel, balloons would be inflated and transferred to the towing ship requiring it. A few men, a rigger and at least a Petty Officer would go along. To keep this system going, bases were formed for the purpose at Sheerness, Shotley, Lowestoft, Milford Haven, Menfield (Davenport), Tipnor (Portsmouth), Berehaven and Lathmullan (Lough Swilly).

H.M.S. Campania, an aeroplane carrier, was fitted out to carry an inflated balloon at Fleet speeds and later in the following year slow balloon ships were used as seaborne hangars from which balloons could be transferred to light cruisers. As the war at sea progressed and the balloons proved their reliability, the Navy and R.N.A.S. conducted different forms of towing experiments. In the autumn of 1916 H.M.S. Chester carried out trials in the Firth of Forth. The success achieved instituted an extensive programme to supply kite balloons to Fleet vessels in 1917, with a consequent improvement in anti-submarine escort standards. Bases were installed at Scapa Flow and North Queensferry, Rosyth.

Meanwhile, how were those air mechanics coping who were operating in the Eastern theatres of war?

The year of 1914 saw the new air service begin to distinguish itself in other theatres. First to take part in land operations beyond Europe was a small R.F.C. detachment sent to Egypt on 14th November, to help defend the Suez Canal against the Turks. Defeating the Turkish Empire was to be the main preoccupation of the Allies in the Near East. This Empire, in 1914, covered a great part of Asia Minor and the Near East, from the Suez Canal and Sinai in the South—including what is now Israel, Jordan and Syria — to Iraq, (or Mesopotamia), in the East. To the North the Turks had subjugated Bulgaria, Albania and Greece.

Total manpower of this R.F.C. detachment was three officers, 37 N.C.O.'s and men. They had three Maurice Farmans but shortly after arrival acquired two Henri Farmans from Heliopolis. After they moved up to what was to become a semi-permanent base at Ismailia they took over two more Maurice Farmans and a BE2c from India Command. The Indian aeroplanes, less engines, had arrived from Situlpur in December, along with an engineer officer and a few air mechanics, as reinforcements for the R.F.C. unit. Two Renault engines and spares were sent out from the U.K. and were soon installed in the Maurice Farmans. Extra pilots were sent out.

The climate of Egypt is normally near perfect, equable and generally healthy. On the mechanical side the fine sand and dust clouds blown up by the propellers from the untreated surface of the aerodromes infiltrated into everything in its path. The effect on the engines, unfiltered as they were, was extremely serious from the abrasive quality of the sand and dust. Everything mechanical was susceptible to a rapid wear effect and this problem remained a major one until the fitting of elementary filters alleviated the engine wear. Hinges and pulleys were susceptible to clogging, particularly if oiled or greased.

First task of the detachment was to get the aircraft into action. This they did to such effect that the aircrew were quickly able to report the Turks massing for an attack on the canal in February 1915, which was repulsed. In April, the riggers fitted up four aeroplanes with bomb racks, each aircraft to carry three bombs, for a long range attack on El Murra. All aircraft returned. The R.F.C. was on the offensive.

* * * * *

Another small detachment had commenced operations in the southern hemisphere of a far away and little publicised theatre of war—Africa. Their campaign was short and the

Air Mechanic Welsh in RFC uniform, 1916. A. Welch.

71

aeroplane played a busy but not decisive part; the air service was to remember the operation more for the extremes of climate and the conditions and difficulties of operating aircraft in such primitive country.

The detachment in West Africa had two BE's and four Henri Farmans and with these did a creditable job, relying implicitly on the reliability of the Canton Unné engines, impeccably maintained by the engine fitters. There were no landing strips available; the first engine failure would have been the last. There was only one failure.

When the unit received its Henri Farman and Caudron aircraft they were dismantled and in cases which had to be taken from the supply ship to the beach on lighters, with the aid of native labour, who dragged the 2 ton cases through the surf and then pulled them a further $1\frac{1}{2}$ miles by primitive transport through the jungle.

One of the notable facets of this campaign was the recognition of the destructive effects of the climate on the wooden aeroplanes. The humid atmosphere played havoc with them, warping the most seasoned woods, causing droop and bow where it had no right to be. Within a short time the riggers were finding it difficult to re-true an aeroplane to rid it of the flying faults caused by the bowed and distorted wood members. Here was real proof of the need for all-metal aeroplanes. Insects enjoyed eating the glues with consequent detrimental effects on the joints and then proceded to try and eat the aeroplane. One aircraft broke up in the air from the effects of the wood-eating ants. This was a country of jungle and desert scrub, of heat, humidity and dust and the armourers, particularly, had the tricky job of bombing-up with bombs that were very unstable as a result of the humid conditions.

The first part of the campaign came to an end in July, when the Germans in West Africa capitulated. The reconnaissance information brought in by the R.F.C. aircrews from long flights had proved to be very accurate and had made an important contribution. The R.F.C. unit was split, one section to the German East African area, the other section, the lucky one, sent home to the U.K., with elements of the South African Aviation Corps on its strength, to refit to become 26 (South African) Squadron and return to Mombasa, East Africa, in January 1916.

At Mombasa the cases containing the squadron's aircraft and spares were opened, to give the mechanics an unpleasant shock. Some bright storeman had omitted the original propellers but had thoughtfully sent six different types for eight aircraft instead! One of these was broken. The five that were serviceable had to be bored out to fit the BE2c's. Which left three aeroplanes without propellers.

From April to mid-May 1916, the rainy season clamped down on all flying and the ground crews spent a few uncomfortable weeks in the humid air catching up on their servicing and repairs. The aerodrome was like a swamp which soon became an attraction for clouds of malaria-bearing mosquitoes. But in general aircraft and mechanic bore up to the strain reasonably well, although the mechanic suffered more. Aircraft parts could be replaced or repaired but it was difficult to cure a mechanic suffering from cholera, swamp fever, malaria or festering sores, or any of the other physical hazards so rife in the days before D.D.T., pencillin, or the sulpha drugs. The cemeteries scattered in the wake of this campaign were mute testimonies to the inadequate medical knowledge of the day and the risks attendant in overseas soldiering.

Organised social relaxation was nil. The centres of civilisation to which they might have gone for a break were too far away and invariably, in 1915-17, had little to offer. Africa was too far to send out concert parties.

In March of the same year, four mechanics had engaged in a hazardous journey that was as adventurous as any fiction. With a thousand porters they had marched to Koanda Irangi to build an aerodrome; on the journey three of the porters were eaten by lions. On arrival, and unfortunately, a number of mealie fields had to be cut and burned to provide the necessary flying field. A similar journey to that by the four mechanics was made by Air Mechanic E. W. Nelson of 26 Squadron in December 1916. He had been sent from Irangi to lay out a landing ground at Ubena. As the 130 mile journey was unsuitable for cars or lorries he had motorcycled to the area. With the helpful assistance of local engineers he managed to create a reasonable aerodrome, including constructing a hangar whose roof was a tarpaulin and sides grass. The first BE2c landed there on 20th December.

Unit armourers had their problems. As mentioned previously the humid conditions had a highly dangerous effect on the bomb fuses. Evidence of this is related in one of the bravest deeds of the campaign, carried out with cold-blooded courage. Air Mechanic E. R. d'Ade was an armourer attached to the Aircraft Park supplying bombs to the forward units. Because of the heat only 200 bombs out of 1,600 were serviceable, the primers having deteriorated. For four months d'Ade, using his own chemical formula, reprimed the primers, making serviceable 500 bombs. He insisted on working on his own in an isolated hangar. He was killed by an explosion while working.

At the beginning of the new year 1917 the Naval squadron was withdrawn to Zanzibar and it is a tribute to the R.N.A.S. air mechanics that the squadron had operated without a serious breakdown of serviceability. From February until June A Flight of 26 Squadron stationed at Ubena received no supplies of fuel, spares or bombs. That did not deter the flight. Guided by the armourers, who played the leading part, bombs were made by filling paraffin tins with nuts, bolts, nails and scrap iron and topped up with dynamite. A sort of do-it-yourself shrapnel bomb kit and most effective, too.

Supplies of petrol had to be transported across a 6,000ft. (2,000m) pass through Mount Livingstone. When it arrived its use could have proved disastrous, if a thoroughly dangerous trick practised by the porters had not been discovered in time. The crafty bearers were part emptying the 8 gallon containers at the beginning of the porterage and topping up with water at the end. As a result the fitters had to double check the filtering of fuel through chamois leathers. This practise by the porters was never entirely stopped.

Much ingenuity was shown by the R.F.C. mechanics on the Rufyi front in keeping the aeroplanes in the air. At one time all the tyres burst from the effects of the heat penetrating the worn covers. The inner tubes were replaced by Ford car inner tubes which just fitted; the old, worn covers were once again patched and replaced.

*   *   *   *   *

The first air operations mounted in Mesopotamia were under the aegis of the Indian Government. This force was truly representative of the Empire forces engaged in this theatre, Indian, Australian, New Zealand and British. A comparatively well-equipped base, which included an Aircraft Park, was laid down at Basra where, on the nearby River Euphrates, a steamer and barges were used for accommodation, workshops and stores. With the air base established the air unit became mobile and in August 1915 was raised in status to A Flight of 30 Squadron, which had been formed in Egypt on 24th March 1915.

The dreadful consequences of any major siege, that of starvation, turned the thoughts of the military to the air as a means of succour and a decision was made on 10th April 1916 to drop supplies to the beleagured garrison of Kut, which had been besieged the previous December. The garrison was now rationed to horse meat, the minimum quantity of food to sustain life being estimated at 5,000lbs (2,273kgs) a day.

Food dropping in earnest started on 15th April and carried on until the 29th when Kut capitulated. During that period 19,000lbs (8,637kgs) of food was dropped, of which Kut actually received nearly 17,000lb (7,727kg). The food was of good variety and included flour, atta, sugar, salt, dhull, gin and dates. But it was not enough to sustain life. In addition a large variety of other items were also delivered, which included medical supplies, wireless equipment, launch engine parts, mail for the garrison, 70lb (32kg) millstone dropped by parachute and £10,366 in gold, silver and banknotes.

With a disposable load of only 150-200lb (68-91kg) a great many trips had to be made and part of the reason for the failure was the harassment by an enemy aircraft which, partially successful, required the diversion of earmarked supply machines for escort duties. But the supply drop was a brave attempt and gave both ground and air crew valuable experience and data for future operations of this kind. After Kut capitulated the aircraft moved back to Shaik Sa'ad.

Many of the men who served in these campaigns have passed on. The great majority of them have never recorded their experiences, regarding what they did as no more than what they joined the service to do. Had they been told that it was their dedication that enabled the aircraft to take off to perform their tasks, they would have made some deprecating remark. Most of them would have said, '... what about the infantry, the fighting troops? ...' and they would have been right. But their modesty does not detract from their own saga.

Air Mechanic Hague was posted direct from Reading to his first operational aerodrome, Shaik Sa'ad, to join 30 Squadron, which he reached after a long journey often interesting, sometimes exciting, mostly boring, via South Africa and India.

During the advance the aeroplanes had suffered severely and at Kifri some of the battered RE8's used by the Squadron began to wilt under the strain. At this aerodrome their worn old tyres finally succumbed to the effects of landing on stony ground, sand and thorn scrub. Additionally, tough grasses on this ground wound around the axles between flange and wheel washer and simply sheared off the axle split-pins.

The torn inner tubes were repatched with ordinary bicycle repair patches. The covers presented a more serious problem. This was solved by the sailmakers who made new outer covers from four thicknesses of Willesden Green canvas, a particularly tough material. Used on sand the covers were quite satisfactory. To prevent the possibility of the axle split-pins shearing again from a similar cause, a steel collar was made to fit over the end of the axle and the original soft split pin replaced by a steel bolt. This job entailed working through the night and as Hague wrote '... But what a job. The Sergeant and I, still a 2nd A.M., worked on these drillings from 6 p.m. until 7 a.m. before we got them done. We had only a hand drill with a drill in it which our nearly worn out files would not touch. It had taken us turn and turn about to get the work done with one (drill) ...'

The great heat and humidity caused much loss of body moisture by perspiration which had to be replaced. To help quench the thirst 'chatties' were placed at different points for personnel to use. Chatties were unglazed earthenware pots, the porous nature of the material allowing water to seep slowly through the walls and the evaporation of which created a cooling effect on the contents. The water used for drinking was heavily chlorinated and for good reason, for much of it for use by service units was drawn straight from the Tigris, and on a number of occasions that same river carried dead Turks and British from the fighting up river. Disease was rife, the major killers being Asiatic cholera and dysentery, the latter carried by clouds of flies, one of the greatest single nuisances encountered in desert or bush, almost impossible to get rid of. To take food and drink without ingesting a persistent fly was, at times, distinctly difficult.

Sunstroke, sand sores, sandfly fever, malaria and septic sores were lesser ailments, and aspirin and 'pinky parny' (permanganate of potash crystals in water to sterilize food) did little to alleviate the complaints. It was entirely typical of the outlook that when one reported sick he had to make the effort. Hague had to walk four miles to the nearest hospital which took him two hours in his state. He spent two isolated weeks in the hospital, feeding all the time on Glaxo; the doctor diagnosed him as a suspect Asiatic Cholera. What were the miraculous powers of Glaxo? Better rations and a controlled salt intake would have helped tremendously, but this is in hindsight.

A contributory factor to the complaints was that the very hot days were followed by exceedingly cold nights when fuel was at a premium, so much so that organised searches were made for it, even for dry camel dung which was very good.

Despite the influx of more modern aeroplanes, however, the squadron mechanics still had their servicing problems. Air Mechanic H. Anthony, who served on 63 Squadron,

RFC armourers fusing a 50kg bomb mounted on a primitive bomb rack IWM.

75

revealed that the Beardmore engine in the Martinsyde was particularly unreliable, being prone to leaks from its copper water cooling pipes. Because the R.A.F. engines had been found to have 'loose items', which included spanners, in the sump, every new R.A.F. engine was stripped on arrival and inspected before installing into an aircraft. In view of the efficiency of the Aeronautical Inspection Branch (A.I.B.) one wonders how such foreign objects could have found their way into these engines.

Like the majority of engine mechanics who had the doubtful pleasure of working on rotary engines, Anthony found the smell and effect of the castor oil fumes on the stomach the hardest to bear. No laxative problems here. But one of the best moments of his technical career was running up the Rolls-Royce engine of a visiting Bristol Fighter after rectifying a snag — a sticking magneto brush. He writes '... We gave the engine a run up and what an engine after what we had been used to, it was like the sound of music and plenty of power. Of course, out came the Sergeant and took the credit for finding the fault. ...'

Ah, well, it was ever thus.

A British aircraft had made a forced landing on ground between the British and Turks. Anthony, with a rigger and a sergeant in charge, were sent to recover the engine, if possible. Because of the effective covering given by the Infantry, the R.F.C. mechanics were able to retrieve not only the engine, but also the instruments and wings. In the process Anthony got a right telling off from the Sergeant as, unable to remove the split pins effectively in the dark, they chiselled through the attachment bolts. The resultant noise brought the blast from the Sergeant, sensitive to possible reaction from the Turks. For this episode and for several other acts of devotion to duty, Anthony earned the Meritorious Service Medal.

One of those contributory 'acts of devotion' was going out on patrol with a group of Australian Camel Corps troops who were sent out to destroy Turkish wells. As his squadron was working with this unit Anthony was sent along, 'towing' three camels, which carried aircraft spares that might be needed in the event of a forced landing by the co-operating aeroplanes. He was in the desert for four weeks and came back full of praise for the Australians, all men from the outback.

To complete the campaign against the Turkish Empire it was decided to mount a direct drive against his homeland with the aid of Britain's superior sea power. The epic, notorious and disastrous Dardenelles campaign was begun. The first phase of the air operations was carried out by waterborne aircraft which operated from the aircraft carrier, Ark Royal, a name hallowed in the Royal Navy.

While the land forces were preparing for the landing on the Gallipoli peninsular, No. 3 R.N.A.S. Squadron, with a mixed force of six types of aircraft, arrived. Improvisation was the order of the day. The supply of spares created quite a problem, but fortunately the relatively simple construction of the aeroplanes made the replacement of a non-available item not too difficult a task for the highly skilled tradesmen in the workshop lorries and on the Ark Royal.

The landings commenced on 24th April under heavy defensive fire from the Turks. The soldiers suffered terribly, but by the end of May some aeroplanes were able to use an advanced landing ground at Helles on the southern side of the peninsular. But not for long. The ground was within range of the enemy guns and was finally given up at the end of June.

* * * * *

After the Bulgarians had capitulated and the Armistice was signed, on 30th September 1918 the Allies sent a small force into South Russia for an exploratory exercise. The object, to make contact with their former allies and gauge the situation, for Russia was being torn apart by the Revolution and its civil war aftermath.

Included in the party that travelled from Batoum to Baku was Air Mechanic J. Massine, a photographer who had previously served in a photo section near Salonica. The Russian trip provided the men with sufficient adventure to satisfy most. The original intention of the party, to evaluate the situation as it affected the Allies, was undertaken in the prevailing atmosphere of all revolutions, of chaos, distrust and bitterness.

The party was supposed to be attached to General Deninken's Army at Batoum, but was finally attached to another group headed by a General Rycroft. This good General halted at every station of importance. At Tiflis, Massine saw the Russian Bolsheviks clearing people from the station so that they could not hear the propoganda talks. Tiflis was the home of Josef Stalin.

Shortly after this their train was sabotaged by sand in the axle boxes, which caused the train to burn out, and with it the supplies it was taking to British troops in Baku. At Baku the party were given 12 hours to leave, but with typical British arrogance of that time they did not leave for two days. The return was uneventful and Massine went back to Salonica. He was again sent to Russia, this time to join a training mission at Novorossisk, equipped with a mobile photo and darkroom lorry which was never used.

When due for demobilisation Massine was recalled to Novorossisk and ordered home to the U.K. on his own! Which provided him with another set of experiences, for these were dangerous times and after the catastrophic war and revolution life was very cheap indeed.

Of the photographic work that Massine did, and he said he did very little, none of it was associated with aircraft, being ordinary ground photography, using panchromatic plates and bromide papers. So, if this account of one ordinary mechanic's experience has been a digression from the aviation scene it makes a change; tradesmen have their share of adventure, even if most of it has never been recorded.

Novorossisk was reinforced by 47 Squadron and remained the centre of Allied operations in South Russia until mid-1920, when the resistance of the White Russian forces collapsed and the town was evacuated.

In Northern Russia Britain had sent a seaborne expedition to Murmansk and Archangel as early as May 1918 to prevent Germany from establishing U-boat bases there. Secondary aims of the force were to help the Czech forces in their drive on Vladivostock and to deny the resources of Western Siberia to Germany. This North Russian Expeditionary Force was reinforced by a contingent of French troops in July 1918.

June 1918 saw the arrival of a flight of DH4's and the following month the seaplane carrier H.M.A.C. Nairana arrived with five Fairey Campanias and two Sopwith Baby seaplanes and a Camel. During operations which followed the R.A.F. took an active part, which culminated in the occupation of Archangel in August 1918. The R.A.F. were also occupied further afield against the enemy at Oberzerskaya. In December 1918 the R.A.F. was organised into two commands, one with Elope Force at Archangel and the other with Syren Force at Murmansk.

It was not until June 1919 that another seaplane carrier, H.M.S. Pegasus, arrived at Archangel, one of seven that arrived in that area. On board was that observant chronicler,

H. Vale, whose description, a large part of which is quoted verbatim, affords a contrast to Massine's experience in the south.

All the R.A.F. unit were volunteers, about 60 ground crew of all trades. Before embarking they had been on rifle and revolver drill courses at Blandford, and boat drill and elementary seamanship with the Navy. All had been inoculated against the possible diseases; cholera, typhoid, malaria, smallpox and tetanus. At this time the official R.A.F. uniform had not been introduced and both officers and men wore a hybrid variety of uniforms.

To cope with the expected cold weather all ranks had been issued with special kits which included knee length boots, fur lined greatcoats, fur hats and extra thick-and-heavy underwear. Mosquito nets designed for wearing over the head were found to be essential during the short Russian summer. Webley revolvers were also issued, but were not often worn.

Vale writes, '... The task of the R.A.F. was to co-operate with Naval and Army forces who were operating inland along the course of the Dvina River for the purpose of protecting British interests in that region, with Archangel as a base; the R.A.F. operated from the Dvina River using two large special service barges, known as SSB1 and SSB2. These had been towed under ballast to Archangel from the U.K. All other ranks had to join in the task of preparing the barges for their journey inland, drawing stores from the Fleet store ship and taking all the necessary equipment aboard the barges. SSB2 was an observation balloon unit and was loaded with cylinders of hydrogen and had accommodation for the balloon crew, whilst SSB1 was equipped for the seaplane unit.

'The aircraft consisted of Fairey and Short seaplanes which were stowed on seaplane lighters towed behind the barge. SSB1 was equipped with living quarters below deck and any essential repair work was carried out on deck as there was no room below for workshops. For major repairs the aircraft were towed back to the base ship where a crew of specialist tradesmen had been retained for this purpose.

'The work of the ground crew consisted chiefly in launching and retrieving aircraft, daily and minor airframe and engine servicing, refuelling from 8-gallon cans of petrol, loading 112 and 220lb bombs, minor repairs to fabric, airframes, floats and cowlings. The wooden 2-blade (Fairey) and 4-blade (Short) propellers often had to be replaced after damage from floating logs and/or lumps of ice coming down the fast flowing river. The midnight sun in the Arctic regions made flying possible almost 24 hours a day, but this was not often necessary'.

Special Service barge No. 1 used as an observation balloon unit on the Dvina River during the North Russian Expedition in 1918. Vale.

Chapter 5
On The Home Front

Not all servicemen go to war, however enthusiastic they may be. Far from it. Under that all-enveloping phrase 'exingencies of the service', many keen types, anxious for action, found themselves spending their war on the home front. However, fret as they might, in their minds they must have known, particularly in that period of static warfare, that there was little chance of actual contact with the enemy. The advent of long range bombing did of course, become the great equaliser insofar as involvement in war was concerned, but during the First World War bombing was comparatively negligible.

So, many air mechanics of both services by force of circumstances, or service compulsion, served at home. These men may not have won campaign medals; they certainly helped those who did. They should feel no sense of guilt. For they served.

The U.K. was, however, the base for a number of operational units; the R.N.A.S. anti-submarine units; the night fighters waiting to engage the Zeppelins; the coast patrol airships. In addition there were the necessary back-up units of flying and training squadrons (these were not the same); the repair and assembly depots and the development and experimental units.

When the R.F.C. left the U.K. for France at the outbreak of war the air defence of the country was given to the R.N.A.S., which had approximately 90 aeroplanes and seaplanes, about 50% of these serviceable. The air units left in the U.K. consisted of:

No's. 1 and 6 R.F.C. Squadrons — in the process of forming
The Military Wing
The Central Flying School at Upavon
The R.N.A.S. Flying School at Sheerness
R.F.C. Reserve Squadron
A detachment of the Aircraft Park at Farnborough
Airship station at Kingsnorth with seven airships
R.N.A.S. units at Eastchurch, Isle of Grain, Westgate, Clacton, Cromarty, Felixstowe, Yarmouth, Killingholme, Calshot, Dundee.

The majority of operational flying from U.K. was by the R.N.A.S. with their U-boat searching patrols and convoy and Fleet escort duties, albeit confined to coastal waters. Not all aeroplane or seaplane stations on this work were situated near towns. One such place was the flying boat station in the Scilly Isles, to which Air Mechanic G. Clarke was posted in 1916. The nearest town was Tresco and across the channel was St. Marys. While the station was being completed a skeleton crew stayed on the station, the remainder of the personnel commuting by boat every morning from St. Marys. The flying boats were kept in a constant state of readiness armed with four bombs, two under each wing.

Mechanics resting in front of a 504K F. J. Hardwick.

The bomb carriers were not too reliable and it was not uncommon for a boat (short name for flying boat) to return with a hung-up bomb, that is, one half released. The tricky job was to release it without dropping it with its fuse already primed, and from an unstable dinghy bobbing up and down under an equally unstable wing presented quite a feat of skill for the armourers. Clarke says that one of the C.P.O.'s invented a means of releasing the bombs by a system of copper tubing and compressed air which proved effective. He does not go into technicalities.

The boats, probably Felixstowe F5's, were powered by two Rolls-Royce engines which were returned to the makers for overhaul after about 100 hours. After every flight all wires and controls had to be checked, probably as a result of the buffeting these lightly built boats received on take-off and landing.

One amusing yarn Clarke relates concerned his Commander, Hope Vere, who had a wire-haired terrier, by name Henry. The Commander was not the desk flying type and when he got fed up with office routine he would suddenly exclaim, 'Oh, balls, where's Henry' and go stalking out. The remark became a catch phrase.

A seven days leave was granted every 12 weeks. This meant being taken by drifter to the mainland, and if the weather was bad and the drifter was late one lost that much leave. But, Clarke says, the drifter crews made every effort and took many risks to get the men over to the mainland, often 30 men at a time crammed together for an eight hour journey.

Clarke describes the examination procedure for promotion or reclassification as he saw it, '...You were recommended by your superior if you showed initiative and had to go before a travelling examination board, lined up before a Sgt. Major, drill, drill, and out you go one at a time and into the exam room, draw outlines, give names and makes of planes, and say what timber was used, what engines and one or two daft questions by the President to judge your character and you always passed, and an extra few bob a week. . .'

In the West Country Air Mechanic H. Vale was having his first experience of an operational station. Mountbatten, near Plymouth, was to be one of the most well-known Fleet Air Arm and Coastal stations in the R.A.F., but when Vale arrived it was an established ex-R.N.A.S. base known as Cattewater, operating Fairey 3D and Short seaplanes and flying boats from three large hangars.

To quote Vale's account '... All these types were launched from beach trolleys which were lowered down slipways into the water until they were able to float off. All tradesmen not on essential work assisted in these operations and some had to don rubber suits and walk down the slipway steadying the aircraft at the wing tips and the stern post until it could be floated off the trolley with engine(s) already running, and pushed out into the stream. At this stage the water was usually waist high when dealing with flying boats but seaplanes floated off when it was knee high.

'Some of the first 'aircraft carriers' were submersible seaplane lighters shaped with a slipway in the middle, somewhat like a barge with one end open. A folded-wing seaplane or flying boat was mounted on a trolley on rails lashed to the deck of one of the craft which would then be towed by a destroyer near to the point where it was to be taken off. A motor boat would then take the ground crew and the pilot and observer out to the seaplane lighter, the wings would be unfolded and secured, the engine run up and when all was ready a sea-cock would be opened to flood the chambers and the lighter be semi-submerged to enable the aircraft to float off. The men would then return to the ship until the aircraft returned from its mission. The men returned to the lighter and guided the aircraft on to the trolley, blew out the chambers with compressed air to raise the lighter to its normal level. The aircraft's wings were then folded and secured, the aircraft lashed down to special ring bolts in the deck of the lighter and the destroyer would tow the unit back to base.

'There was no special training for ground crew on this type of work, it was usually done under the direction of an N.C.O. of experience who would give orders and signals as was required. The aircraft engine(s) were started up with small cylinders of compressed air and if this failed there was a hand start mechanism fitted to the Rolls and Sunbeam engines. It took two men to operate this, one kneeling on the wing-pad reaching downwards and one standing on one of the floats reaching upwards.

*   *   *   *   *

What was it actually like to serve on the 'aeroplane ships?' What was the routine in these revolutionary vessels? The conditions for operating the aircraft? There are few of these hardy sea-going airmen left from those historic days. Let Air Mechanic Mansfield, who served in H.M.S. Campania, and Air Mechanic Vale who served in H.M.S. Pegasus describe in their own words.

Mansfield, '... I did not know when I was well off until I was drafted in September 1917 to H.M.S. Campania which, when not at sea, anchored in Scapa Flow about three miles from Kirkwall.

'The Campania was an old liner converted into a seaplane carrier by having the forward funnel divided into two sections, a flight deck between extending down to the bow. Getting airborne from the flight deck was not easy. The ship sailed into the wind about 25 knots and even then the seaplanes on leaving the flight deck dipped badly towards the sea before getting away. The man at the wheel of the carrier was alerted to swing the helm over should the seaplane hit the water.

'An axle was placed under the floats. This axle was fitted with rubber tyred wheels, I cannot remember the construction of these axles or the method of fitting them to the floats, but the aircraft were released from the floats as soon as they were airborne, and the floats picked up from the sea later.

'We carried three heavy machines, one a Short and two Campanias which were built specially for the ship's holds. Each had a single engine, the Campania's Rolls-Royce and the Short with a Sunbeam engine. All machines were fitted with large wooden floats.

Lifting a Short seaplane from the hold of a seaplane carrier (possibly the Campania) prior to placing it into the water. IWM.

Hoisting a Sopwith Pup from the hold of an early Aircraft Carrier. IWM.

'The Rolls-Royce engines were started by a handle situated at the side of the engine which was geared at 6 to 1 of engine speed. While the engine was being turned by the handle a booster magneto was operated by the person in the cockpit, which was not an easy operation. The Sunbeam engine was started on compressed air from small bottles which were in the cockpit.

'We also carried a number of Sopwith Pup light seaplanes with rotary engines, Gnome or Le Rhone. These planes were also fitted with wooden floats. All machines were carried in what were the ship's holds (now called hangars) and were hoisted out with derricks. There was sufficient room to stand two of them on their floats, one either side of the hangar where we started engines prior to hoisting them on to the flight deck or into the water as required. Repairs, as required, were mostly done in the hangar. It should be noted that owing to the small amount of flying these machines did, little repairs were needed. The heavy machines had fuel for four hours only.

'Although I may have given the impression that a number of these deck take-offs took place, in fact they were few and far between. During the 9 months or so that I was aboard Campania there were no more than three occasions when this operation took place. To anyone aboard a modern aircraft carrier the whole thing was ludicrous. By the time we had hoisted the seaplane from the hold to the flight deck on the derrick by steam winch, fitted the axle under the floats, spread the wings (this was the Chippy's job) started the engine and got the machine away, most of the morning had gone.

'We used to go to sea from time to time usually for four days. It was on one of these occasions that I experienced one of the finest sights I shall ever see. We were sailing alone at dawn when over the horizon came the Fleet, battleships and cruisers sailing in line astern and surrounded by destroyers, a sight that made me proud and one never to be seen again.

'The day following the return to harbour meant 'coaling ship'. We used to take on about 400 tons each time, and the R.N.A.S. boys were given the worst job of filling sacks down in the colliers hold. There were four teams in each hold and as we filled sacks to a total of one ton, they were roped together and hoisted on the Campania. We were only working for a short time before it was hardly possible to see the other teams owing to the coal dust. After coaling ship our washing facilities were not what might have been expected on board an ex-Atlantic liner. Two of us would share a tub in which we would get boiling water from the galley tap and carry this some distance to obtain cold water and take it in turns to wash down in the hangar. . .'

'I was loaned for about two months to the light cruiser Cassandra. R.N.A.S. staff aboard was one pilot, one mechanic and one carpenter. She carried a land plane with folded wings and a Gnome rotary engine, probably Sopwith Pup, housed in a hangar built alongside the bridge. When the plane was required to fly, which was only once while I was aboard, it was pushed out onto a framework of girders in front of the bridge. The ship was steamed into wind at about 25 knots, and swinging the propellers whilst standing on a metal girder was not easy.

'As we were liable to come under enemy fire I was ordered to empty the aircraft of fuel into cans and put them at the side of the deck so that the aircraft could be pushed overboard, with the tins. This was a long job as the only way the tank could be emptied was by syphoning with a rubber tube. When in the Kattegat we were only a few miles from Kiel and the First Lieut. was pacing the bridge muttering, "I hope they come out. . ." and I was thinking, "I hope they don't". I think we were a decoy to bring the German Fleet out. We stayed in the Kattegat for about two hours and then steamed at high speed for Scapa.

'Although we experienced hard times it was something I would not have missed, if only for the comradeship under those conditions'.

* * * * *

Mansfield had served on one of the most distinguished carriers of the early years, the ship being part of the Grand Fleet. In August 1917 the Home Fleet was joined by another seaplane carrier to swell its already large total. H.M.S. Pegasus, originally named Stockholm, incorporated several of the improvements initiated by Campania. Aboard her was Air Mechanic H. Vale. Let him continue. . .

'Pegasus was constructed with a large box-shape hangar built aft for storage of seaplanes and a similar hangar under the bridge to hold two small single-seater scout aircraft. Aircraft could not land on her but there was a small moveable flight deck at the bows which enabled the scout aircraft to take off. For this operation the flight deck was moved forward, the aircraft taken out of the hangar and hoisted with derrick, the flight deck was then moved back and the aircraft lowered on to it. With the ship full ahead into the wind the aircraft was able to take off; the aircraft were usually of the single seater Pup or Eastchurch Kitten type, with a limited range of operation. To return to the carrier they had to land on the sea nearby and be hauled aboard with a derrick.

'The aft hangar contained four folded-wing seaplanes. Rails were let into the deck of the hangar extending out on the poop deck and the seaplanes were wheeled out on trolleys running in these rails. The wings were then unfolded and secured and after the engine had

84

been warmed up the aircraft was picked up by a crane and lowered over the side with the engine running. It was then released from the crane, taxied away and took off.

'The Short and Fairey seaplanes were fitted with a hoisting ring above the top centre section, with four wires leading from the ring and attached to the centre section struts. The crane hook was fitted with a quick-release eye pin. As the machines were two seater open cockpit types it was the man in the rear seat who had the job of pulling the toggle which

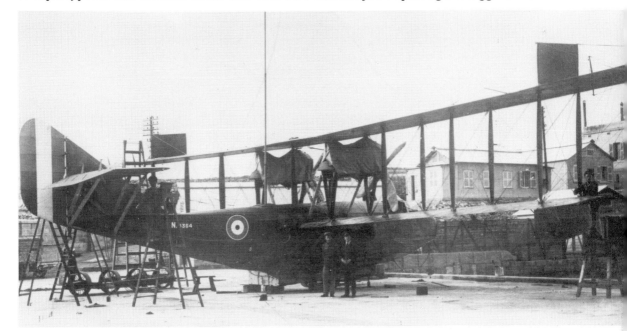

Servicing a Felixstowe F5 flying boat of an RNAS unit in the UK. G. Hawlett.

released the pin when the pilot was ready to cast off. On returning to the carrier the pilot would touch down astern of the ship, the crane would be swung outboard and the pilot would taxi up until he was under the crane hook. The man in the rear would meanwhile stand up and grab the crane hook and engage it in the hoisting ring attached to the centre section. These operations could only be carried out whilst the ship was stopped and required the very closest co-operation of the ground crew.

'There were two men known as the 'prodder kings' who were armed with long bamboo poles with pads on the end, whose task it was to ensure that the wings and tail of the aircraft were kept from being damaged against the side of the ship if the weather was gusty and the sea choppy. Another man had a separate line attached to the crane hook in order to yank it well clear the moment it was detached, as there was always the possibility that the seaplane might drift backwards with the tide and the crane hook would foul the seaplane's propeller'.

* * * * *

The repair of damaged aircraft in the war years fell on the shoulders of the Aircraft and Repair Depots, which eventually became gigantic workshops geared for mass rebuilds and repairs of the scores of damaged aircraft received monthly. Each Depot was divided into sections, each responsible for the repair, inspection, replacement and test of a major system of the aeroplane or airship.

Farnborough had become the largest single service factory, producing army or R.F.C. aeroplanes and was in direct competition with civilian firms, which did not always make for efficient production of the right kind of aeroplane. Much waste and duplication was entailed, a feature of this terrible war. To maintain the momentum of output, special clocks were installed showing the rate of output of each day, targets which were aimed at and then exceeded. In time of war, when your chargehand is a Senior N.C.O. and the foreman is a Sergeant Major, a sustained effort was maintained.

Part of the Farnborough Factory complex was No. 1 Salvage and Repair Depot in which Air Mechanic Armitage was employed in the gun fitters shop, installing guns and firing gear. He worked on two types of gun gears; the 'Scarff' a mechanically operated interrupter gear and the 'Constantinesco', a hydraulically operated synchronising gear. The Scarff was not a very successful type; over a period, locking nuts would loosen and ball joints would wear, causing mistiming of the gear with consequent loss of the propeller.

The Constantinesco was more successful, employing the principle of an impulse from a cam on the prop shaft transmitted hydraulically to operate the gun gear. Accuracy of fitting was essential for there was little margin for error. Inefficient cartridges excepting, if a propeller blade was hit by its own gun on a test flight and the fault was traced to bad workmanship, the fitter was court martialled.

After a short period of fitting Armitage was promoted 1st Class air mechanic, signed for a £50 kit of tools for which he was responsible, given a junior mechanic and they were on their own.

Armitage said that conditions at the Depot were bad, the work was filthy with inadequate cleaning facilities and no hot water, having to remove grease and oil with paraffin or petrol. This became a natural cleansing method in the R.A.F. Accommodation was tented all the year round, with the men having to raise the floor boards of the tent to prevent the mud oozing up between them. During the only time they had lived in huts they had been forced to evacuate them shortly afterwards to hand them over to the W.A.A.C.'s who were coming into the R.F.C.

*   *   *   *   *

Air Mechanic Cornish was posted to 18 Wing Aeroplane Repair Section at Northolt as an under-training sailmaker, but he was put to work sweeping out the carpenters shed. The sweepings were used to keep a smoke fire going on the aerodrome to act as a wind direction indicator. Then he was detailed for bath and boiler house duties and C.O.'s orderly. It was not until Cornish was posted to 56 Training Squadron at London Colney that he finally pursued his vocation, and was kept very busy. Cornish enjoyed his work, even if he saw more crashes than he would have wished, including being too near a couple of them.

His description of covering a wing with fabric remains virtually the same method used down the years, until the advent of more sophisticated methods such as geodetic wing covering or medappolam fabric on wood. '. . The wings were placed on trestles. The fabric was then positioned, either by sections or in the form of a bag and temporarily tacked in place. Any metal strips under the fabric, usually part of a rib or bracing, would be bound with fabric strip. A section or bag would then be sewn together at the rear of the plane (to be covered). Afterwards it would be secured to the ribs at nine inch spacing by waxed thread 'padded' around the rib by a large curved upholsterers needle, each stitch locked with a knot.

'Frayed tape, about three inches wide, was then doped over the rib stitching. The whole section or bag was then doped with three coats of PC 10 khaki dope and the roundels, etc., painted on as required. . .'

Cornish remained with this unit until he was posted back to Farnborough, along with thousands of other now surplus mechanics, and transferred to the 7th Queens Own Royal West Kents and was wounded during the final Allied attack in August 1918.

A contempory of Armitage, Sergeant T. Missenden, was another who spent his war in a Depot, on armaments. In Missenden's case his was a 'rest' posting after hospitalisation, for he had previously seen action in the Dardenelles and had been invalided home with enteric fever and dysentery.

He was posted to the Royal Ordnance Factory at Greenwich, and being a skilled armourer was employed in checking and inspecting Vickers and Lewis guns and ring and bead and telescopic gunsights. He also worked on synchronising gun gears but did not actually work on aircraft. One of his tasks, which gave him a break from routine, was to visit the makers of Power Bomb Teachers to inspect the product and their packing in special crates for overseas shipment, which were lined with tin and made airtight to float if the worst happened.

The Bomb Teacher was an ingenious aid to teach aerial bombing, and consisted of a mock cockpit secured above a flat section of a floor, on which a moveable map could be laid. A pilot under training would press a lever as the map unrolled to simulate flight, and a spot of oil was released to hit the point where theoretically the bomb landed. The system was purely mechanical, the Power part of the name coming from a Lt. Power. It was, in effect, one of the first simulators.

Missenden tried to become a pilot but was physically unsuited. After his return to the Depot he was put on clerical duties, which he resented and said so. The following day it appeared on Daily Routine Orders that 'Sergeant Missenden reverts to the rank of Corporal at his own request'.

At No. 5 Aeroplane Repair Depot at Henlow, Beds., Air Mechanic F. J. Hardwick served throughout his service and found the hours of work long, 7.30 a.m. to 8 p.m., and of great monotony. A number of the repaired aircraft were destined for Karachi and preparing them for the long sea journey broke the routine somewhat. The aeroplanes were dismantled and packed in huge crates (some crates accommodated an entire Handly Page 0/100 fuselage), which had to be manhandled from the workshops to a lifting point along the camp road. Of 17 lorries which left Henlow in convoy for the docks only four returned without trouble, the others breaking down or crashing.

Hardwicke sat a trade test for his Leading Aircraftsman reclassification while at Henlow. His task was to rig an aeroplane without instruments, using his eye and experience only, a task which seemed rather strange in view of the increasing higher technical standards required. He passed.

An airmen who had a rare distinction in a technical sense, was Air Mechanic C. G. C. Kelsey who, with a Corporal Taylor as his rigger, formed the ground crew which serviced the 504K used by Princes Albert and Edward during their flying lessons at Plough Lane, Croydon.

Narrow escapes from death or injury were commonplace in this war, and with these old aeroplanes many an air mechanic had the proverbial close call. Air Mechanic Nicholson was one of them.

Having little to do one day he asked a Lt. Young if he could accompany him for a flight in a DH6. He was told to get a helmet, which was compulsory. As Nicholson had some difficulty in obtaining one the pilot became impatient and took off alone. There was a stream at one end of Stamford aerodrome at that time and as Lt. Young was taking off a pupil pilot was coming in to land. They crashed head on, falling one each side of the stream. One machine caught fire and the burning petrol ran across the stream and set fire to the other. Both pilots were roasted. Nicholson might have been involved.

Stamford was a training aerodrome with DH5 aircraft and Nicholson was rigger to the C.O.'s aeroplane, an RE8. During one Easter holiday the Major asked him to come in and see him off in the RE8 for a trip to Cambridge. Nicholson got the machine out of the hangar with the help of some Americans and reported to the Major, who said he would do one circuit and land and then when he took off again he, Nicholson, could go.

The machine did a circuit, landed with the throttle too far back and the engine stopped. Nicholson ran across to help but before he arrived the Major tried to start the engine himself. He gave the engine too much throttle and the RE8 started to move. On these aeroplanes the tail skid was bias sprung at right angles when at rest. The aeroplane started to taxi in a circle with the Major trying to reach the cockpit, finally the machine hit a bump and went up on its nose. When Nicholson finally reached the scene he saw a lovely girl trying to console the Major, saying, 'Never mind'. 'Never mind, be buggered,' replied the Major, 'If anyone else had done it I'd have had him court-martialled'. The Major told Nicholson he had tried to start as he didn't want him to come across.

*　*　*　*　*

Life in the service for a boy mechanic could be frustrating especially when that boy was keen to go on active service. Boy J. Webb completed his technical training with No. 10 Training Squadron at Shawbury, under the supervision of a 1st Class Air Mechanic. His first job was mainly refuelling and washing down the Camels of the unit; he could thoroughly recommend getting thick castor oil from the surface of an aeroplane.

On 1st April 1918 Webb was classified a 2nd Class Private in the new R.A.F. ranking. Unfortunately, Webb became a victim of the occupational risk attendant on all mechanics who swing propellers. He was hit by a 504K prop while swinging it and sustained a broken arm and leg, resulting in two months at Prees Heath Military Hospital and two more months in the camp hospital. He was lucky at that. When he was mobile again and was posted to operational squadrons he was excused prop swinging.

The hazards of starting loomed large in the everyday life of a fitter or rigger, the majority of tradesmen who were involved with aircraft making this point. Until the advent of mechanical/electrical starting systems this was to remain one of the major risks of the ground crew, until the propeller was finally superseded by the jet, which brought its own problems.

Boy Fitter R. P. Fair who was posted to a Handley Page 0/100 squadron at Andover was no exception and said that of all the aeroplanes he was involved with, the SE5A (Hispano Suiza and Sunbeam Arab) was the most difficult to start with its outside hand starter. The Handley Pages were started from a standing position on the wing by cranking.

He did some flying in the 0/100's and on one occasion whilst in the air an external petrol pipe fractured, spraying petrol over the wing. Fair was instructed to shut off the fuel supply to the damaged pipe, and pump petrol to the engine with a hand operated rotary fuel pump until the aeroplane landed safely.

*   *   *   *   *

It is obvious that other necessary back-up trades be included in a book of this nature. One such trade, if it can so be called is that of hospital orderly. Air Mechanic A. E. Evans was made a hospital orderly on the strength of his civilian occupation, an apprentice pharmacist, without service training. When he reported to the sick bay at Northolt he was given a St. John's Ambulance First Aid book to read; this was his course.

Evans was then put on airfield ambulance duty, often from dawn to dusk with just a break for meals. The ambulance, a Crossley, was poorly equipped by today's standards, carrying two Minimax fire extinguishers which, Evans said '... made no impact at all on a blazing machine. . .' The engine of the ambulance was swung and run for a few minutes every half an hour to keep it warm for emergency, the petrol pump having to be pumped by hand to maintain pressure for supply to the engine.

When a fatality occurred Evans would help the N.C.O. i/c the sick bay to lay out the body for the local undertaker, who gave the Sergeant £1 and Evans 50p. The smell of burned flesh would remain for several days. Treatment for burns was a picric acid solution which was not very effective, of course there were no antibiotics available. Prop swinging produced its own crop of fatalities and serious injuries and Evans witnessed both. He also helped bury the results of the Camel's unforgiving reaction to inexperienced pilots who could not control its vicious spin.

Evans witnessed an incident which he regarded as a great act of courage. He was watching an Avro 504 flying at about 1,000ft. (300m) when he saw a puff of smoke come from it. Immediately, two figures appeared on the lower wing, one each side of the cockpit. They edged along the wings, holding on to struts and bracing wires changing position at times to keep the aircraft level. When the nose dropped they both moved quickly to the cockpit, where the pilot plunged his hand into the flames to pull the stick back.

As the aeroplane levelled out close to the ground the two men jumped from about 20-30ft, rolled, and sustaining no injuries, got up and ran to the ambulance to get treatment for the severe burns to their hands. Evans said to the air mechanic passenger, '... You had courage to get out on the wing up there. . .' The airman, an A. C. Carpenter, replied, '... When you find a fire raging under your seat you don't think about courage, you just get out quickly'.

*   *   *   *   *

Flying Training Schools and Squadrons, where necessary, were using any available land that was suitable for an aerodrome. Racecourses were ideal sites. One such well-known course that was converted was at Doncaster, to which Air Mechanic A. M. Merrix and three friends were posted in mid-1918. Their arrival on the squadron was quite spectacular in a most macabre way.

An RNAS canteen of 1918 at Manston during the winter. Primitive but needed. H. Wood.

They were walking across the square to the Orderly Room when they became aware of the roar of an aero engine and moments later a 504 crashed in front of them. It immediately burst into flames and the shocked new arrivals watched helplessly as the pilot was roasted. As Merrix said, '...We couldn't do a thing for him as all the cross bracing wires formed a kind of cage. . .' to make it even more memorable another aircraft crashed, even as they watched, into a tree on the Doncaster Road. As Merrix put it, '...quite a sensational start we thought. . .'

The training squadron was composed of three flights, each with a hangar and 10 planes. Routine consisted of wheeling the aircraft out and filling up with 'aviation spirit' and castor oil. The fuel capacity was about 10 gallons, supplied from a mobile 30-40 gallon (135-180L) tank fitted with a semi-rotary pump. The castor oil was in drums which were hoisted up to the tank.

What Merrix considers his worst experience was when he was ordered by the pilot into the rear cockpit of his aeroplane for a flight. 'It was bitterly cold and I was only wearing my overalls. My fingers were so numb I couldn't fasten the safety belt and had to let it dangle. The pilot climbed to 1,500ft. (460m) and was above the clouds. Suddenly, without warning, he started to loop. Ordinarily the strain would have been taken by the safety belt but of course, it not being around me, for a few seconds I seemed to be hanging in space with my hands gripping the coaming of the cockpit. It was only for a few seconds then we were upright again. After he had straightened out the pilot turned and pointed to the joy stick in the rear cockpit. After a few gesticulations (we had no phones) I realised he wished me to fly the plane. Why, I never knew. Anyway after I took the joy stick the plane performed like crazy. I was very relieved to get on the ground again. . .'

Another time, '... there was the case of the Plane with the Twisted Fuselage. Most of the pilots gave this plane a miss and said she should be written off. But the Station C.O. thought otherwise. He came down to the aerodrome one day about 6 p.m., we had just washed out flying for the day and told me to get the plane out. I took her outside the hangar, filled up and swung the prop. Once again I was told to jump in, only this time in the front cockpit. Pretty soon we were looking down at the hangars — and I for one wished I was still in them. After a time he opened up the throttle to its full extent which was about 90 m.p.h., practically its full speed. The C.O. then asked me to look along the fuselage and as I looked I could see that the bottom right longeron (one of four) was whipping very badly. It was causing the whole fuselage to twist and I thought this will never stand the strain.'

'We didn't have parachutes in those days and I didn't fancy our chances much. However the C.O., one of the best pilots of the day, nodded after I had pointed out where the trouble lay and started on the way back. He shut the throttle and glided down towards the field and finished up a few yards from the hangar doors. I was out like a shot. He never said a word and was off. Next day the aircraft was in the A.R.S. for a real overhaul and a new longeron fit. This was a case of a fault not showing until it was in flight. . .'

Another, who wrote home describing his experiences with the R.N.A.S. and R.A.F., was Air Mechanic W. K. Turner who gives us an illuminating glimpse of a mechanics life at Netheravon, a Flying Training Station in Wiltshire.

Turner had been remustered from his R.N.A.S. trade of engine fitter to fitter general during the changeover to the R.A.F. The training aeroplanes included Henri Farman (80 h.p. 8-cyl. Renault), DH6 (120 h.p. V8 R.A.F.), FE2B (160 h.p. straight eight Beardmore) and the Avro 504 (90 h.p. Clerget). Also on the station were Handley Page heavy bombers (two 350 h.p. Rolls-Royce) which were used to train night flying crews.

Night flying was still in its infancy although being mastered from the experience gained by the Independent Air Force, operating its night bomber squadrons in France. The usual flare path was normally marked out on the aerodrome with paraffin flares.

Quote from Turner's letter of 2nd July 1918:—

'When taking off and landing at night, electric lights glow under each wing, with another underneath the body and one on the tail. Also all the instrument dials and a compass are illuminated. When the pilot wants to land he fires a white flare from a Verey pistol and if all is clear, the Ground Officer fires a similar flare.

'When the plane has dropped to within 100ft or so of the ground the pilot fires his landing lights, which are like Roman Candles, fastened underneath each wing. How they don't set the thing on fire I don't know. A few weeks later they did and Flight Cadet Fisher, on his first solo flight (at night) was burnt to death. Of course all the landing grounds were grass, the tarmac apron being only in front of the permanent hangars.

'Many other types of aircraft used to call at the Station including BE2s, RE8s, DH4s and 9s, and Sopwith machines. One of these, the Camel, was so well balanced that one man could lift the tail and wheel it about. One day two brand new Bristol Fighters, on their way to the front, put in for the night. They were placed in a Bessoneau hangar, but a terrific storm blew up, wrecking the hangar and causing the machines inside to be complete write-offs. It was the worst storm I had ever seen, and all the men on guard that night were put under open arrest for allowing the storm to do such damage! I happened to be one of them. We were all soaked to the skin, or nearly so, as some planes were left out all night for lack of accommodation and we had been endeavouring to secure these to piquets screwed into the chalky subsoil. After hours of work securing an old "Rumpety" (Farman Biplane) without an engine, a sudden squall blew it into the air to strike some overhead electric cables. Talk about fireworks! A Handley Page was blown across the downs towards Upavon'.

25th May, 1918

'A Major and a Captain were killed yesterday while trying to loop-the-loop in a DH6, which is not built for stunting.

'In these the engine was liable to fall out if upside-down flying was attempted, as it was only secured to the framework by four perforated steel clamps each bolted to the slender wooden frame by two $\frac{3}{8}$" bolts. The frame was further braced by a sheet of thin plywood! With only 80 or 90 h.p. pulling, it was essential to keep weight to the minimum.'

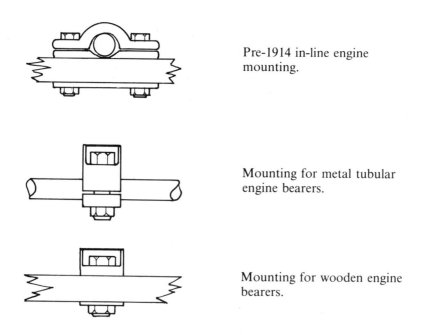

Pre-1914 in-line engine mounting.

Mounting for metal tubular engine bearers.

Mounting for wooden engine bearers.

Sketch showing typical in-line engine installation.

'In the height of summer we worked two shifts — 3 a.m. to 1 p.m. and 1 p.m. to 11 p.m. or whenever the machines were washed and stowed away in their hangar. By the 1st September the respective hours were — 5 a.m. to 6-30 p.m. and 8 a.m. to 9-30 p.m. with staggered breaks for two meals. As the hangars were a mile and a half from the cookhouse we had to step it out. There was no mechanical transport for us. By September 16th the times were again altered — Shift 1, 5-15 a.m. to 8-30 a.m., 10-30 a.m. to 12-30 p.m., and 3 p.m. to dusk. Shift 2, 9 a.m. to 12-30p.m. and 2 p.m. to dusk. The workshops also worked long hours. The Yanks however worked only from 8 a.m. to 11.45 a.m. and 2 p.m. to 5 p.m. and then went to supper! As soon as their whistle sounded they dropped whatever they were doing — and if it was urgent we had to finish it off. This and other differences (particularly pay) didn't make for very good relations.

'Work in the flights was rather heavy as the tails of the aeroplanes had to be lifted — by two men if they were strong enough or three or four if they were not — and the tail skids placed on a two wheeled bogey having a long handled shaft held by another man. The machine could then be wheeled on to the aerodrome, where it was supplied with petrol and oil — and water if the engine was water-cooled. There were no petrol pumps then. The best aviation spirit at 5/6 (27p) per gallon came in 2 gallon cans (9 litre) and had to be funnelled through gauze and chamois leather to ensure freedom from grit and water. The tanks were sometimes under the pilot's seat or sometimes attached to the fuselage. After sixty hours flying the engine had to be removed and sent to the workshops for overhaul, and a new or reconditioned one replaced.

'You may have seen inside the cockpit of these old machines. The rudder was controlled by twisted wires running from a pivoted piece of wood worked by the feet. The joystick was a vertical lever rising from the floor between the knees which could be moved in an arc in any direction. This controlled the ailerons behind the wingtips and the horizontal rudder. There were about four or five instruments, compass, altitude recorder, wind speed indicator, oil pressure gauge and sometimes an ammeter. All the engines were magneto fired.

'There were two workshops, the A.R.S. where all repairs were done to the craft itself and Headquarters Workshops where the engines were repaired and overhauled. The fittters worked in gangs of three or four to each engine and when an engine came in for overhaul it was completely dismantled, the separate parts washed in a bath of paraffin, wiped or drained dry and placed in a wooden box with compartments for each cylinder and its components.

'The senior fitters would scrape and refit the white metal main bearings and connecting rods, whilst the others replaced little end bearings, lapped in and fitted up new cylinders and any other new parts required. Everything had to be just right before it left the workshop. There was no such thing as near enough and hoping for the best. I had several weeks in the workshop — Hours 7-30 a.m. to 8, 9 or even 10-30 p.m. with time off for two meals.

'When the pilot was seated and had checked the ailerons and rudders, a little dialogue ensued:— Mechanic — 'Petrol on, switch off, suck in Sir'. Pilot:— 'Petrol orn, switch is orf, suck in'. The mechanic would then give the two-bladed prop a few turns in the direction of engine rotation and then call 'Contact Sir'. On receiving the reply 'Contact' he would grasp the horizontal propeller facing him on the right hand side near the tip and standing as clear as possible, give it a mighty swing and move quickly backwards. Chocks of wood were placed in front of the the wheels to prevent the machine moving forward. If one was swinging a prop after a forced landing, chocks might not be available then one had to be very wary. There were no brakes on the machines as they were too light and top-heavy, and anyway the axles were only tied to the undercarriage with elastic. Some wouldn't swing props if they could help it and others never really learnt how to.

'Trapped fingers and broken wrist watches often happened and if the engine backfired, one had to sense it immediately. A certain middle aged recruit would duck his head forward when he swung and was frequently warned about it. Unfortunately he did it once too often and was killed. Some makes of engine turned clockwise, some anti-clockwise and some had to be sucked in clockwise and swung the other way for starting. One day one of the latter landed at our station and as I was near when the pilot was ready to 'take off', I had to give him a swing. I was unaware of this little variation and swung it clockwise. Had it fired I might not have been writing this now'.

13th September 1918
'Yesterday we had only three machines serviceable in our Flight and two of those crashed in the afternoon. In the first case the engine went 'DUD' so the cadet volplaned down. When he got near the ground the engine suddenly picked up and buried its nose in the earth. The afternoon was spent taking the plane to pieces and bringing it home on a trailer. In the second case, another cadet was taken ill while in the air and made a bad landing about four miles away across the downs. Neither of the pilots was hurt and in the second case only the undercarriage was broken, so we took that off and lifted the plane on to a trailer. It was almost dark by this time and we only had the distant lights of the 'drome to guide us. It was the most exciting ride I've had. The grass was so long in places and the ground so rough, that the tender (a 30 h.p. Crossley van) stuck. We had to keep getting off to push. The planes' wings were hanging over each side of the trailer and rocking violently, so three of us had to hang on to the wing tips to steady it. We were advised to run behind, but the other two preferred to run in front and were bowled over several times when it was pulled out of their hands. I hung on to the extreme end and behind. One minute I would be lifted into the air, the next bumped down to earth, and at one point the wing lifted a footpath signpost out of the ground and laid it carefully down as though it were done by human hands. When it got quite dark we took it in turns to run in front of the tender with its only headlamp. (either oil or acetylene, I forget which). At last we reached the hangar, dumped the lot inside, mounted the tender and made for the cookhouse and tea. You can bet we were ready for it at a quarter to ten'.

'We had two forms of transport for bringing home crashed machines. There were the large standard sized Leyland, Dennis, Albion, Guy or other make of lorry, and the 30 cwt Crossley tender which was a truck with a van-like canvas hood. These could tow a fairly long two-wheeled trailer capable of carrying a DH6 or any make of similar size across the downs; but if the public roads had to be used, the machine was dismantled and loaded on to one of the lorries. There were no cranes on the lorries so everything had to be lifted by manpower.

'In all these camps we were housed either in draughty huts, usually with leaking roofs and a coke slow-combustion stove in the middle; or in bell tents. The beds in the huts consisted of three planks, with two cross pieces to rest them on. There were also three "Biscuit" mattresses — if you were lucky — and three blankets. If you got a position in a

Typical balloon section near the Meaulte-Bray road, showing operational balloon on its bed with 'nurse' or storage balloon and gas cylinders and screen. Mechanics are filling the main balloon from the nurse. IWM.

good hut not too near either the door or the fire, you weren't too badly off, but the Irish were always having a 'Barney' and breaking the Euralite lining panels, making the place very draughty, as well as making an entrance for rats. In the tents we had three blankets and slept on the earth. I had six weeks in a tent and the man next to me was an all-night snorer. He nearly drove us all mad, as we slept 9 or 10 in a tent. I believe 16, even up to 22 (in 1908) used to be the usual number, and if they slept without any ventilation — they died.

'I did get three or four days in October and the 6 days at Christmas or New Year, granted to everyone that year.

'Flight pupils were drawn from all branches of the Army, chiefly commissioned ranks, although there were a few Sergeant pilots and former civilians. The array of uniforms was weird and wonderful, every style and shade of khaki, from green to brown. We were decked in discarded infantry and cavalry clothing and every kind of headgear, the silliest of which was the R.F.C. Forage Cap which drained water down your neck when it rained and fell off when you bent down. It wasn't long before I had changed all the brass buttons for new Air Force brown ones which didn't need cleaning, and bought an Air Force peaked cap with cloth badge. They were well worth the expense. My feet were nearly deformed by the wretched army boots'.

Saturday, 9th November, 1918
'The war is finished. Germany surrendered unconditionally last Thursday. That came through from the Air Board last Thursday night and was confirmed by the War Office

yesterday. (The Armistice was officially signed, of course, on Monday the 11th.) Everyone so inclined got blind drunk that night and a long procession headed by the Yankee Band marched round the village. Many of their instruments have since been consigned to the scrap heap.

'It was another 'Mafeking night', troops coming down from the many camps on Salisbury Plain did much damage in the villages. I and another chap tried a week later to get a 'posh tea' in the village, but all doors were bolted against us. It was only by announcing who we were and which camp we came from — through the closed door — that a lady eventually admitted us and provided us with a plate of ham and some apple pie. They hardly dare go out to buy food as the troops had run amok, especially the Colonials.'

'After the war, educational classes were started, but although they got off to a good start, people soon tired of them.

'At the end of January 1919 I was 'demobbed'. I remember travelling from Salisbury to London by train — 17 men in one compartment — all with kit bags, greatcoats and parcels of every description. I could only get one foot to the floor as I stood in the middle of the compartment holding on to the crowded racks — and the journey took 2½ hours.

'As I have said, I was only in the Service the inside of a year, but my short sojourn was an invaluable experience and (now it is over) one that I would not care to have missed.

'The quickest way to get out of the Forces after the war was to ask your former employer to apply for you.'

* * * * *

Women's services at home were ordered to replace men by the following percentages:

Vulcanisers	75%
Clerks and Sailmakers	70%
Batmen, Cooks, Draughtsmen, Drivers M.T.	66%
Tailors, Telephonists, Painters, Storeman	50%
Instrument repairers	26%

First official enrolment of women with the R.F.C. was under Army Order 711 of 28th December 1917. In this the first idea of local training was put forward, together with other suggestions and information.

A woman would have to work with, and receive training from, the man she was eventually going to replace. In this context it was anticipated that top grade fitters would not be replaced by women. It would not be possible to divert special tools or equipment, except for certain cases, to use for training.

Probably the girls who can claim to being the nucleus of the W.R.A.F. tradeswomen were M.T. drivers who had enlisted in 1916 into the Women's Legion and who had subsequently been attached to the R.F.C. They were allowed to wear suitably adapted R.F.C. uniforms with badges. The girls were specially selected by virtue of being qualified drivers. They had to be self-reliant and confident in their technical abilities, for they had the full responsibility of their vehicle and its maintenance. After the W.R.A.F. came into existence a number of Women's Legion pioneers were merged, at their own request, into this service as fully qualified drivers.

The Women's Royal Air Force (W.R.A.F.) was formed on 1st April 1918 and disbanded on 1st April 1920. In that time the success achieved by the women ensured the rebirth of their service when it was needed for the next world war, and its continuation after that war was over. In its two years existence the W.R.A.F. grew to a total of 21,700.

The W.R.A.F. was formed from the Women's Royal Naval Service (W.R.N.S.), the Queen Mary's Army Auxiliary Corps (Q.M.A.A.C.) and the Women's Legion Motor Drivers. A number of the girls from the latter service had been seconded to R.A.F. units and their experience proved invaluable.

The recently formed R.A.F. had been divided into five organisation and administrative areas, North-Eastern; North-Western; Midland; South-Eastern and South-Western; and a separate No. 11 Group, Ireland. The W.R.A.F. hierarchy appointed an Inspector to each area, but overall control was maintained by the Air Council.

Compiling regulations for the new service was comparatively easy as the other womens services were used as a basis and women rushed to join this service as enthusiastically as the men had flocked to join up in 1914.

The principal aim of the W.R.A.F., to train women to take over the work of the home based mechanics and so free them for service in the combat areas was only in part realised, as the cessation of hostilities soon after its formation prevented that aim from reaching fruition. The authorities decided on the secondary aim of replacing airmen by women to speed up demobilisation of R.A.F. mechanics.

Terms of recruitment were for one year or the duration of the war, whichever was the longest, from a minimum age of 18. The members, as they were known, were placed into one of two categories, according to their wish. These categories were mandatory and independent of trade choice, and were:

Mobiles— To serve in any part of the U.K.

Immobiles—To serve only locally from their own town, but required to serve a four week training course before being posted back to a local unit.

It was a peculiarity of recruitment that in the beginning the girls were enrolled at their local Labour Exchanges under civil contract, and not enlisted. This contract was backed and strengthened by a Defence of the Realm Act (D.O.R.A.), which proved a highly unsatisfactory arrangement for the R.A.F. When the girls went overseas they came under the Air Force Act which made their control and discipline much more effective. Recruiting through the Labour Exchange Boards, on which sat an officer of the W.R.A.F., continued up to March 1919. After that date recruiting was through a W.R.A.F. officer stationed at each large R.A.F. station or unit. At the time of the Armistice both W.R.A.F. and R.A.F. were engaged in recruiting campaigns for women.

It was not easy to enlist. There were quite a number of reserved occupations which automatically ruled out the girls enlisting, unless they could produce written permission for their release. They were also required to produce two authentic references from reputable people, one of whom had to be a woman and must have known them for at least two years. The girls had to be entirely British and pass a medical examination.

A few brief examples of the work these trades entailed will give some idea of the standards required:

Rigger

This trade was one taught by R.A.F. riggers on an 'on-the-job' basis and was graded in stages. Proficiency in wire or cable splicing was followed by training, under supervision, on actual aircraft. Some of the girls became quite good to the extent that they were allowed to dismantle damaged aircraft and carry out minor repairs.

Fitter (aero engine)

Another vital job which was taught specifically by R.A.F. engine fitters. The women did not do any servicing, being employed mainly in cleaning parts after an engine had been stripped. However, as in the case of the riggers, some of the members proved so competent that on several units the women helped to reassemble engines.

Painters and dopers

The dopers carried on where the fabric workers left off and their job was unpleasant and potentially dangerous. This trade was one of the success stories of the W.R.A.F. as some dope shops were staffed entirely by women. Although the early methods of doping and the cellulose materials used were well able to cause poisoning, happily, there were relatively few cases, but the danger from the cellulose fumes was always there.

Recognising this, the authorities gave the members permission to 'brew-up' more frequently to help combat these fumes (the antidote quality of milk was not then known). The word soon got around and the natural popularity of the girls increased dramatically! Until the mechanics were told to make their own tea.

Painters and Signwriters

This was an allied trade to the painter and doper, to mark the service aircraft with its roundels, squadron markings, serial number and any other identification or marks.

Although this book emphasises the technical types, it would be foolish to overlook the equally valuable work carried out by those whose talents were not directed, or influenced, by aircraft. Like the men, the girls filled the necessary posts here just as efficiently as they did at the hangar or workshop.

The so-called non-technical types were doing as important a job within their own field. For instance:

Pay Clerks and Store Clerks

These tradeswomen were probably in the majority and were employed in practically all units where the W.R.A.F served, and were able to assist in the release of a number of men for more vital duties in the R.A.F. The famous, or notorious, Blandford Camp in Dorest was staffed administratively by these tradeswomen. Against the emotive background of this camp the women clerks helped to keep the large numbers of men flowing in and out for demobilisation.

Pigeon Women

No, this was not a woman who looked like a 'pouter', but one employed on the airship base at Pulham St. Marys to look after the messenger pigeons. She was required to record all the data, flights, time of departure and arrival of the birds, where released, state of weather and other relevant information.

Motor Cyclists

It was pretty arduous work driving the tenders and cars of the period, but whoever could handle the motor cycles of those years, unreliable, prone to skidding and bone jarring in their suspension, must be even tougher.

The so-called weaker sex were employed as despatch riders, mail collectors and chauffeurs for sundry V.I.P.'s and were trained by R.A.F. M.T. sections. Of course, the 'bath tub' passengers didn't have such a good ride, either!

Pay was quite good but varied according to a rather complicated system of grading. All the major categories were broken down into sub-categories, up to six of them. All other ranks of both groups received a standard consolidated allowance of 14s (70p). The lowest trade grade in the technical group, a painter worker, received 25s (£1.25p) and the highest, a Chief Section Leader Technical, got 42s (£2.10p). Mobile members received 1s 6d (7p) a day for laundry expenses. The pay rate compared very favourably with the airmen's rates of pay.

Strangely enough the highest paid member in the W.R.A.F. was the shorthand typist, who could receive up to 45s (£2.25p) depending on typed words per minute (a maximum of 100 is given). All other categories received correspondingly less, until one arrived at the poor General Domestic Worker who got the princely sum of 9s 6d (47p).

The system of posting after recruit training was for individual Unit Commanders to indent for the replacements they required to Area H.Q. who informed the Depots, who carried out the posting routine. The members were posted direct from the Depot to their units, irrespective of any trade they had opted for. Except for M.T. drivers there was no technical training school for the W.R.A.F. until October 1918.

New drivers-to-be were trained at No. 1 M.T. Depot, Hurst Park, where they were initiated into the technicalities of Ford, Crossley and Leyland. The course was short and intensive, but varied, and the end results of great credit to the school and valuable replacement drivers for the R.A.F. drivers awaiting demob. On successfully passing out they were awarded proficiency certificates.

In the first month of the W.R.A.F.'s formation the girls were issued with uniforms made for the Q.M.A.A.C., an ugly shapeless frock coat design, relieved only by the words 'Royal Flying Corps' embroidered on the sleeves. The next uniform to be issued was the new khaki tunic and skirt pattern, much improved, with an R.A.F. badge in black and white, worn on the cap, the tunic and the greatcoat sleeves.

In November 1918, the new blue uniform was issued on the authority of an A.M.O. and was a retrograde step, in that it reverted to the old R.F.C. pattern, the tunic buttoning-up over the chest on the left side. Other ranks received a free issue kit every year, but as this proved unsatisfactory the authorities decided in 1919 to put the issue on the same basis as the R.A.F. i.e., renewal when worn out. The uniforms were worn on all occasions and the girls were proud of them, but at times they found that 'uniform only' was a trifle irksome, and endeavoured to brighten them up with strictly unofficial accessories. Regimental badges of boy friends would be prominently displayed, the top button of the tunic was often removed and the collar turned down to show more neck—very daring! The more fashion conscious substituted the official black stockings for the then fashionable beige ones.

As a result of these unofficial attempts to cheer up the drab uniforms there were often snap inspections to check for deviations from the standard. The Immobiles were often caught out as these girls, living at home, would often be unable to acquire the article of clothing they needed in a hurry.

The food was never up to the standards to which most of the girls were accustomed. However, examples of menus served on one camp have been left for us to judge if complaints were justified. Here they are:

Stews. Sausages. Cottage pie made from bully beef.
Unsalted potatoes. Half cooked and gritty tapioca without sugar.
Biscuits. Rice with tea leaves, etc. in it. Slabs of bread and jam. Tea.

It would appear from this list that the major and common, fault lay more in inefficient supervision in the cook-house before the food was cooked, and the cooks themselves being insufficiently trained to prepare meals for large numbers. These complaints coupled with, in 1918, a great shortage of cooks and an equally great demand from the R.A.F. for their services, decided the W.R.A.F. to institute its first School, of Cookery, which was based at Berridge House, which opened in October 1919.

Berridge House was an independent unit within the W.R.A.F., the Commanding Officer, or Administrator, as she was known, being responsible only to the Air Ministry. Three large kitchens were equipped for training, each under the command of an Assistant Administrator. Each course was of two weeks duration followed by an examination, the successful cooks being awarded a certificate. The members and air mechanics who received these trained cooks subsequently rejoiced. Unsuccessful candidates were given another chance at the discretion of the C.O.

Such was the success of this course that the establishment was expanded to include courses for P.T. Instructors, Mess Orderlies, Domestics and Patrols in its curriculum. In December the original school was renamed W.R.A.F. School of Instruction.

In many units, working long and hard on a surprising variety of technical tasks, skilled and semi-skilled members, either service or 'on-the-job' trained, or bringing their own special skills, gave the W.R.A.F. the solid base of work output achieved which was to be such a dominant feature in favour of its reforming in 1938. The members set high standards for their daughters.

The W.R.A.F., in common with other women's services, had its own military patrols to keep a disciplinary eye on its members. A stringent standard was laid down and kept by those who volunteered for this unenviable, but necessary task. The job of these girls was to see that the high standards of the W.R.A.F. were maintained in the public eye and be seen themselves as examples.

The patrol members had to be young, under 23 on enlistment, fit and good at games, and be tactful in dealing with members of their service in the pursuit of their jobs. This was to patrol the W.R.A.F. camps and all public places used by members, who were not allowed to smoke or drink in pubs and bars, or be seen loitering—which created a false impression — and the patrols enforced these regulations. The patrols had to see that all local or standing orders were carried out, escort prisoners, meet drafts, escort visitors and if necessary supervise the carrying out of minor punishments. All the girls were not angels.

The only distinguishing marks worn by the patrols was a dark blue armband with the words 'W.R.A.F. Patrols'. When on duty they usually patrolled in pairs.

Minor breaches of discipline were often dealt with by Hostel or Technical Administrators by stopping leave or restricting privileges. Serious disciplinary charges were dealt with by the General Officer Commanding personally, referring only to the Commandant if he thought it necessary. From these cases the defendant, if not satisfied, could appeal to the Air Council within 14 days. Subsequent decisions by the Air Council were final.

Some charges were treated on an entirely different plane. A member could be prosecuted under the Defence of the Realm Act (D.O.R.A.) on the authority of the Air Council. For example, if she was:

Absent from duty without leave or lawful excuse.

Refusing or wilfully neglecting to perform any of the duties allotted to her.

Wilfully impeding or delaying the due performance of any work on or in connection with which she may be employed.

With little synthetic amusement available in those days, social entertainment was limited and usually of the do-it-yourself variety, enlivened by the station dances and shows and invitations to functions.

At work, during the tea and dinner breaks, the members generally provided their own amusement; one popular form was the reading of cards by the resident fortune teller. She was listened to with rapt attention as she forceast the tall, dark men, the hint of fame, the affair of marriage. In their own rest room, or hut on the station, as a break from routine, or bound to the station by bad weather or a chronic shortage of cash, the girls often held impromptu dances, spoiled only the lack of male partners. For it was strictly forbidden to invite men to their quarters. But when one considered that the girls wore army type boots, dancing the Lancers must been a bit of hazard for the spectators let alone the partner.

It was rather hard on the girls, too, when they went to shows, or were invited to dances, as regulations insisted that all members had be in their huts for roll call. Many a male partner must have been browned off at being abruptly left in mid-dance.

Along with social entertainment, participation in sport was enthusiastically entered into. Most of the women taking part found the opportunity to express themselves in sport, so often frowned on in their homes as 'not the thing'. It was found that the women of those days were not keen on solo sports, possibly because of the political flavour of those times towards emancipation of women. In any case, the individual coaching of women was a new art.

Team events was a different kettle of fish. This gave them the opportunity to prove they could compete with the best in the most practical way, for example, competing as a representative team in R.A.F. and Inter-Service Athletic meetings.

At station level the fun of joining in games was the thing, playing the traditional women's games of netball and hockey. As a fun break they were often challenged to a game of cricket by the airmen who, to help even up the disparity of skills, played left-handed. Presumably left handed airmen played right-handed! The resultant game must have been hilarious and provided some of the light hearted relief needed as an antidote in those grim times.

WRAF pushing out what looks like a Bristol Scout in 1918. IWM.

Chapter 6
The R.A.F. Rebuilds

The Great War was over. The airmen were going home. They had had enough of hardships, long hours, squalid conditions, mud, dust and blood. They had gladly endured the conditions to gain victory. Now they wanted to get back home and resume the life of peace they had known.

The majority of airmen were totally unaware of the part they had played in the rising concept of the new strategy—air power. Most accepted their status, thinking the aircrew were all important. Which, up to a point they were, but even aircrew needed serviceable aircraft; both types were complementary.

Demobilisation was geared to the rapid discharge of the millions of men and handful of women who had so valiantly served and fought. To handle this flood of impatient manpower, numbers of boys and men under training were switched to clerical duties and posted to former recruiting depots, such as Blandford and Crystal Palace.

Demobilisation procedure involved the clerks in much form and document filling, all necessary records for their return to civilian life. The beginnings of the modern disease of 'forms for everything' is apparent in the number required for each man, six in all.

After the initial euphoria of the coming of peace the need was to build up the Royal Air Force. Despite the fact that the Great War was over and most major powers were fast reducing their armed forces, Britain was engaged in the Russian misadventure and was quickly embroiled in operations in Afghanistan, Egypt, Somaliland, Iraq and Kurdistan. Because of these brush war commitments the R.A.F. was forced to retain the four year men to the limit of their engagement as a temporary stopgap. At the war's end the R.A.F. comprised a small nucleus of other ranks (O.R.'s) serving on regular engagements, and a very large number of Hostilities Only (H.O.) men.

Rebuilding the greatest air force of its time, was a task that required a man of iron will and foresight, with ability and the term of office needed to accomplish the job. That man was available in Sir Hugh Trenchard, to whom the Government of the day gave the necessary power.

The Royal Air Force had played a major role in the victory of the Allies over Germany. Now, in peace, it was to be involved in another battle — that of survival — which, while not as bloody, was equally as savage. Sir Hugh Trenchard now began the final phase of his service career which was to make him immortal. His 'finest hour' was to last for many years, as he fought his running battles against the First Sea Lord, Chief of the Imperial General Staff and the Treasury, to keep the R.A.F. in being.

Broadly, his objectives were to:
Keep the R.A.F. an independent service
Raise the standards of training and efficiency
Develop and foster an Air Force spirit.

To achieve these ends his proposals were to:

Create an Air Force Staff College and Cadet College
Introduce a Central Flying School
Introduce short service commissions
Create an apprenticeship scheme for boy mechanics.

It is the last item with which this Chapter is concerned.

The Air Council, guided by his dedicated hand, began its task of creating a peace time Air Force that was to be the envy of the military aviation world and a source of comfort to many thousands. To create the famous R.A.F. esprit de corps they began by retaining in service a number of famous war time squadrons, and they introduced the boy apprenticeship scheme.

Trenchard's avowed intention of having the finest trained air and ground crews ensured that instruction would be first class. However, it would take 3-5 years before the apprentices would begin to make their presence felt on the squadrons and depots. During those years the service was going to have to rely on men service; those already on war engagements, re-engagements and new recruits. The men service was the wholemeal bread upon which the apprenticeship scheme was the butter. The R.A.F. was desperately short of skilled men but it wanted the best, and in fact began to immediately raise the standards of quality and entry of its other ranks.

Airmen re-enlisting would receive any existing bonus being issued to the R.A.F. of the Occupation Forces. In the question of bounties this was on a sliding scale according to the airman's term of engagement:

For 2 years — £20 payable in three increments of £6.67p (£6.13.4d)
For 3 years — £40 payable in four sums of £10
For 4 years — £50 payable in five sums of £10 at approximately yearly intervals.

Extra leave entitlement was also offered as a further inducement to re-enlist. A final factor, important so far as the R.A.F. was concerned, was that no airman could purchase his discharge.

The diversity of trades then considered necessary for the R.A.F. of 1919 were:

Technical

Acetylene welder	Armourer	Blacksmith
Boat builder	Camera repairer	Carpenter
Coppersmith	Draughtsman	Driver, motor boat
Driver, petrol	Driver, steam	Electrician
Fitter, aero engine	Fitter, general	Fitter, M.T.
Instrument repairer	Kite balloon telephonist	Millwright
Machinist	Magneto repairer	Moulder
Motor body builder	Motor boat coxswain	Pattern maker
Rigger, aeroplane	Packer	Painter
Photographer	Propeller maker	Vulcaniser
Rigger, airship	Tinsmith and sheet	Upholsterer
Turner	metal worker	Hydrogen worker
Winch driver and	Wireless operator	
fitter	Wireless mechanic	
Fitter, jig and tool maker		

Non Technical

Assistant armourer	Blacksmith's striker	Butcher
Caterer	Cook	Coppersmith's mate
Deckhand	Fabric worker	Hospital orderly
Labourer	Motor cyclist	Packer's mate
Seaplane wader	Shoemaker	Tailor
Telephone operator		

Clerks, Storemen and Administrative

Batman	Clerk, general	Clerk, pay
Clerk, shorthand typist	Clerk, stores	

After four and a quarter years of a war with the greatest killing rate in history to that date, this particular recruiting drive, mistimed to come in the demobilisation period, was not a success.

Only 1,106 men enlisted in the first two months, of which 243 were technical tradesmen. Some trades were impossible to fill. For example, Drivers, M.T. were 2,500 short of establishment and civilian drivers were employed as a stop gap, a state of affairs which lasted until the next war. Another example of the shortage of skilled tradesmen was given

Three recruits to the new post war RAF at Halton North Camp. Note that the uniform still has RNAS cap badges, button-up belts, and slacks with turn ups.

F. Marchant.

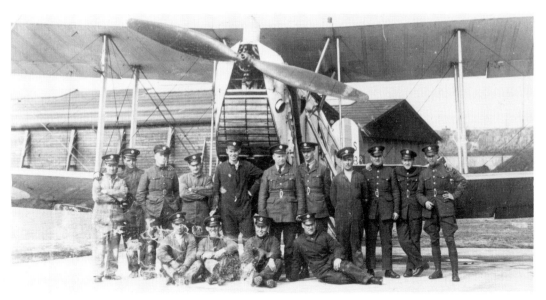

Airmen of a towed target flight based at RAF Gosport pose in front of a Blackburn torpedo bomber, about 1926. F. Marchant.

in the maintenance and repair of Rolls-Royce engines, of which there were stocks for 4-5 years. There were so few airmen competent to service these engines that the work had to be contracted back to the parent company. This set a precedent for future policy.

Recruits began as Aircraftsmen (A.C.2) and rates of pay were the latest, plus war bonus, which ranged from 1/8d (8p) for a technical Leading Aircraftsman (L.A.C.) to 9d (3½p) for a Boy. Periods of service were later set at:

    4 years with 8 years Reserve
    6 years with 6 years Reserve
    8 years with 4 years Reserve

A DH10 crashes at Abu Siren, Egypt, 1920 as a result of port engine cutting on take-off, a fault to which these aircraft were prone. F. Marchant.

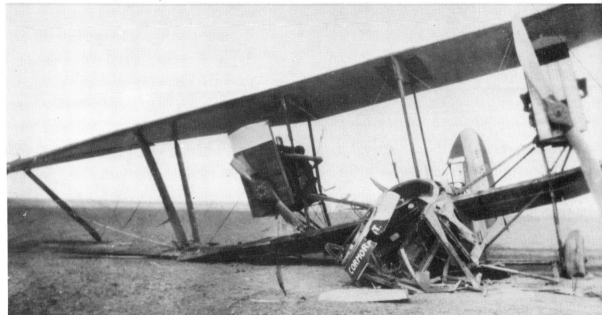

Potential recruits were sent to Halton for medical, trade test and, if successful, attestation. Those who failed the Selection Board had three choices: A.C.2 Administrative, A.C.2 Non-Technical, or were sent home. A month's disciplinary course followed on the same station, after which the non-technical men were posted to their various units. Technical men would change their huts to do a course in the Training School, still on the same camp.

A Siemens-Schuckart D3 (160 hp Siemens-Halske Sh3 rotary) of Jasta 15 found by the Occupation Forces 1919. Note 'ground movement' wheels and aircraft in hangar. G. Hawlett.

As the R.A.F. absorbed new recruits and began to recover from the effects of the demobilisation it also began a long overdue revision of its trade structure. Many trades, necessary for the past war, were pruned out.

Pay was also stabilised after the war, when it is interesting to note it was virtually the same as the Air Battalion rates of 1912, and remained stable until well into the Second World War. In addition to normal trade pay an erk could increase his daily rate if he was eligible for non-substantive pay, which was given for possession of certain qualifications or for performing special duties.

An air gunner 6d (2½p), and a service policeman 6d—1/-(2½-5p), received this daily rate when authorised on establishment. An A.C.H. G.D. airman on sanitary duties was rewarded with 4d (1½p) a day for his unpleasant duties. When teaching, a schoolmaster was awarded twice as much as the A.C.H. G.D. On the rare occasion when an interpreter was required to ease communications between guest and host the interpreter was entitled to 1/- (5p) an hour up to a maximum of 5 hours after which the rate was reduced.

In 1919 the standard kit was two each grey Army shirts, grey socks, long woollen underpants, woollen vests, a khaki cardigan, two pair 'ammo' boots, a pair of canvas shoes, a khaki 'dog collar' tunic and a pair of slacks. Nothing fitted or was tailored. Cap badges were similar to Naval P.O.'s, with an albatross instead of the anchor; some airmen like D. B. Waight, were issued with three cap badges, one each of R.F.C., R.N.A.S. and R.A.F.! When a blue uniform was issued it originally had black buttons and included the famous, or notorious, pantaloons and puttees, a baggy type of breeches which looked terrible in their original state, and were laced up at the knees before puttees were put on.

The puttees were wound round the leg from ankle upward to knee and taped in place. Because the puttees were not cut on a bias they presented a stepped appearance when worn. Also they were not conducive to good blood circulation if tight. The pantaloons were often illegally tailored to present a smart winged appearance, which on inspections were liable to be rejected, which meant their owners faced the cost of a new pair or being charged with illegal alteration.

* * * * *

A.C. Smith joined in August 1921 from Portsmouth, as a result of a recession in the boat building trade and listening to the tales of ex-R.F.C. mechanics. He found joining the men service quite easy, the entrance exams comprising an oral test, a short essay and a maths paper. The airmen who passed the test were accepted for trade training, others who did not make the standard were—according to Smith—offered Aircraft hand General Duties with the implication that refusal would mean that they would have to pay their own way home. It is difficult to believe that this was so. The attestation was at Uxbridge but Smith and his new friends stayed only a few days there before going to Manston; this was before Uxbridge became the recruiting Mecca.

DH9A's of 3 Squadron on the aerodrome at Bereznik North Russia August 1919. IWM.

At Manston the new recruits were put on disciplinary training, fatigue and guard duties while waiting to commence the course. On his first ever full guard duty Smith encountered a typical Senior N.C.O. of the old school. He was detailed for No. 1 post, main gate, and was, he thought doing well on his first stint, when a certain W. O. 'Timber' Woods, ex-guardsman, walked past on his way to his quarters. The W.O. turned into the guardroom and Smith overheard him asking the guard commander, 'who was the bloody fool outside?' Smith stamped his way vigorously through his stint but it was not enough. The next morning he was charged with being slovenly on duty and awarded three extra 24 hour guards.

Discipline was strict but despite his first brush with authority on guard Smith reckoned it did them no harm. True words. Regular P.T. was taken seriously and one lanky lad who liked running 'failed' to hear a recall signal on one P.T. session from the instructor, but was back before tea.

As vacancies became available recruits were sent to the particular workshop or hangar to commence technical training and were issued with tool kits and a book on carpentry, which might have been the same 'The Aeroplane Speaks' with which A.C. Waight was also issued. Among the training aircraft was Avro 504K, Bristol F2B, DH9A., Sopwith Snipe and Salamander, Nieuport Nighthawk and a Fairey wooden hulled flying boat.

Lectures on subjects other than basic workshop were normally held in the large hangar, with classes grouped around a blackboard and sitting on their issue toolboxes and surrounded by the training aeroplanes. Passing out from the carpentry course meant the ordeal of an oral, a written and practical examination. The practical tests were a wood joint and the perennial wire and thimble splice (usually from 5 cwt 7-strand control cable). Smith passed out in March 1923 and was posted to 5 F.T.S. Shotwick (later Sealand) near Chester.

A.C. L. G. Gardner enlisted in June 1924 and was posted to Uxbridge where life for raw recruits not yet 'squadded' was pretty fearsome in those long gone days. When in the canteen they were warned not to mix with any uniform staff but to keep to the civilian party. '... the first time in my new hut was murder ... lights out at 21.30; in the darkness came the snores, groans and moans of the lost tribe ...' He lay on a sagging spring bed under threadbare blankets with his head on a hard packed bolster.

On his enlistment interview Gardner had had what was for him (this was 1924) the embarrassment of appearing nude for the first time, in front of three doctors, '... after what seemed ages and dozens of acrobatics, I was told to dress and wait downstairs for results. ...'

Practically every recruit had the same experience when they reported for the first time at the recruiting office. Waiting around for a few hours, surreptitiously eyeing each other, striking up aquaintances, drinking tea — and waiting. Then the group of lads, expectant, eager or apprehensive, under the control of an N.C.O. were walked to the railway station.

A.C. Taylor gave up four years of his apprenticeship as a sheet metal worker to join the R.A.F. in May 1925, and was sent to West Drayton for educational and trade tests and then on to Uxbridge for the rigours of recruit training. From the recruit depot he went on to Manston for a 12 months trade course.

The Manston syllabus allowed one day per week at school, the rest of the week was on workshop practice, which included geometry, development by the triangulation method, radial line and parallel line. Taylor admits it was stiff work and not everyone mastered all the syllabus but all the course had a go. Complete exercise articles were marked with number and name, displayed on a wall and judged at the end of a phase. Among the articles made were pots and pans, square and round funnels, brazed joints and copper pipework. A petrol tank was made with filler cap, sump, drain cock and baffles. Another exercise was a complete radiator of the honeycomb type with tubes from an old car radiator. The rad. was removed from the car, separated, re-turned and rebuilt in a block.

The General Strike occurred whilst he was at Manston and the airmen were kept on standby but were not called.

*   *   *   *   *

Knowing that for many years he would have a small Air Force, Sir Hugh Trenchard decided to concentrate on making the R.A.F. into an elite force with emphasis on the highest quality of flying and technical training. Should the service be required to expand rapidly he wanted to have a cadre of highly efficient technical officers and N.C.O.'s. His approach was to develop a boy service to the ultimate standard, technically, educationally and mentally.

Boy service was not a new idea. It was of long standing in the Navy and Army and had been introduced into the R.F.C.

As a measure of the need for imposing economies that faced Trenchard, a brief review of the Air Estimates of that period might give some idea of the tightness of the strings around the national purse.

It had been decreed by Lloyd George's Government that, based on calculated assumptions, there would be no major wars within the next 10 years. This enabled the Treasury to keep defence commitments to a minimum. It also ensured that the Services would have little new aircraft and equipment made available to them.

The only flurry of panic spending that did occur to spoil this neat solution was in 1923-24, after it was discovered that France had been spending many millions to build up a large Air Force of 3,000 aircraft. With Britain's natural reaction to any military goings-on on the other side of the Channel it was policy to assume that France could pose a threat, so the Government authorised the raising of eight new squadrons — which took many years to materialise. Money suddenly became available and the Air Estimates jumped from £15,666,500 in 1922 to £18,605,000 in 1923-24 and £21,445,000 in 1925.

After the mild crisis they then dropped back to the uneconomic average level of £16-20 million for the next 10 years and despite the brush wars in which Britain seemed almost continually to be engaged, no incentive was shown to pump more money into the services. Successive Governments constantly brought forward the commencing date of the 10 year rule, applying its principle as an excuse for not developing the services. Until 1933.

Despite all this, Trenchard showed his foresight by concentrating on what he considered the single most important factor in his long term rebuilding programme — recruiting the right type of man. He reasoned correctly that with enthusiastic volunteers from a higher social level than was normal for the services in those days, and with the right training, he could produce a technical minded, adaptable man, who retained his enthusiasm in the R.A.F. and who could be relied on to operate on his own initiative. For this type Trenchard decided that a selective boy service would give him the time to train the new airmen of the post war R.A.F. into the elite force that he envisaged.

The preliminary proposals for recruitment was the subject of a leaflet issued to Local

Education Authorities (L.E.A.) in October 1919. Boys would be between 15 and 16 and be trained for three years. On reaching the age of 18 the boy was expected to sign on for eight years. In addition to the method of entry by open competition, a system of limited competition held twice yearly was introduced by the L.E.A.'s or governing bodies of certain schools and associations. Open competition exams became a yearly event with L.E.A.'s providing high quality recruits.

Exams for the 1920 intakes were held in the preceding November at Aberdeen, Belfast, Birmingham, Cardiff, Dublin, Edinburgh, Exeter, Glasgow, Hull, Leeds, London, Manchester, Newcastle, Norwich and Southampton and included papers on maths, experimental science, English composition and general matters. Boys had to be sons of British born parents.

By the 1921 competition the scheme had settled down. The boys were now required to sign on for 10 years man service plus two on reserve. A total of eight hours per week were devoted to study of educational subjects, English language and literature, history, geography, civics, practical mathmatics, general science and drawing. Nine hours were given to physical subjects, drill, physical training and organised games.

The religious instruction was also in good hands, with Chaplains of several denominations being appointed. But leave was not as freely organised, being restricted to the periods organised by the School, unless exceptional circumstances warranted otherwise. The rate of pay was 1/6d (7½p) per day up to age 18, when it was doubled.

The psychological touch was that the boys should not be cajoled by the usual recruiting publicity, but that they would want to put 12 years of their life on the line. And by insisting on a stiff educational and physical exam Trenchard ensured he got the best.

Boys successfully passing the course would pass out as Leading Aircraftsmen (later modified) with a certain number of exceptional boys selected for an additional six months course for promotion to Corporal. From the latter a number would be selected for commissioning to the Cadet College at Cranwell.

In the words of the Air Council:- Only those boys would be nominated who, in opinion of their Local Education Authority were suitable in character, able to undertake the entrance examination and possessed the energy, keenness and initiative essential to a successful career in the Royal Air Force.

While the groundwork for the boys training scheme was being laid, negotiations were in progress to turn Halton into an established apprentice school. The Air Council applied to the Lords Commissioners of H.M. Treasury for permission and cash to build accommodation on the site of the wartime school at Halton, accepting that this was a heavy item of expenditure and pointing out that the R.A.F. had no permanent peace time barracks, having been born in war. To help even further to make the boys competitive with their civilian brothers, they would be encouraged to take recognised engineering exams and gain technical certificates.

Halton became No. 1 School of Technical Training and was geared up for three-year courses and staffed by 35 officers, 500 N.C.O.'s and airmen and 100 civilian instructors. With the urgency of war removed the syllabus planners were able to adopt a more leisurely approach to technical training. They deleted obsolete subjects and included others which had been previously curtailed. The latest advances in aircraft technology were studied and the lessons incorporated into maintenance subjects, i.e. methods of construction and repair schemes.

Fitters servicing Napier Lion engine. MOD.(Crown Copyright reserved).

Every effort was made to give the men and the boys the best that was available within means and circumstance.

* * * * *

On a September morning in 1925 young Ken Marshall left his Kingston-on-Thames home and, accompanied by a proud father who had been a long serving rifleman, travelled to Baker Street station to join a new intake of would-be apprentices for Halton. The batch of boys, mostly of middle class background, entrained for Wendover, arriving in the early evening. Like the great majority of recruits their first real impression of the R.A.F. was through their first meal and bed. In 1925 the latter were of the hard 'Mac Donald' variety.

Selected for training as Fitter Aero Engine, Marshall and his new class mates of 6 Entry were put under the administrative control of Squadron Sergeant Major 'Toby' Farlow who proved the point that N.C.O.'s were specially selected, '... Tall, thin, slightly bent with service, he was a strict administrator of the rules, but on the other hand no boy went to him when in trouble and was turned away ...' Insofar as their trade was concerned the School did its utmost to have permanent instructors, each taking a clas of 10-15 boys. The instructor stayed with his class for the first year, which was devoted to foot drill, basic workshop practice and theoretical application.

The second and third years were applied to aircraft and service requirements, workshop application involving welding, brazing and blacksmith work and the study of ever increasing complexity in maths. On the square, rifle drill was introduced but in the last two years the real emphasis was on the technical side.

111

The instructors, as Marshall maintains and most ex-apprentices endorse, '... were experienced R.A.F., N.C.O.'s and ex-service civilian instructors. I feel that we were taught to a very high standard which set the pace for the rest of the service. Some said it was too high, but I think the ability of the R.A.F. to expand its maintenance organisation for war was borne on the backs of the ex-apprentices and through them the people who taught them. ...' An accurate statement. The eight hours a week on educational subjects were under civilian teachers who all held a degree in their specialist subjects and were specially selected for their personality and practical engineering knowledge'.

*   *   *   *   *

Accommodation at Halton was inadequate for the 3,000 boys per year under training that was planned, so until new buildings were ready R.A.F. Cranwell became an overspill station for the trainees. To this No. 2 School of Technical Training went A.C. G. F. McConnell who had enlisted under the 1921 Competition.

The first nine months was devoted to basic workshop practice, the syllabus included use of tools, filing and a working knowledge of allied trades (blacksmithing, machine shop practice, metallurgy, welding, brazing, etc.) Much emphasis was put on accurate filing, with such exercises as male and female cubes, hexagons, dovetails and so on. This was necessary in view of the amount of hand fitting that was needed on aircraft and vehicles, for in those days airmen were enlisted and trained as craftsmen to do a craftsman's job. The system of repair by replacement had not yet become service procedure and damage was repaired by tradesmen—professionally.

Sgt. Hawkes at R.A.F. Upavon in 1926 in uniform of the day and wearing WW1 ribbons. Hawkes.

After basic training the boys were offered a choice of trades on the fitting side, Fitter Aero Engine; Fitter Driver Petrol or Fitter Armourer. McConnell became Fitter D.P. and went into workshops for a first class training under extremely competent N.C.O.'s.

The trainee Fitter D.P.'s were taught on Leyland heavy lorries and Crossley light tenders. Driving instruction was given about one day in 10 under a F/Sgt. Joe Hammond. Along with the practical and theoretical lessons (engines, automobile engineering) educational needs were taken care of by a curriculum which was designed to further develop the boys as tradesmen.

McConnell found the sports facilities were good but this may have been due to the close proximity of the Cadet College. Cranwell also boasted the rarity of a swimming pool which was highly popular. Compulsory sport was almost always cross country running, not very popular on a cold, wet and blustering day. The highlights of the trainees life at Cranwell was centred on a weekly visit to Sleaford, the nearest village, with a visit to the cinema and high tea in the local cafe which cost around 5/- (25p).

From the boys pay half was retained for 'credits' which went towards their leave and barrack room charges. On reaching the official service age of 18 the 10/6d (52½p) weekly pay was doubled, but half was still retained. Money however, at that time did have real spending power and boys were even able to make an allotment home.

A paper was issued in 1922 detailing the expenditure of the Boys Wing at Cranwell on training aids and equipment, which revealed a few interesting examples and comparisons. It was estimated that the overall cost per boy was £262 per year; the figure was derived from dividing the number of boys for 1921/22 (1,045) into the total cost of expenditure and depreciation (£274,437).

The value of aeroplanes and engines at the school is informative in its revelation of the difference in cost between an operational and an instructional aeroplane. For example: a complete 504K was valued at £851; two instructional 504K's at £16 total. Likewise an operational Bristol Fighter cost £1,600 but instructional types were valued at £16 each.

It was the same thing in the cost of aero engines. A serviceable 100 h.p. Monosoupape cost £633; a training engine £6. A Rolls-Royce Eagle VIII was valued at £1,375 complete but a training engine cost £14. There were some interesting figures given in the Articles-in-Use Schedule. The barracks were valued at £24,667, the machine and technical workshops £7,842 and the carpenters A.R.S. at £3,036. But the figure for the boys wing was only £19. The fitters shop was worth £3,148 while the Sergeants Mess and shoemakers were on a par at £62 and £43 respectively.

In one year the boys used up £11,950 of clothing against £2,297 for the airmen and were paid £76,041 against £41,716 for other ranks. Unintentional or not, one could assume from another set of figures that airmen were not too literate, for £548 was spent on the boy's library; the airmen received £6.

The boys also got quite dirty, the cleaning of their clothes and overalls costing £1,179, but the airmen got a little of their own back in a masochistic way by eating £100 of guards suppers.

The permanent buildings of course had a higher value with only 3% depreciation against 7½% for corrugated iron and wood construction buildings. For teaching and looking after boys that year the civilian educational staff were paid £8,644 — an average for each instructor of £445.

From the success of the apprentice scheme it appeared a natural extension to include an important non-technical trade, that of clerks, a trade vital to the organisation and administrative running of the R.A.F.; the authorities realised the importance of highly trained clerical staff.

The clerks training was run on the same lines as other boy entrant trades; entrance was by an exam, equally as severe as for the technical apprentice. Particularly ambiguous was the maths paper which, strangely, was strongly biased technically, with such subjects as Euclid, calculations of areas and volumes, algebra and trigonometry. The remainder of the exam followed apprentice practice and the course was for two years.

In 1925 the pay per day was:

Aircraftsman 2nd class	3/- (15p)
Aircraftsman 1st class	3/9 (19p)
Leading Aircraftsman	4/6 (23p)
Corporal	5/6 (28p)
Sergeant	7/- (35p)
Flight Sergeant	8/6 (43p)
Sergeant Major 2nd Class (This rank was abolished in 1938.)	9/6 (48p)
Sergeant Major 1st class (This rank became W.O. in 1938.)	10/6 (53p)

The first, general part of the course, was carried out at the R.A.F. Records Office at Ruislip. At the end of the period the top marked boys were selected for specialist training in pay and stores accounting and sent to Depots for further training. At the end of the course, recruits who had shown special aptitudes, and were recommended by the C.O., were selected for an advanced course to take them to the rank of Corporal. These were future commissioned officer material.

Another boy trade which ran on similar lines was that of Electrical Fitters, the boys being recruited on similar terms and trained at Flower Down, near Winchester. The course was three years, and the school staff comprised 40 officers, 350 N.C.O.'s and airmen and 10 civilian instructors.

By 1934 the apprentice and boy clerk schemes were well established and virtually unaltered from the original conditions. The intake of boys had been widened to include the Commonwealth countries, Australia, New Zealand and South Africa. The boys sat the exam in their own country but if successful they had to pay their own passage to the U.K.

The apprentice trades had been extended to include Fitter Armourers for a small number of apprentices who, having completed the first year, might wish to specialise in this skill. Also a new trade had been introduced, Fitter II, which combined the trades of Fitter II Airframe and Fitter II Engine and was originally meant to specialise in maintenance. The scheme was altered by the requirements of war to Fitter I, able to do both the work of Fitter Aero and Metal Rigger.

Because of the number of boys who had sat and passed the exams but could not find a place at Halton, the Air Ministry extended the apprentice scheme and introduced the Boy Entrant scheme in the early 1930's and offered them training as armourers, photographers and wireless operators. The boys signed on for nine years from the age of 18, with a limited number of selected boys allowed to re-engage for 24 years. The scheme followed closely that of the apprentices except that the training period was shorter, the trades were Group 2 and there was little possibility of being earmarked for rapid promotion or a commission.

But the scheme was successful and many boys who would otherwise have been lost to the R.A.F. were now given their opportunity; the three trade courses were trained at:

Armourers — Air Armament School, R.A.F. Eastchurch
Photographers — School of Photography, R.A.F. South Farnborough
Wireless Operators — Electrical and Wireless School, R.A.F. Cranwell.

With a nation-wide awakening to the merits of a Royal Air Force apprenticeship and the kind of life the R.A.F. could give, letters began to arrive in their scores at recruiting offices throughout the country. For the Boy Apprenticeship scheme was a success from the beginning. It still continues.

* * * * *

F/Lt. Ward, an ex-clerk gives an interesting sidelight in an incident he describes. '... During the summer of 1935, I was in the Accounts Section at R.A.F. Halton. The apprentices of No. 1 School of T.T. were paid only 3/- per week of their pay-the rest was compulsorarily saved for them until they went home on leave. Pay parade was held in one of the workshops and required a large amount of silver (one florin and one shilling per boy) and this had to be carried through the workshop to the pay table.

'I can well remember the occasion when one of the large silver bags burst on the shoulder of the N.C.O. who was carrying it, and the silver cascaded all over the workshop floor around the various machines. It says much for the honesty and discipline of the apprentices that every single coin was returned to the pay table within minutes. These 15 and 16 year old lads of course passed out a few years later just in time for the start of World War 2 ...'

Deservedly, the apprenticeship and boy entrant schemes paid off. Almost all the boys of Halton, Farnborough, Eastchurch, Cranwell, Ruislip and Flowerdown that were in the R.A.F. at the outbreak of the Second World War, if not already so, were subsequently promoted or commissioned. The high standards of technical training they brought to units, once they had 'settled in' and gained experience paid great dividends, for despite the stringent financial policy of 'make do and mend' the 'ex-brats' reimbursed the cost of their training many times over.

Many ex-apprentices and boys became aircrew and did just as well in the air as their compatriots on the ground, many reaching high rank, some even air rank. For they had this one common bond, a genuine dedication to, and for, the Royal Air Force. No direct entry airman, however they might denigrate the 'quick promotion' that was part of the ex-brats heritage, will deny that the R.A.F. was able to expand smoothly and efficiently as war became imminent because this cadre of highly trained tradesmen slipped smoothly and efficiently into the positions of responsibility. Sir Hugh Trenchard was to be fully vindicated in his policy.

Chapter 7
Station Routine

When the great day arrived in the lives of the trainees — the completion of their training — and postings were put up on the notice boards, conversation became a buzz of excited speculation. Where was the unit? What did it do? What aeroplanes did it fly? What sort of a Depot was it? Who was the S.W.O.? Where was the nearest town? Who was the C.O.?

Posting day was one of suppressed emotion. The long hard grind of training was over. The concentrated technical instruction, intermingled with parades, inspections, fatigues and guard duties, was behind them. As they gazed around room, hut or billet at the spit and polish of burnished coal bins, polished lino, blackleaded stoves, kit lockers scrubbed and displaying meticulously laid out brushes, mugs, knives and forks, there must have been some emotional thoughts. There were. To get away from it all. Perhaps the only emotion shown was in their farewells to their friends who were not going with them.

Popular stations in the U.K. between the wars were near London; Northolt, Tangmere, Kenley, Martlesham Heath. The most disliked, those that represented isolation, such as Wick for a Southerner or Mountbatten for a Scotsman. It has been a more than coincidental saying in the R.A.F. that if one applied for a preferential posting near home it was an almost certain guarantee for a posting to the opposite side of the country.

Whenever possible, postings were a group affair but quite often an airman would have to travel alone in full kit, carrying one or more kitbags across country, hoping that he would arrive at the nearest point to his new station in time to catch any service transport and arrive before the cookhouse was closed. Invariably he arrived too late.

At his station he would be shown to a strange hut or room and a bed on which to dump a kit. Under the interested stares of the occupants he would begin to unpack, but if he was experienced he would unpack the minimum, for it was probable that on reporting to the S.W.O.'s office in the morning he would be allocated another hut. The R.A.F.'s esprit de corps being what it was the newcomer would soon be made to feel at home and be given all the local information. If there was still time he would probably go, or be invited, to the canteen and have a long awaited meal and perhaps a few beers. Conversation soon flowed. As a new recruit he might be kidded a bit on the (supposed) fearsome character of certain N.C.O.'s but usually he was given sympathetic treatment.

His canteen meal would probably be sausages (bangers, dogs or growlers) with mash, or steak and kidey pie with veg. which with tea would cost around 6d (2½p), a pint of canteen beer would set him back about 4d (approx, 1½p) and taste, according to his new friends, nowhere as good as the local brew.

Every station had its own Station Warrant Officer who was, and is, the senior Disciplinarian 'other rank'. He was responsible only to the Station Commander and Adjutant for all administrative matters pertaining to discipline, parades, guards, station

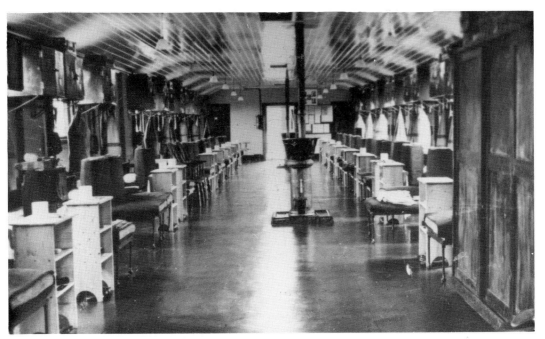

A typical barrack hut of the early 1930's, in this case at RAF Manston which was used as a Technical Training School. S/Ldr Grout.

hygiene and the general running of the station. He was a man of great power and the station's reputation as a happy one, or otherwise, depended largely on his temperament. The new man would report to him.

Having officially arrived, the new man would report to his Flight or Section disciplinary N.C.O., who introduced him to the N.C.O. in charge. That N.C.O., usually a Flight Sergeant, had a chat with the new arrival, after which he was kitted out with necessary tools and overalls. He was then detailed to his new job. It was the usual practice to try and place the newcomer under the wing of an experienced airman if the new arrival was fresh from a training school.

By comparison with the years immediately following the Second World War, the conditions and pressures of the years 1918-33 might possibly be said to be much easier but that is a relative supposition. Both periods had similarities; traumatic in the sense of demobilisation; the country, after being geared for war, trying to get into the routine of peace; the need to rebuild the services from manpower which had the natural post-war antipathy to the services, and the ever present world-wide unsettled conditions.

Having said that, the reader must not think that slackness prevailed, far from it. Working hours were often long and hard, particularly in the summer, or during the numerous war exercises, but normal routine work began with a working parade on the square at 0800 hours and finished at 1630. How much work was put in during those hours depended on the weather, flying programme and the amount of aircraft unserviceability. It has often been said that the pre-war R.A.F. was the 'best flying club in the world', which may well have been true for the flying types, but was certainly inapplicable to the ground crew. They were the servants of that club. A typical routine day of the late 1920's would be this:

Reveille was normally around 0630, with the necessarily noisy arrival of the Orderly Sergeant and the Corporal stamping through the huts or rooms arousing the men with raucous shouts or banging a stick on the stove, and uttering threats about 'last man up would be charged, etc., etc.' There would follow the usual rush or crawl to the ablutions, hoping, if it was winter, that the water would be hot.

Breakfast was usually 0700 to 0730 and was plain and wholesome, or unappetising, according to one's stomach's point of view, or the cook's temperament. After enjoying/dismissing the meal, untensils were cleaned and then it was back to a short concentrated period of each man carrying out his room job, cleaning windows, stoves, ablutions, spare bed spaces, and so on until, with all the Macdonalds (beds) in position and blankets folded correctly the room looked like a typical service room of the 1920's. The term Macdonald used for the rigid, two piece iron beds was because they, like the supposed characteristic of the Scots, had no give in them!

Then it was outside on parade by huts, or Flights, and marched to the parade ground to be sized and positioned by Senior N.C.O.'s until the S.W.O. took over. The parade commander would arrive and carry out an inspection on haircuts, shaves, cleanliness of boots and uniforms, the S.W.O. hard on his heels ready to take the names of any airman who offended the parade commander's standards.

After the inspection the C. of E. padre might hold a short service, but in case his religious background offended other suppliants, the Roman Catholics and Jews were ordered to fall out and stand on the edge of the parade ground, facing outward. Then followed a march past in Squadron or Flight order past the saluting base, the march being continued along to the place of work, where the airmen were dismissed.

After changing into their blue overalls the men took a quick look at the Flying Programme, and the aeroplanes would be given a Daily Inspection. The Form 535 would be signed by the tradesmen concerned and checked and cleared by a technical Senior N.C.O. of an aircraft trade.

With shouts of 'two-six', the rickety, corrugated-iron clad doors would be pushed noisily open along their tracks, ending with a rattling thump against the stops. Those aeroplanes detailed for flying would have their tails lifted and the skid lowered into a box fitted on a steerable wheeled trolley and pushed onto the tarmac, or grass, outside the Flight Commander's office.

Once lined up, any warlike stores required for an exercise would be fitted, practice bombs, ammunition, along with any special item such as cameras, or W/T sets. On these aeroplanes, where it could be done, the engines were started by swinging the propeller, the man on the end of the prop praying loudly that the fitter wouldn't make a balls of it by under or over doping the engine with the ki-gas pump and so give him a lot of hard and unnecessary work.

As engines became more powerful the job of swinging propellers against the higher cylinder compression became a muscle-wrenching and stomach pulling exercise. To ease the physical strain, first two and then three airmen were employed in chain formation to provide the power to pull the propeller over. All that power was applied through one set of fingers! Some variations were used, such as placing a stout bag over the propeller blade and pulling a rope attached to the bag. However, another positive solution was sought to

Bristol Fighter prop swinging by the chain method, the strain of which led to the development of the Hucks starter. MOD.(Crown Copyright reserved).

.... Hucks starter starting a Sopwith Snipe of 5 FTS. A major advance in starting high powered engines. MOD. (Crown Copyright reserved).

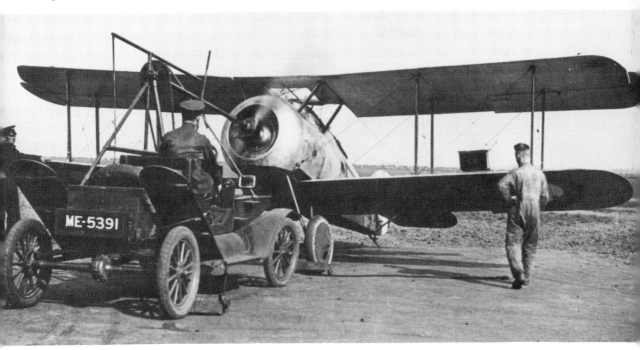

Sequence of removing a Short S8/8 Rangoon flying boat, of which only six were built, for major inspection or repair. Probably 210 Squadron at R.A.F. Pembroke Dock. Kevis.

120

cut out this often exhausting task; overseas, a Liberty engine in a DH9 would often have to be started in a 100°F plus temperature.

The inertia starter was only available to certain aircraft and to assist the starting of higher compression engines the Hucks starter was devised. This consisted of a built-up structure on a Model T Ford chassis, on which was mounted fore and aft along the top of the structure, a shaft driven by chain and clutch from the car engine. At the front end of the shaft was a dog clutch which, when the Hucks starter was driven up to the aeroplane, engaged with a similar dog on the propeller boss.

When all was ready the driver engaged the chain drive, the shaft spun the propeller until the engine fired, when the dog clutch automatically disengaged. The starter's use was restricted in its limited adjustment to the heights of different aeroplanes, and as a result was generally used only on single engined aircraft, or twins with low set engines. But it was a useful interim device which saved a great deal of physical effort and was looked on with some affection by the ground crew.

As the engines fired, blowing great puffs of rich black smoke from the exhausts, the quiet morning air became filled with their chattering clamour which settled into a steady roar as the fitters throttled them into a high rev rate to warm up as quickly as possible.

The aircrew would stroll out, unless a panic exercise was on, clad according to season or type of operation and clamber aboard, the pilot replacing the fitter, the rigger helping the pilot to secure himself to parachute and aeroplane by straps, Sutton harness and oxygen and W/T lines as applicable. Once settled the pilot signalled the ground crew to the tail, one to each side to bend over the tailplane, backs to the slipstream. The pilot 'opened up' the engine checking each magneto for a drop in revolutions and giving a brief burst to maximum revs.

The full power effect could then be seen as the aeroplane swayed and strained at the chocks, the ground crew pinned against the tail, the engine note now a deep bellow. As the engine was throttled back the ground crew quickly moved to the wheel chocks picking up the attaching ropes and watching the pilot. A criss-crossing wave of his hands and the ground crew pulled the chocks, quickly threw them behind the aircraft and ran to the wing tips.

To directional movements of the pilot's hands, and with helpful burst of engine power to assist control of the rudder and to help the airmen pulling and pushing on the wing tips, the aeroplane was taxied to the point where, with a dismissal by the pilot and an acknowledging salute by one of the airmen, it could proceed unassisted.

Back at the hangar, work would be continuing as other aircraft, grounded for periodic servicing, were thoroughly checked or those which were unserviceable as a result of malfunction, defect or damage, were put right. The hangar would be the scene of organised bustle, snatches of song occasionally breaking out above the generated noise of mechanical operations. At this period the fabric covered biplane was king and the air in the hangar would be redolent with the intoxicating scent of dope and fabric, oil and grease, a combination that was as a beautiful drug to the tradesmen of the day. Outside, when all immediate work was completed, and one's aircraft was in the air it was possible to lay on the grass and wait for its return with the nostalgic fragrance of new cut grass and the sweet, earthy smell in one's nostrils, the warm sun beating down creating a somnambulant state enhanced by the drowsy hum of an aeroplane droning across the blue sky, these were halcyon years, probably the 'Golden Years' to many.

When an aeroplane had been inspected and serviced, an aluminium black painted folding board was hung on the propeller boss; the facing side would read P.O.W. (initials for Petrol, Oil, Water) indicating the machine was ready for flight. If the aeroplane was unserviceable the board was reversed to show the letters U/S in red.

Inside the board was a Form 535, the first aeroplane servicing record. This form was ruled off with columns to show amounts of fuel, oil and water, initials of tradesmen who had carried out the servicing, and a column for checks by the N.C.O. in charge of trades and Flight. There was a page to show causes of unserviceability, the rectification work carried out and signatures of tradesmen carrying out the work. It was a most useful record bringing a regulated and planned procedure to aeroplane servicing. Minor and major inspections due were shown and flight time was recorded to keep a check of hours flown. The Form 535 became insufficient to record all the necessary servicing details as the aeroplane became more complex and was superseded by the Form 700.

The servicing cycles in the R.A.F. were regulated in hours flown for an aeroplane or airborne equipment, to miles run for an M.T. vehicle, and were scrupulously maintained. The general servicing cycle for aeroplanes and engines was 120 hours, working on 10 hours for a minor inspection up to a major at 120 hours, which was extended as aircraft became more reliable.

As each aircraft taxied from its position the time was noted down in a book by an airman of the watch located in the Watch Office overlooking the aerodrome. When the same aircraft returned, the time of placing the chocks in position was noted and the deducted times from these two figures constituted the flight time.

The ground crew of the departed aeroplanes would tidy up the chocks and other gear, clean their own aircraft's drip tray and, if they caught the eagle eye of the Sergeant, be detailed to other routine job consistent with keeping the flight in top operational and presentable shape. The latter description was liberally interpreted by the erks as 'bullshit', and might consist of painting, cleaning, greasing and oiling, marking out lines on the hangar floor for individual aircraft and ground equipment. The ground equipment was maintained impeccably; it had to be, it was invariably so old.

A general buzz of engines in the sky usually heralded returning aircraft. Airmen would move out of the hangar if they could, for the sight of a flight of biplanes landing was still exhilarating to men who had seen it over many years.

As each machine taxied near to the hangar it was met by its ground crew, who helped the pilot to taxi on to a probably crowded tarmac to the refuelling point. This was a moment of intense concentration as aircraft passed close to each other, prop whirling, as pilots endeavoured to park as closely to one another as possible. And mostly without any brakes. This was possibly why airmen of the day wore heavy boots that were studded and tipped, as they would be required to act as brakes at times. The possible spark hazard from those same boots seems to have been ignored.

Work and flying would continue until 1200 when the main party would be marched back to the domestic area to be dismissed. A few airmen might be left at the hangar to refuel late arrivals, or this might be done by the duty crew, or duty Flight.

In workshops, tradesmen followed a different routine, in that almost all were specialist trades not all directly concerned with aeroplanes and engines. The majority of their work was in station maintainance but sections were allocated for aeroplane and engine repair beyond the capabilities of the Flights. The hours of work were similar and instead of aeroplanes to manoeuvre they had workshop machines to operate, specialist equipment such as welding gear and forges, to maintain. The ancillary trades, wireless, armourers and electricians, usually had their own separate sections and their routine was closely allied to that of the hangar and workshops.

For the M.T. drivers, however, routine was quite different for, except for the standard deliveries and collections, they never could be sure of finishing work at the same time as the rest of the station. The drivers were often on a shift system to ensure that someone was always available to answer the call for collecting a new arrival or deliveries. The exception were the civilian drivers, of which there were usually a high proportion on each station because of the difficulty of maintaining an establishment in this trade.

In Station Headquarters, the clerical, administrative, pay and disciplinary trades were housed in permanent offices and did not move around so much as the technical trades. S.H.Q. usually kept strictly to their hours of commencing and finishing work. The exception to this rule were the Station Police, who followed a modified shift system with its own clear routine.

The police were responsible for the security of the station, prevention and detection of crime and the observance of the rules and regulations laid down in Station Standing Orders (S.S.O.'s). They patrolled the camp and in the evenings patrolled the nearest town and village, particularly at week-ends, when they would meet the train arrivals to dissuade disorderly conduct. It would be easy to spot an airman for he should be in uniform as only Senior N.C.O.'s were allowed out of camp in civilian clothes when off duty; regulations which remained in use until the early 1930's. Of course, not all airmen observed this rule and their detection depended on the sharp eye and accurate memory for a face of the service police.

On duty the police wore a white blancoed belt and white cap cover with, occasionally, white gaiters, which uniform gained them the name of 'snowdrop'. And this in the 1920's. Their guardroom would be spotless. As well it might, cleaned and polished daily by the sweat and endeavour of 'jankered' erks. It was also a mecca of bull in the full service

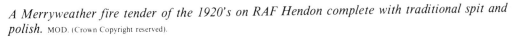

A Merryweather fire tender of the 1920's on RAF Hendon complete with traditional spit and polish. MOD. (Crown Copyright reserved).

meaning of that much used term. Linoleum floors would literally gleam, and to prevent even a speck of dust landing the police walked across it on pads of felt so maintaining its polish. Any airman who had the audacity to walk across that hallowed floor without pads became an instant enemy of society!

The stove would sit, black, smug and largely unused, ensconced in its white painted surrounds and imperiously flanked by scrubbed white brooms and burnished coal bin. Very few airmen visiting a service guardroom felt at ease in this atmosphere and, with an occasional abuse of power by young policemen intent on making their mark, most avoided it, but in general the police did a fine job of work for very low pay and much maligning on the part of the rest of the station.

At the billets (barracks or huts) the dismissed airmen would grab their 'irons' (knife, fork, spoon) mug and plates and walk to the dining hall for their meal. Corporals coming in for their meal strode to the head of the queue. After the meal and washing their crockery and cutlery the airmen usually sauntered back to their billets, to relax on their macdonalds; lunch time was usually the unofficial time when they could disturb the neatly folded blankets laid out on the beds. Others wandered over to the Naafi for a cup of tea; others checked on Station Routine Orders (S.R.O.'s) to see if they were detailed for duty.

At around 13.15 the airmen would be 'fallen in' by one of their N.C.O.'s and marched back to their place of work, there to continue the rest of the day's activities. At approximately 16.30, depending on the programme, work would cease. But before the airmen left the hangar, aeroplanes had to be properly parked in their own space and cleaned of the day's grime, machines and equipment cleaned and the shops and sections left tidy. The duty key orderly would lock up and hand in the keys to the guardroom.

After flying ceased the fire and ambulance crews would depart, the fire engine to its shed normally sited near the Watch Office or control tower and the ambulance back to Station Sick Quarters.

Fire incidence in the service had become a costly business. The highly inflammable material that went into the making and operating of aircraft created considerable fire risks of high intensity burning, and despite sterling work by the rather outdated fire services during an emergency, once an aircraft caught fire it usually burned out. For some reason the fire fighters were accepted as a low grade trade. Maybe this was derived from their eternal polishing of their appliance — a time honoured theme of most fire services — but when fire service was required many an aircrew were grateful for their prompt action. Saving only one aircrew would justify their entire pay for their term of service.

A duty crew was detailed for each week by successive Flights of resident squadrons or flying units, usually a Corporal and a fitter and rigger, whose duty it was to refuel and service visiting aircraft and late arrival aircraft of the station. If a new type of aircraft arrived it quickly had its small crowd of technically interested airmen.

Tea was normally a relaxed meal at which the days events or the evening social programme might be discussed. For those going out of camp early it would be a quick meal.

Because of the remoteness of most aerodromes, most stations made provision for airmen to park their cars and motor cycles. This did not mean there were plenty of vehicles. Far from it. Finances did not normally go to such luxuries. But, conversely, second hand vehicles were also very cheap in those days and a respectable 'banger' could be picked up for a fiver. So a few airmen would share and buy a car for their personal transport and, when the opportunity arose, for private 'snogging'. In the main, because of cheapness of maintenance, motor cycles were the most popular, in addition to their sense of speed and freedom.

For those left on the station for the evening there was little to do. There was the Naafi for a few beers and sing song, or earnest conversation on all manner of subjects. Radio sets arrived in the Naafi in the early 1920's '... Their 'query' type horns became a prime target for the men', wrote A.C. Marchant, 'who threw their old buns into the horn as a protest against the harsh sound of the speakers. ...'

Those airmen inclined to athletic pastimes had the gym or sports field in which to display their prowess. Or there was the pleasure of just lazing on their beds reading the latest book, or writing home. The evening passed pleasantly for those off duty.

For those on duty it was somewhat different. Most stations of the time had a 12 hour guard duty, usually from 1800 to the following 0600. The employment of tradesmen for guard duties had long been a bone of contention in the R.A.F.

A man detailed for guard duty would be allowed to leave work earlier to allow him time to prepare, cleaning buttons, boots, skeleton web equipment, rifle, bayonet and scabbard, have an early tea and change into 'best blue' with pantaloons and puttees. He would be on guard duty parade around 17.45, there to be inspected by the Orderly Officer. Invariably the guard mounting ceremonial would incorporate the lowering of the ensign to the accompaniment of a bugle. All in the vicinity of this ceremonial would have to stand to attention.

As the guard fell in they might be joined by one or two sorry looking airmen clad in best uniform and wearing full pack, who would fall in to one side of the guard. These would be men on 'jankers'. Jankers is the old R.A.F. term for men on punishment parade. Discipline, although fair, was usually strict and most airmen of those times were punished for some service misdemeanour. Those that did not were not necessarily more virtuous, they were just undetected.

A punishment of seven days Confined to Barracks (C.B.) meant that the unfortunate airmen had to report to the guardroom several times a day, usually the most inconvenient, in his best uniform and wearing full pack. After work he would report as indicated and then be dismissed to change into working clothes and report back to the guardroom, there to be detailed several hours of fatigues which could be anything from scrubbing or polishing the guard room floor (usually) to cookhouse fatigues. Early on a winters morning he would be detailed to clean out and light the 'black horror' stoves in H.Q. offices. The airman was very glad when his punishment period was over.

The guard would be dismissed into the guardroom where they found themselves a spot on the floor to sleep or, if they were detailed on the roster for the first two hours, they would fall in outside. Here the Sergeant would read out the 'Riot Act', the guards duties, in a loud voice, issue the ammunition and see the rifles were correctly loaded. On most occasions in the U.K. no ammunition was issued. The Guard Corporal would march the first shift to the guard posts. The men not immediately on detail would be allowed to go in twos to collect blankets from their room or hut.

The guard period would usually pass without incident, or occasionally with, such as an airman not being as alert as an over zealous Orderly Officer would like, or the visit of the Station Commander, or a senior officer, which meant calling out the guard at whatever hour. Very rarely an airman might be caught dozing off or actually asleep, and for this latter offence there was no escape. He was relieved of duty immediately with the almost certain prospect of a court martial and the 'glasshouse' facing him.

Trying to snatch a few hours sleep in the guardroom could be a tiresome chore. With airmen arriving to book in from their evening out, guards changing shifts, it would be nearly midnight before the men could settle. To Marshall it left a vivid memory. '... To this day the smell of coke and paraffin reminds me only too vividly of a cold winter's night ... when, despite being wrapped up in greatcoat and blankets, the cold woke you up before your time to go out, the smell of the fire, just dying out because no one was awake to make it up, caught you in the throat and you lay and shivered, and wondered why you had been such a mug as to volunteer for a life in the R.A.F. if this is what it meant. ...'

But healthy, tired young men soon made light of the discomfort and had to be shaken quite heartily when their turn came for duty. The guard would be dismounted at 0600 and the first light of dawn was never more gratefully welcomed. Tired, weary, unshaven and feeling the need for a bath, the guard would march to the dismissal point and then to their huts. Except for a shave, the other requirements, rest and a bath would have to wait, for the men had to be at work by 1000 hours. But they still had to do the essential hut cleaning tasks before they could rest on their beds for a couple of hours.

If the new day was a Wednesday, then our ex-guard could reasonably expect to make up their lost rest. They had only to work from 1000 to 1230, emergencies excepted, when the whole station ceased work for the day. For Wednesday afternoon was the weekly sports afternoon, when all available N.C.O.'s and airmen were expected to participate in some form of organised sport. Our airmen just off guard had quite the best excuse for getting their heads down after dinner.

Generally, most men did participate in sport, but with the experience gained from increasing knowledge, together with a natural disinclination to take part in anything involving physical effort, some airmen would dodge the sports. The scrounging to do so could involve much mental effort; various subterfuges were employed to avoid turning out in the regulation white vests, blue shorts and gym shoes for organised P.T., cross country running or for field sports, inter-Flight football, rugby or cricket. If there were more men than sporting activities the surplus would be detailed to the sidelines to support their teams. At the worst they might be employed on fatigues.

Team sports were greatly supported in the early days for various reasons. The station, or camp, as previously mentioned was usually miles from a town or village and public transport was both sparse and infrequent. The low pay inhibited visits to the outside world to a minimum. Supporting a team gave the advantage that on away fixtures it was often quite easy to travel to the venue in the team service lorry as a supporter, and there meet old friends. After the match there was the prospect of an evenings entertainment in the nearby town.

While the W.R.A.F. was still in being, for those in the vicinity there was the chance to see the girls in action on the sports field. Team events gave the girls the opportunity to prove they could compete with the best in the most practical way, for example, competing as a representative team in R.A.F. and Inter-Services Athletic meetings. In the 1919 Inter-Service event at Stamford Bridge, the W.R.A.F. relay team won in the excellent time of 55.5 seconds. So there had been some fast girls in the W.R.A.F.!

After the games were over the living-in airmen wandered back to their quarters. The living-out types would probably cycle to the nearest village where they had their digs.

126

Older married airmen were probably in married quarters.

For the young married airman there was little chance of occupying any of the small 'married patch' on the station. For obvious reasons few had been built during or immediately after the war for the new service, and what there were would be occupied mainly by N.C.O.'s and older airmen with largish families. So the young airmen would seek accommodation in the nearby town or village. On average, however, they were not so young, for the age at which the R.A.F. considered a man suitable for marriage allowance and other benefit was 26. To make this point the erk had to apply for permission to marry from his Commanding Officer.

On several days a week the married airman, whether living in quarters or living-out, would go to the ration store and draw 'dry rations'. This was his due and consisted of meat, tea, sugar and bread. On pay day he drew his Consolidated Ration Allowance (C.R.A.) which was a money allowance to assist him and his family. Remember, he would in all probability still only be an Aircraftsman First Class on a minimum daily rate of 3/- (15p). The food, C.R.A. and marriage allowance would be just sufficient, even in those days when an old penny could still buy quite a few things. He would not really feel the benefit of pay and allowances until he had attained Senior N.C.O. rank.

Every few months the airmen were subjected to an inspection known by its medical name as Free From Infection, or F.F.I., and which was aimed at checking the men for

This photo of a Siskin 3A being serviced epitomises the role of the erk. From the shadows it appears to be the end of the flying day but the erk's boots still gleam as much as the aircraft. The mechanics are topping up with oil. Flight International.

blanket rash, although V.D. symptoms were also looked for. The incidence of V.D. even in the 1920's was rising sufficiently fast to cause concern and in the services, having apparently more opportunity to catch the disease, a rigidly applied inspection was put into being.

F.F.I. was not for the modest. The airmen undressed in a hut or room and followed each other in a queue to the waiting medical officer, holding up their slacks. Arriving in front of him they dropped their slacks, held up their arms and were subject to scrutiny, the M.O. lifting the dashed thing with a rod or ruler and using a torch to inspect more closely. In the days before bed sheets were issued it was common for an infectious rash to develop in the sensitive areas. The inspection was more generally known by the airmen as a 'short arm' inspection. Sufferers from V.D. were rare, but if found and sent to hospital could expect the treatment then in vogue to be painful. Woe betide any man that contracted the disease, refused to reveal it and was found out. Punishment was severe, indeed.

Friday was the day most welcomed because it was pay day and there were few airmen for whom it meant little. Pay was still at W.W.1 rates and was to remain so for many years, and most airmen were scratching for money before Friday. Pay parades were usually held around midday, either in one of the hangars or the station gymnasium. The airmen were paraded and placed in the an A to Z queue for their surnames. The pay clerk and witnessing officer would sit at a trestle table covered with a blanket and the parade would await the arrival of the Pay Officer and his service police escort. When he was ready after stacking the notes and coin, the first airman's name was called out by the pay clerk, the airman answering with a loud, 'Sir, 216', or whatever the last three digits of his official number was, and then advance to the pay table, salute smartly and collect the amount the pay clerk called out.

On these parades the S.W.O. or his deputy, usually took the opportunity to check the airmen for haircuts and general turnout. There was also another table nearby, presided over by an N.C.O. who collected weekly dues, such as garage fees.

About four times a year pay day coincided with the ever welcome credits pay out. This famous mythical term must be familiar to all airmen, and was the cause of much misunderstanding and argument at the Pay Office. Many airmen thought that the generous government of the time paid them all a sum of money each quarter known as 'credits' and when this was not forthcoming many arguments arose, and the poor old pay clerk was subjected to all kinds of accusations and abuse.

The fact is that during normal pay parades it was not possible to pay everybody to the exact penny of their weekly rate of pay, and pay was issued to the nearest 2/- (10p), i.e. a man on 4/6d (22½p) per day earned £1.11.6d (£1.57½p), but for convenience of coining he drew only 30/- (£1.50p) on pay day. Thus the odd 1/6 (7½p) went to his credit. Another man, however, might perhaps be on 4/- (20p) per day; he would draw the full correct rate of 28/- (£1.40p) but nothing would go to his credit. Shortly following the end of each quarter (three monthly periods) the accumulated balance (or credit) was paid out to each airman. The first example quoted would receive a little extra spending money that week, but the other man would get nothing, hence the arguments.

In addition a Clothing Allowance was granted quarterly, which was intended to be spent at the Unit Clothing Store on the replacement of clothing and necessaries. If, however, a careful and prudent erk looked after his kit, he did not need to spend all the allowance. In this case the balance was added to his credits and paid to him each quarter. It was not unknown for a rogue to draw kit at the store in another airman's name, especially during W.W.2, and one can imagine the argument that this caused when the balance was paid out on 'credit day' and caused the pay clerk much wasted time in turning out the appropriate vouchers and checking on signatures, etc.

After pay those lucky enough to have a chit signed by their O.C. or Flight N.C.O. i/c, allowing them to leave work early to go on long weekend would hurry to their huts to have a meal and change. Long weekend F295's were normally from after duty on Friday until 2359 on Sunday, often extended by individual stations to 0700 on Monday.

After changing, the airman, if he was one of the fortunate few, would collect his personal transport from the garage and go on his way, almost certainly with a maximum passenger load. For those not so fortunate it might mean a dreary wait for the local bus or a walk into the village for the same reason, unless, like one or two stations it had its own railway halt.

In those golden years, because of low pay, and the uncertainties of the inefficient transport, not all availed themselves of weekend leave, preferring to wait until the 'grant' periods, which were extended Bank Holidays, usually of five days duration.

Most evenings of the week the majority of the airmen stayed on the station, but should they wish to go out they were free to leave the station from after duty until 2359. All airmen carried a permanent pass (P.P.) which they had to produce at the guardroom.

One of the delights of an erk's life was the annual Air Officer Commanding (A.O.C.'s) Inspection. The visit by the A.O.C. lasted one day, the preparation for the inspection as soon as the date was known, often several months. The inspection was a thorough check into the efficiency and running of the station. All the organisations, administration and technical procedures in use were checked by a team from Command H.Q. which preceded, and accompanied, the A.O.C.; in fact a number of the team spent several days on the on the chosen station.

Very much like an annual spring clean, the inspection was also an opportunity to clear out the accumulated rubbish of the past year.

Hangar floors were scrubbed of any oil or dirt and 'bull' was sometimes taken to extremes by emptying the hangars and scrubbing and then brushing a fine layer of cement dust into the surface. The parking spaces for each aeroplane would be repainted, chocks and ropes refurbished, and drip trays polished to near mirror finish. Aeroplanes were scrubbed and polished even more than they were normally and, where it was necessary, redoped and repainted. Every effort was made to attain maximum serviceability. Hangar surrounds were cleared, approach paths tidied, white lines repainted and the aerodrome itself mown just prior to the visit.

All aircraft log books and technical records were brought up to date and rescrutinised for errors by the Engineer W.O.'s and section Senior N.C.O.'s. The aeroplanes were fitted with their correct equipment according to the particular operational standard detailed by the log book. Outstanding modifications were incorporated as much as possible. The squadron's 'Christmas tree' was checked of its Aircraft On Ground (A.O.G.) demands. The Christmas tree was an aeroplane which had been grounded for a long period by major unserviceability, and from which items had been cannibalised to service another aeroplane quickly.

Ground equipment received the same treatment as the aircraft in cleaning, checking, polishing, servicing and painting and all important certifications were brought up to date.

On top of this agony the airmen had the job of bringing their clothing, equipment, hut and drill up to the same standards. This was the time of the year when an airman could lose most, or all of his clothing credits, and was often put into debt, for at all costs his clothing and equipment must be seen to be clean, serviceable and complete. So kit inspections and clothing parades were numerous and many a faithful dog collar tunic, or cap, or a favourite pair of pantaloons, privately tailored to give a dashing winged effect, were ruthlessly declared worn out or illegal by the squadron or section disciplinary N.C.O. Overcoats were free issue and so sometimes given the benefit of the doubt.

This arbitrary handling was probably a blessing in disguise. With the credit scheme many erks made their clothes last as long as possible in order to draw unused credits and as a result some clothes, particularly socks and underclothes, looked distinctly second hand. All kits had to be marked with the airman's number, either by metal stamps, stencil or sewn on white tape. Boots had to be correctly studded and tipped; all items laid out for kit inspection had to have its allotted space and position on the bed.

Concurrently with kit inspection was equipment cleaning — blancoeing the web equipment and polishing its brasses, using cobblers wax on bayonet scabbard and burnishing the bayonet. It was so much more considerate for an airman to stab an enemy with a polished blade.

The men drew little enough pay but they still had to supplement the barrack room or hut cleaning materials by collectively buying more floor, stove and metal polish and scouring powder from their own pay. The floors were made to gleam, the stove was placed out of action for the day and glistened ebony black in its white painted surround. The scene was repeated in all the offices.

Truly the phrase, 'If it moves, salute it, if it doesn't, paint it,' complied with for these A.O.C.'s Inspections was inspired and apt.

Practice drills gradually increased in intensity and were held several times a week, culminating in full scale dress rehearsals with the airmen wearing full equipment and carrying rifle and bayonet. There was a touch of the old army influence here, for the airmen carried full waterbottles and the rucksacks held their quota of clothes all neatly arranged in correct order. The side pack carried knives, forks, etc. and the mug was slung on the belt. (the earlier issue mugs were enamel). It was better to have an A.O.C.'s in winter for at least the greatcoat was worn and not carried in the pack on a hot day. During all this preparation a normal flying programme was carried out.

The night before the visit was 'all go' for the erks after an exhausting final day in flight, workshop or office and a last drill rehearsal. They had to set-to after their tea to re-blanco and the final bull, with a possible quick visit to the Naafi, working through until 2200 and crawling into bed knowing they had quite a day to face on the morrow.

That day began with a very early reveille and breakfast, followed by a final clean up of the room or hut; they laid out their kit for inspection which was checked under the eagle eye of the discip. N.C.O., after which the men then changed into their best blue. When all was well and before parade time the men gave a final polish to their equipment, helping each other to 'fit', and formed up outside to march to the parade ground where they were marshalled in Squadrons and Flights and sized, under the command of the S.W.O. who, when satisfied, handed over the parade to the Station Adjutant. While the parade was assembling the officers had been walking backwards and forwards at the side of the parade ground — a Naval throwback tradition from walking the quarter deck?

The Adjutant called the parade to order, ordered officers to fall in and handed over the parade to the Station Commander. Afterwards, the whole parade usually awaited the arrival of the A.O.C., when the parade was called to attention, the band played the General Salute and the visit was on.

The A.O.C. commenced by carrying out an inspection of the ranks. If he was a bit of a stickler he would choose a few unfortunate erks to fall out on the edge of the parade ground where the contents of their packs would be examined for content, cleanliness and correctness, water bottles for water and so on. These unfortunates would then have to quickly repack and rejoin the ranks.

Then came the march past in Flights and Squadrons to the music of the R.A.F. March Past, with the A.O.C. taking the salute. The parade marched off the square to their dispersal point where they were dismissed to their huts and rooms to change into working blue, rearrange their uniforms and equipment to complete the kit layout and then march to the place of work. Sometimes the order was varied and the airmen remained by their beds while the A.O.C. inspected the kits.

At the place of work, at the hangars anyway, the aeroplanes were pushed outside if the weather was suitable and lined up. Because everyone was loth to disturb the show window appearance little actual work was done and N.C.O.'s and men kicked their heels until either the order was given to stand down, or it was decided to put on a flypast, or the A.O.C. inspected the hangar and its environs.

Dinner in the spotless dining hall was rather better than average. The afternoon passed in a rather apprehensive air as the A.O.C. and his retinue toured the various sections and offices. Finally it was all over and in a vaguely traditional way the A.O.C. usually allowed the rest of the day off for the men. It was much appreciated. Tea was greatly enjoyed and that evening the Naafi canteen wet bar was much busier than usual.

It would appear that the advent of an A.O.C.'s visit was the signal for an increase in that fine old service custom known as bull. Unfortunately this was too often the case, for it was very prevalent in the years between the wars. Why it should have been is given in several reasons. It may have been inherited from the Air Battalion/R.F.C. days from the ex-Guards N.C.O.'s who remained in the R.A.F.. It may have developed from the necessity to maintain buildings, clothes and equipment longer than was intended because of the economy measures, and overdone. Perhaps it may have originally been a form of discipline imposed by higher authority upon the men to keep them occupied in periods of inactivity, possible an accentuated form of visible efficiency that evolved through Trenchard's decree for his Air Force to be seen to be efficient. Whatever the cause, there was plenty of bull during the inter-war years and at times, under a sadistic officer or N.C.O. it reached ridiculous proportions, with an often degrading effect on the men. This type of bull was often practised in the 'glasshouses', the military correction detention centres, or prisons.

In these establishments a few sadists were given their head to devise methods of a heartbreaking nature and it was a tough serviceman who did not finish his sentence profoundly affected, or indeed broken, in a few cases.

On occasions the genuine bull could be beneficial. In those years there was a tremendous pride in squadron, flight and machine, and much energy was voluntarily expended in 'bulling' the aeroplanes, equipment, hangar and offices. Technically, as a machine was being bulled up the mechanic was also automatically checking the

131

These three airmen seem to be enjoying the life at RAF Upavon in 1926. G. Hawlett.

mechanical aspects, for example, in cleaning off oil streaks over a cowling what caused the oil leak?

Bull could also be having one's regulation issue pantaloons, which in their issued state looked remarkably like a pair of Edwardian drawers, tailored to give a dashing winged effect, complemented by a pair of Fox's puttees that gave a more natural shape to the leg. But the bull carried on unabated until the Second World War, holding on firmly in the training centres. With the outbreak of that war and the influx of hundreds of thousands of civilian-orientated recruits on 'hostilities only' engagements, the hallowed concept of bull took a hammering and was relegated to its proper place in the scheme of things. The post-W.W.2 R.A.F. became all the better for it.

Possible an offshoot of bull was the prevalence of swearing in the services, unique in the sense of being almost universal among N.C.O.'s, and men but rarely used by officers. Swearing was almost an extension of service language. The meaning was not in the word, but in the tone of voice, and a man soon knew if it was meant. The language was applied whole-heartedly to his songs making them fit only for service stag nights. Among the songs:

Salome	Abdul La Bubu Lamir
That great big wheel	Quartermaster stores
Somersetshire	Bless them all

Because the majority of R.A.F. stations were, of necessity, away from large centres of population, efforts were made by the airmen's entertainment committees to invite the local people to station dances and concerts. These were usually a great success and every effort was made to ensure it would be, for the dances were also the opportunity to meet the local 'crumpet'.

Where possible the band would be from the station personnel, but if there were insufficient musical talent a local band would be engaged. Many an airmen met his steady girl friend and future wife at these dances. To reciprocate local 'hops' were held weekly in the nearby villages to which the erks were welcomed.

Any trouble between the two factions, airmen and villagers, usually had beer and girls as its epicentre, possibly with some cause, depending on which side you were on. The erks were isolated on stations several miles from civilian life and when released wished to make the most of their social life, which included girls and drinks. Womanising in the R.A.F. was less than civvy street despite the often puerile, imaginative boasting of some airmen.

A major reason for this, besides the lack of cash, the distances from station to town or village and a normal 2359 hours curfew, was in the number of illustrated V.D. lectures given to the airmen, which while in no way denigrating the local ladies, tended to make the airmen more than careful with casual female aquaintances.

Romance and passing affairs there certainly were, but not many erks could keep a girl friend for long on 28/- (£1.40p) per week. Sex was certainly discouraged even if by so doing it tended to encourage promiscuous affairs. Generally, the purpose was achieved against all the natural urges of young, healthy airmen living closely among their own sex and deprived of female company for long periods.

Life in the services was never smooth and predictable for long. Perhaps as a result of a love affair gone sour a man would be involved with the police, perhaps in a moment of forgetfulness a technical man might make a serious error in his work, resulting in an aircraft being damaged. Perhaps the Dutch courage from a skinful of beer might provoke a man to strike a N.C.O., or maybe a bad type might start stealing from his comrades.

Whatever the major offence a man was invariably destined for court martial action. Courts martial, the service equivalent of a civil criminal court, were held in some dread, an emotion which the services did little to dispel. Possibly the dread was engendered from the old days by the air of stiff military discipline in which the proceedings are carried out, its imposing array of senior officers, the stamping of the court orderly and the general starkness of the court. Whatever the deterrent effect it did not alter the course of justice.

That same justice had to take its course and after the first charges were made a Court of Enquiry was set up to sift and record the evidence. All witnesses were interviewed and their evidence recorded and signed by them in the presence of the officer detailed. The evidence was then sent to the Provost Marshal's H.Q. where a decision was made if the seriousness of the crime warranted the convening of a court martial.

In most cases the court martial itself was over in a day. Officers detailed (sometimes defence officers were especially asked for by defendant) for the court martial carried out their unenviable tasks, being guided in legal queries by a representative from the Provost Marshal's office. The defendant and all witnesses were marched in except civilians — to the accompaniment of commands and stamping feet by the court orderly, usually a Senior N.C.O. It is worth recording that many officers were against this unnecessary drill.

As a general rule, for all charges except those concerned with security, a limited number of airmen and N.C.O.'s were allowed in to see justice being done. The sentence, if a man was found guilty, was usually subject to confirmation by the A.O.C. in C. and when confirmed the airman was sent off to serve his sentence in the delegated detention centre. Where an N.C.O. was the subject of a court martial it normally either meant a reduction in rank or reduced to the ranks, and the serving of a period of time in the detention centre. N.C.O.'s punishment was correspondingly more severe.

The foregoing describes something of the routine and conditions of life that erks experienced on the average station during the Golden Years. Despite the few grievances and complaints the accounts may convey some of the very real assets that the greater majority of pre-war airmen and airwomen enjoyed, and who would not have changed this period of their lives when the R.A.F. carried very few passengers. With its almost diminutive size it could not afford to. There was a saying in those days that service numbers were not used, everyone knew each other by their first name. Every man was virtually hand picked.

After the first World War the R.A.F. contributed a number of squadrons to the Army of Occupation. Under the intensive demobilisation programme and the economic plight of the R.A.F. the number in Germany shrunk from 44 squadrons in 1919 to one squadron in 1920.

There was little recruiting for women as it was probably envisaged that the W.R.A.F. would be run down as soon as the R.A.F. was at sufficient strength to dispense with their services. Meanwhile a large number of mobiles fufilled the condition of their service and served on the continent in 1919 when, in March of that year because of the fast thinning numbers of airmen, the authorities were induced to send out W.R.A.F volunteers, who arrived in France in April and in Cologne in May.

The travel arrangements were primitive and the members endured some of the conditions that service troops had taken for granted, piled into railway carriages with full kit, or crammed tight into bone shaking lorries for the journey along the atrocious roads to their new units. The reception they received made up for the hardship.

The women were well received and at some units they shared the men's canteens. But they had to work hard during the long hot summer, which contributed its own problem in a water shortage at some units. The girls made the best of it and their company was much appreciated by the erks.

The women who went to Germany experienced the two extremes of being received with cheers by the occupation troops and rejected with hatred by the local populace. Such was this hatred that there were one or two ugly scenes when the members were out walking. As a result their freedom was controlled and they had to be in camp by 2130, and armed guards were put on their quarters.

At least the 500 or so members who served overseas had the satisfaction of breaking new ground and setting a precedent, and although their tour was but a few short months they had the satisfaction of seeing a new country and creating a favourable impression among the Allied forces.

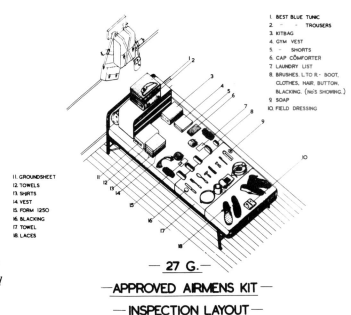

1. BEST BLUE TUNIC
2.   "   " TROUSERS
3. KITBAG
4. GYM VEST
5.   " SHORTS
6. CAP COMFORTER
7. LAUNDRY LIST
8. BRUSHES. L.TO R- BOOT,
  CLOTHES, HAIR, BUTTON,
  BLACKING. (No'S SHOWING.)
9. SOAP
10. FIELD DRESSING

11. GROUNDSHEET
12. TOWELS
13. SHIRTS
14. VEST
15. FORM 1250
16. BLACKING
17. TOWEL
18. LACES

The view the Inspecting Officer wished to see and the erk hoped that he would.

— 27 G.—

—APPROVED AIRMENS KIT —

— INSPECTION LAYOUT —

It was most frustrating to the W.R.A.F. members on all these units that, as soon as they had got their sections running smoothly so, inevitably, came the order to reduce establishment, and the unit was run down and the members sent home to be demobbed. In all, the W.R.A.F. served on 10 units in France and Germany, doing the work for which they had been brought into being, efficiently, cheerfully and without complaint.

At home the demob of the W.R.A.F. continued until it finally ceased on 1st April 1920, two short but valuable years of contribution.

*   *   *   *   *

From Cranwell, A.C. McConnell, a newly qualified Fitter Driver Petrol was posted to the M. T. Repair Depot at Shrewsbury, a station noted in 1922 for its hard work and bull. The unit was the major Repair and Overhaul Depot for the R.A.F. in the U.K. and also acted as a stores depot for issue of vehicles for overseas use.

McConnell found that the hard work notoriety of the unit was true but it was well organised. Vehicles were overhauled on a flow line system, one of the earliest examples of this method in the R.A.F. As McConnell describes, '... and each unit, i.e. engines, gearboxes, back axles, etc. were overhauled in a separate department and finally reassembled, tested, stored or issued to units. Body overhauls were done by Carpenter Coach Builders and Coach Painters, strange R.A.F. trades. . .'

Promotion was exceedingly slow, a spin-off result of the consistently small size of the R.A.F. It was not uncommon for tradesmen to reach L.A.C. rank and stay in that rank for the remainder of their service, however long. An average waiting time for promotion from L.A.C. to Corporal for a Fitter Driver Petrol was 8-10 years, for Cook 10 years or more, for Airframe and Engine Fitters 10-12 years. According to McConnell it was possible for a Group 3 tradesman to be recommended for remustering to a Group 1 M.T. trade, providing there was an establishment and he could pass the trade test. Some of these airmen did remuster and then had to wait years for a vacancy, in the meantime doing fitters work.

This policy, plus the added knowledge that ex-apprentices would be more favoured for promotion, did not encourage airmen to sign on for long terms. The only saving, in economic terms in the R.A.F. was that long service pensions were kept at a minimum.

The knowledge that apprentices would have a degree of priority over direct entry airmen when it came to promotion and the feeling of resentment it caused, is substantiated by several apprentices. McConnell wrote, '... Our function was supposed to be that of improvers, this led to some bad feeling among the skilled men we were put to work with, as promotion was slow in those days, and trade boards and educational tests were not so easily passed by some of the older hands who were nevertheless excellent tradesmen. It was not unusual for an A.C. I to be instructing an L.A.C. ex-boy in the finer arts of the trade. ...'

A situation had developed after W.W.1 which, despite the experience and cause, was to be repeated after W.W.2. Many Senior N.C.O.'s had elected to sign on for pensionable engagements and in doing so had effectively formed a major block to reasonable promotion for the new, keen and eager tradesmen subsequently engaging. It literally became a case of waiting for the N.C.O.'s to retire.

A.C. Waight, a Rigger Aero, had the added qualification of an air gunners course behind him. Because of this he enjoyed every minute of his service which included the Central Flying School at Upavon, a carrier tour in the Fleet Air Arm and a tour on an Army Co-operation squadron. Ground crew had every opportunity to fly as much as they wished — on Flying Training Schools to give experience to trainee pilots. '. . if a rigger or fitter could not fly a 504 within a few months he only had himself to blame. . .' Waight remembers that several of his ground crew contemporaries were natural pilots but were inhibited by lack of rank, qualifications and physical disability.

Waight himself had a singularly lucky escape from death when, in December 1923, with a pupil pilot P. O. Gain, they spun in from 300 ft. The pilot was killed and Waight thrown clear. He attributed his escape to the breaking of a safety belt he was wearing, which caused him to be thrown on to the starboard wing. The rear cockpit, where he had been sitting, closed like a mantrap over the point where his head would have been. After leaving hospital Waight was given 30 days sick leave.

Flying in the 1920's he wrote, and most will agree, was much more thrilling than it could possibly be today. For instance, the 504K with its 110 h.p. Monosoupape engine could be turned almost inside out, '... I have yet to see a modern aeroplane crabbing across an aerodrome. . .' and Waight remembers a song dedicated to that really marvellous little aeroplane on which the vast majority of the early ground crew have worked, and pilots have been trained since 1915, which has left its affectionate mark on their minds. The tune is to 'That old fashioned mother of mine.'

Just an old fashioned Avro with old fashioned wings
And her fuselage battered and torn,
An old fashioned engine that hiccups and sings
Like a gramophone badly outworn.
Though she drinks petrol and rich castor oil
there is something that makes her divine,
For she's quite safe and sound since she won't leave the ground,
That old fashioned land crab of mine

L.A.C. Waight became due for his discharge in September 1928 and transferred to Class E Reserve in which he served until 1935, when he re-enlisted in the regular R.A.F. for a four year term.

Army Co-operation squadrons were evolved from the general reconnaissance and cavalry squadrons of W.W.1 which played an important part in close support work with the troops and supplied valuable information to the Army. This particular branch of the R.A.F. was quite popular with the erks as it was a gypsy existence in the summer, living in tents, eating meals supplied by the field kitchens and often on the move during exercises with their particular Red, Blue or whatever colour Army they were attached. The permanent stations were Old Sarum (H.Q.) and Odiham near Aldershot. Because of the commitments of operation during the summer, leave was hard to come by, and ground crew usually had to wait until the end of the 'season' in October.

The R.A.F. Reserve to which Waight was transferred was a force comprising ex-officers and men, and civilians employed in civilian occupations who had no previous R.A.F. experience. The conditions of service were such that its members were enabled to keep in training, technical or otherwise, without interference from their civilian employer. Ex-airmen enlisted for a period of four years and in the fourth year were required to attend a 12 day training camp for which they were paid full service rates of pay and allowances.

*　*　*　*　*

A.C. Leigh was posted to the Aircraft Repair Section (A.R.S.) at Henlow to be employed on intensive repair work on aircraft which included the 504, Bristol Fighter, DH9 and 9A and Sopwith Snipe.

It was during Leigh's time on A.R.S. that the situation mentioned by McConnell arose when apprentices were posted in for practical training, all of them L.A.C.'s. A distinct 'anti' feeling was aroused to mar what was in effect a happy station, and not the sort of reaction that Trenchard had foreseen. As Leigh put it, '... in our opinion this was very unfair, more so when we found out they were to be given preference in respect of future promotion, no doubt you may realise that just about finished our ambition to improve our own position. . .'

A valid point, indeed, although some will say that it shows a lack of personal drive to achieve that ambition. If a man was determined to succeed he would not let that kind of situation prevent him trying. But these were the days of the early 1920's, a steadily shrinking Air Force and a constantly reducing possibility of promotion.

After trying hard and being recommended for promotion, it is disconcerting, to say the least, to have preference go to an ex-apprentice with far less service and experience but with superior technical training. And this is what happened in scores of cases where more than one man of the same trade was in line for promotion. It created a quite untrue myth that ex-apprentices were superior. They were, usually in a technical sense only; even if their educational standards were higher on average, this did not necessarily make them better N.C.O.'s. The same educational qualifications often applied equally to men service candidates.

No, it was the natural result of a policy to train apprentices as the future N.C.O.'s and officers and broadly it worked, and still does. The next major war, however, was to prove that many men service and direct entry airmen could be, and were, just as efficient

N.C.O.'s and officers. The preferential treatment of apprentices remained a dissident subject while the R.A.F. remained a small force and promotion was limited.

* * * * *

When the advent of the all-metal aircraft into the R.A.F. became a certainty the question arose of suitably trained airmen to service them. In January 1923, a Warrant Officer 2nd Class H. Tatum, a Halton instructor in the trades of Coppersmith, Tinsmith, Sheet Metal Worker and Acetylene Welder, submitted a report giving his proposals and recommendations for a new trade, with his reasons.

W. O. Tatum suggested that the first of the three trades above be washed out and the trade of Aircraft Metal Worker be substituted. He quoted numerous examples of how quickly the four trades could be trained by himself, and certainly lacked no confidence in his abilities. Some of his comments were very sensible in that he pointed out that the practical tests detailed in AP 836 were not wholly geared to R.A.F. requirements.

W. O. Tatum ended his report with a very brief outline of his service, 24 years in all, classes of work in civilian life, Royal Navy, R.N.A.S. and the R.A.F., including eight years of instruction. His Flight Sergeant and Sergeant had 20 and 12 years respectively in similar service.

The report created considerable interest, reaching Sir Hugh Trenchard himself, who detailed an enquiry as to whether the recommendations were feasible. Very senior Air Ministry staff gave this report serious consideration and the enquiry carried out a detailed examination of the report and finally decided that his ideas were generally impracticable. The most important point raised which worried the enquiry was the reference to metal workers 'working' the metal with its dangerous possibilities of setting up added stresses, altering the designed tensile strengths, and that the proposed tradesmen would not be fitters as such.

The enquiry recommended that the basic trades for all metal aircraft be in the hands of fitters, any repairs required to be handled by the specialist trades of W. O. Tatum and that the trades of Coppersmith, Tinsmith and Sheet Metal Worker be amalgamated, with Acetylene Welder as a separate trade. Eventually the new trade of Metal Rigger superseded the old of Carpenter Rigger.

This is a very much shortened version of the report, and its outcome is included to show that the R.A.F. was fully prepared to listen, and investigate, any ideas from its airmen provided that they had something constructive to say. This kind of outlook gave much encouragement to all trades and made them feel, justifiably, that they were in a service in which their efforts were appreciated. Many good ideas resulted to the advantage of the R.A.F. The system is still in use today.

One of the many successful service careers that illustrates the extent that an airman can rise is that of ex-A.C. K. D. Owen, later S/Ldr., who enlisted in 1930 as an apprentice clerk (after failing his eyesight test on a previous attempt in 1929) and retired after the W.W.2 as a Flight Lieutenant.

As he so rightly pointed out, with mass unemployment the R.A.F. could afford to maintain stringent standards and select the best. But, let A.C. Owen give his own version.

'Conditions at Ruislip .. were pretty grim. During the day, apart from the quota of drill and P.T. the apprentices were used as cheap labour ... messengers and office boys in the Records Office. Such 'technical training' as we had (i.e. typing and shorthand) was given in the evening. Living conditions were appalling — stores in huts with an inadequate supply of fuel, no running hot water and a central bath house with specified times of use, poor lighting and dingy accommodation which had long been condemned. The food for growing boys was quite inadequate, particularly at week-ends, and of course we lacked the money to augment our meagre rations. ...'

This description, if near true, indicates to some degree the crippling effect the economics of the country had had on the R.A.F. which had endured this state since 1918, and there was still no let up.

After two years of the rigours of Ruislip L.A.C. Owen was posted to 502 Squadron, a Vickers Virginia Special Reserve unit at Aldergrove, N.I. Such were the conditions at the training school that he still remembers the relief of his posting. He was justified, for at Aldergrove he entered the 'real' Air Force, working as a clerk in the squadron orderly room and enjoying much flying in the open rear cockpit of the 'Ginnies'. Highlights of the operational year was a squadron move to Manston for a fortnights practice camp.

*   *   *   *   *

Part of Trenchard's publicity campaign to keep the R.A.F. in the public eye was the annual Air Display held at R.A.F. Hendon. It was most popular, and part of that popularity was the unorthodox aspects of flying specially put on for the public's benefit, such as tied together flying, crazy pupil and instructor stunts and aerobatics by aircraft trailing smoke.

For the last item a flight of four Bulldogs was formed at Martlesham Heath in 1933 where A.C. Marshall had been posted. The dramatic smoke was produced by gear installed on the aircraft which consisted of a tank holding a mixture of old engine oil and the requisite colour-producing chemicals, red, white and blue, copper pipes which fed to the engine exhaust system and a special jet fitted into the exhaust. The ON/OFF control was from an interconnected cock in the cockpit.

The whole installation created plenty of extra work '... as the mixture clogged .. after every flight in which smoke was used the system had to cleared; each engine fitter who did the work was coloured the colour of the smoke that his aeroplane produced and a peculiar sight we looked with our hands and faces stained red, white or blue as the case may be ... it took weeks before it finally faded' In the autumn of 1933 Marshall and several others were posted overseas to Iraq.

Through the foregoing pages one has had a glimpse of the type of experience gained by the erks which fitted them so much for promotion when expansion was forced on the R.A.F. by European events. Without any doubt whatsoever the erk of the Golden Years, economically repressed as he was, vindicated the training and faith of Trenchard and his Marshals and became the solid nucleus on which the R.A.F. was to rapidly expand.

Chapter 8
Maritime Digression

After the First World War the control of aeroplanes flying from Naval carriers and operating within the Naval sphere of influence came under the R.A.F. and Trenchard kept a firm hand on his units, which of course upset quite a few people in the Admiralty.

Seaplane bases and air stations of the old R.N.A.S. were now fully manned by the R.A.F., many of these men ex-R.N.A.S. who had 'converted' when the R.A.F. came into existence. From this early organisation Coastal Area Command was formed in 1919, which had control of all units working with the Navy until the Fleet Air Arm was formed in April 1924.

Air and ground crew were posted to the F.A.A. for a tour roughly equivalent to an overseas posting, a scheme not too successful, for at the end of the tour the crews reverted to normal R.A.F. service and the F.A.A. lost a great deal of continuity which is essential for an efficient force.

HMT Somersetshire, one of the most well known troopers of between wars, and subject of a service song. Bibby Lines.

L.A.C. Marchant found the naval type discipline very strict, and airmen were detailed to first or second Port and Starboard watches. To all intents and purposes life on a carrier was purely naval, from the tot of rum or its 3d (1p) in lieu, to the cockroaches sharing the original Furious and Argus. Flying was controlled by an R.A.F. Sdn/Ldr. and aircraft servicing personnel were all R.A.F. except for naval telegraphist for wireless transmission (W.T.) duties and a few General Duties (G.D.) deckhands.

Marchant enjoyed his carrier service and found the work interesting. He too, was observant, and relates a few exciting and humorous incidents which typify the life, and the approach to life, on these old carriers, and the way the early Coastal Area Command tackled the job.

A Blackburn Dart torpedo aircraft had its tin fish (torpedo) slip forward on its mounting, as a result of diving too steeply, which struck the propeller, removing a foot from each blade. The rear of the torpedo forced itself into a bottom cross member strut in the fuselage. When the aeroplane landed and lost flying speed both sets of mainplanes drooped, with their wingtips nearly touching the deck. It was a write-off. When the young P.O. was asked by his Flight Commander if he had noticed any difference in the aeroplane's handling the pilot replied, 'No, sir, try it yourself'. He was back in the air within 50 minutes of landing!

A quick repair job. A Fairey 3F flying to H.M.S. Furious from Gosport had made a hard landing on the deck, the pilot immediately taking off and then finding the port undercarriage strut had pulled away. The carrier signalled Gosport informing them the 3F was to land there with a damaged undercarriage. Despite the presence of the fire tender and 'blood tub' the pilot made a good landing for, by a minor miracle, the port strut dropped into position as the aeroplane touched down; the undercarriage was repaired and the 3F was back on board Furious by the evening.

To maintain interest in the work and increase participation, records were kept on the Furious of fastest times in bringing an aircraft from landing on, folding its wings and pushing it on to the lift. Average times were around 33 seconds. The aircraft of Marchant's times were Fairey Flycatcher, Blackburn Dart and Fairey 3F.

Living conditions on a carrier were about on a par with troopers. A number of airmen, when weather conditions allowed, would sling their hammocks in the hangar, where because of space restrictions every aeroplane had its own parking space and with wings folded and locked, was shackled to the deck.

Before joining H.M.S. Eagle in 1924 L.A.C. Price served for a period in 210 Squadron at Gosport, to which he had been posted from training school as a torpedo fitter. The squadron aircraft were Sopwith Cuckoo, Blackburn Dart, Bristol Fighter, DH9A and the ubiquitous hack 504K.

L.A.C. Price was posted to H.M.S. Eagle with 460 Torpedo Flight and served with the Mediterranean Fleet. On the carrier the job was one of enthusiasm and hard work and from the torpedo fitters viewpoint, operating with aircraft was what it was all about. Let L.A.C. Price relate in his own words his job and how he felt about it.

'... The tin fish was secured by a couple of wire strops with a turnbuckle screw at each end and released by a quick release toggle by the pilot, who flew the machine head on to the target and dropped as low to the water as possible to minimise the dive effects on the torpedo. The subsequent running of the fish to the target was dependent on the work of the torpedo mechanic who prepared the fish for running, the ability of its engines and the various functions of the valves, etc., in the torpedo to do their work correctly and, of course not forgetting the gyroscope which kept it on a straight course.

'There were no easy ways of loading the torpedo on to the aeroplane, it had to be wheeled on a truck and wound up by hand, a really backbreaking job to say the least of it, with very little room to move. The Dart went on to H.M.S. Furious in the Med: Fleet and proved itself a good machine with its ability to easily lift off the torpedo from the carrier deck.

'Operation from a carrier was obviously quite different from shore based flying. When flying was in progress things had to be done quickly as only one machine could land at a time. The crews were in the nets at the side of the flying deck, and as soon as the machine touched down were up and back on deck to get the wings folded and the machine on to the lift to take it down to the hangar, so as to be topsides for the next landing. As we usually had six machines on an attack exercise it was very hectic at times.

'When at rest in the hangar the aeroplanes were secured to ring bolts in the deck by a wire strop with turnbuckle screws fore and aft, and often the duty watch of the R.A.F. were called out during rough weather to secure up a bit tighter on the lashings. Although the work was exacting and at times arduous it was worth it to see an efficient striking force growing up'.

Another contemporary, who joined the ship in 1925, was L.A.C. D. B. Waight, also from Fort Rowner, Gosport. The carrier was then operating a mixed bag of Fairey Flycatchers, Blackburn Dart and Fairey 3F aircraft. L.A.C. Waight's experience was that, '... The R.A.F. got along quite well with the Navy men, who soon nicknamed the airmen 'crabfat soldiers'. The term does not sound complimentary but no insult was intended. It was that the colour of the R.A.F. uniform was similar to the colour of paint used on the outside of the ship, which was known as crabfat. . .'

During the Fleet exercises the hours were long and the work was hard when the weather was good, but this was compensated for when going ashore in the Mediterranean bases. There were very few airmen indeed who did not enjoy their tour on one of these old carriers. The establishment of N.C.O.'s and airmen of a Fleet Torpedo Flight in 1925 was:

1 Flight Sergeant Carpenter or Fitter specialist
1 Sergeant and 1 Corporal Carpenter Rigger
1 Sergeant and 1 Corporal Aero Engine Fitter
1 Corporal and 1 A.C. Wireless Operator Mechanic
5 A.C.'s Carpenter Riggers
5 A.C.'s Aero Engine Fitters
3 A.C.'s Aircrafthands (Batmen)

In addition a number of other trades were supplied by the R.A.F. but these were eventually replaced by their Naval equivalent.

*   *   *   *   *

The final outcome of a battle for control of the F.A.A. between R.A.F. and Navy was that in 1937 the Navy won. Although taking years of determined effort to achieve, the unexpected success found the Navy unprepared in a vital field of operations — manpower. So the Navy turned to its former adversary to supply skilled men until it had trained its own.

A.C. Ward was posted to the station workshops at R.A.F. Gosport in 1937 from Henlow and while there his name appeared on the Preliminary Warning Roll (P.R.W.) for posting to the F.A.A. He joined 822 Torpedo Spotter Reconnaissance (T.S.R.) Squadron attached to the new H.M.S. Furious, at that time being re-equipped with a new aeroplane, the Fairey Swordfish.

First quarters of the squadron at R.A.F. Donibristle, although hutted, were an improvement on the 'earth covered forts' at Donibristle, which were 'dank, damp and uninspiring'. Working up exercises with the new aeroplane were hard. Because of its newness the 'Stringbag' had more frequent inspections, at 10, 20 and 40 hours. Intensive training on deck landing techniques were carried out for about a month, practising on a dummy deck laid out on the aerodrome.

Life aboard a carrier had improved little since the days of the original Furious. Meals had to be collected by the duty mess man from the galleys which were far from the mess decks, in fact, the journey might necessitate climbing up to the main deck, with the result that the food could be nearly cold when it reached its destination.

After the long struggle for control of the air side of naval operations was resolved, Ward reports an immediate impact as it affected the R.A.F. at Donibristle. '... At teatime, the last day of R.A.F. Command, in the airmen's mess the tables as usual were laid out with table clothes and flowers, etc. At breakfast the next morning tables were bare and from then on we ate our meals at scrubbed tables. We complained at the time but it was not naval policy to supply table cloths and I believe we also lost out over no sheets on the bed. ...'

The erks were given the option of transferring to the F.A.A. with a promotion in rank, or staying within the R.A.F. but attached to the F.A.A. A number did transfer and accept R.N. pay and conditions.

Except for squadron moves by air, special flights, sickness or a rare opportunity to use civil transport facilities, all R.A.F. personnel posted to an overseas theatre made the journey by troopship.

Between the wars the carrying of troops by sea was given by Government contracts to selected shipping lines. Chief among the carriers was the Bibby Line, with a fleet of ships whose names were synonymous with overseas service and who created their own special niche in service history. One of them, the Somersetshire, was immortalised in song, sung whenever there was a nostalgic drinking session by ex-overseas erks.

The 'Shire' class had a long history of trooping, ranging from the Boer War; further contracts were awarded in 1921 to the Bibby Line for transporting troops to the Levant and India. Four ships were used, the Dorsetshire, Derbyshire, Somersetshire and Lancashire. This small fleet gave valiant service and became well known in the ports of Gibraltar, Valetta, Alexandria, Suez and Bombay, especially during the Iraq and Indian N. W. Frontier operations, when the ship's rails would be lined with white-kneed troops going East, or sun-happy men coming West.

The troopers were jointly controlled by the Army and R.A.F. who also imposed the discipline, and sailed and operated by the Merchant Navy. When W.W.2 started many ships of all kinds were impressed, ranging from flat bottomed Isle of Man steamers to the Queen Mary, but whatever the type the discipline, conditions, food and wet canteen facilities contrived to remain the same. There was of course the odd exception, but that was probably run by a civilian concern.

The Devonshire a new ship, was ordered, and became the first trooper specifically designed and built for trooping duties. Its peacetime capacity was 1,300 troops and 212 first class passengers and it had larger forward deck for troop parades and exercise. The capacity of the other ships, contrary to the view of the many who went through the sardine stage, was 1,100 men, with accommodation for wives and families. Trying to retain control and discipline over large numbers of troops living in restricted spaces and with not a great deal to occupy their minds was always a major problem.

After the normal herding procedure of the troops on arrival at the port of departure, the drafts were taken aboard and detailed to port or starboard mess decks, some of which might be below the water line. On the way down the men would be issued with hammocks. Mess decks consisted of long tables and forms with almost no storage accommodation or locker space for the men, only for the hammocks. The men lived out of their kitbags. Let into the deckhead over the forms and tables were rows of 'ammock 'ooks, with others where-ever there was room.

Shaking down to shipboard routines was commenced by a general detailing of jobs considered essential on board. Men were detailed to guard the fresh water taps, for fire piquet duties, hammock guard, the ship's Sergeant Major's office for runner duties, for fatigues of all kinds. Some, the lucky ones, were detailed to help the wives on their mess deck with the children, which meant more space to move with more congenial company. Those lucky enough to escape duties could still be in line for short term jobs. On each mess deck, orderlies were detailed every day to collect the days rations, to serve, wash up and clean the mess deck.

Boat drill was held daily, the men, collared in their kapok lifejackets, mustering at their allocated boat stations and given instructions, and checked for correct wearing of the jackets. Speed of assembly was also checked.

With plenty of spare time on their hands it was important to keep the men occupied. Most of them would spend their time on deck playing cards or the great troopship game 'Housey Housey', also called Tombola, now bastardised as Bingo. Because the game was run by the ship's crew, stakes were set sufficiently low to avoid financial distress to the majority of its devotees.

Not so with an unauthorised game played in out-of-the-way places, Crown and Anchor. Stakes were as high as its organisers could make it and were the cause of many a servicemen arriving at his destination completely broke. If a game was discovered by authority charges were made against the participants, and all monies were confiscated and later handed over to service Benevolent Funds.

A 'dry' canteen for the sale of tea, biscuits, cigarettes, etc. was opened several times a day and was a boon for the unfortunates who could not stomach the standard messing, or whose stomach could not stand any messing.

Favourite first bogey to overcome was the Bay of Biscay, endowed with a reputation as a bad crossing but not always so, just as any other stretch of deep water. However, if it was rough then it was a **bad** crossing. Down in the heads, which of necessity one had to visit, the conditions were grim. If a man hadn't been sick on deck then, unless he had a strong stomach, he would be here. The nauseating results of overwhelming and uncontrollable sickness swilled to and fro across the troughs and lay in trodden pools on the deck.

In the early years beer was collected in the evening in large dixies by the mess orderlies. After being shaken up in its collection it would arrive on the mess deck usually flat and near ruined but, as old-time airmen would say, 'There's no bad beer!'. Later, a 'wet' canteen was opened for the sale of beer in the evening for about 1-2 hours. Senior N.C.O.'s had their own mess decks and a separate lounge-cum Mess.

The great majority of overseas theatres were so geographically based that practically all troopships entered the Mediterranean at Gibraltar. This place was also a turning point in life aboard, for in the few days sailing most of the men had found their sea legs and were beginning to enjoy their enforced leisure. Also they usually met better, warmer weather and, in summer, it was the point at which the thick blue uniforms were packed away and the lightweight khaki drill was worn.

Many service men had the erroneous idea that the exposure of their pale knees and arms meant they had to be made brown as quickly as possible, to avoid any catcalls of 'get your knees brown' from the experienced men who awaited their arrival. Unfortunately, and despite many warnings, many of these know-it-all types seriously underestimated the power of the Med; sunshine and suffered painful sunburn.

At times the ship could be steaming on a sea like blue molten glass, trailing a wake of viscous regular curves, with barely a trace of pitch or roll. Cruising in the placid blue water could be most relaxing and enjoyable.

Ports of call were normally made en route to disembark drafts or take on passengers bound for a change of station. If the other drafts were lucky they might even get the chance of a few hours ashore at such places as Gibraltar, Malta, Alexandria or Aden. Against a background of commercial bustle—Eastern style—was the skyline of an eastern port with here and there a minaret or temple peering from the westernised dock area. It could all be very exciting on the first trip, and it was.

A humorous description of a trooper journey in the middle 1920's is given by A.C. McConnell on H.M.T. Marglan. '... We left England with more women and children than troops, not that this made our journey any more enjoyable or the food any better ... the days of the long journey were passed in playing Housey Housey, fatigues, P.T. and keeping out of the way of overzealous N.C.O.'s. Passing through the Bay of Biscay ... I for one, hoped the ship would sink. ...

'Our first stop was Port Said — our first glimpse of the mystic East ... oranges and turkish delight were cheap here, the cheapness of the latter had a funny sequel. One of our mess mates was a Scotsman, a blacksmith by trade. He had been fitted out before embarkation with an almost complete set of top and bottom dentures for which he had waited many months — it wasn't easy to get so much treatment or to put the Service to so much expense then. Jock made a pig of himself on turkish delight ... and when the motion of the ship made itself felt entering the Red Sea ... was sick ... over the ship's side, unfortunately his teeth came out at the same time. ... Those of us around him had the greatest difficulty holding him back from following his teeth in their passage to the sea bed. ... Jock was to wait another year before he was refitted and had to pay a substantial amount towards the cost.'

Perhaps it might be appropriate to end this digression with the pre-war airmen's definition of a troopship. 'The ships were painted white with a blue band round them, the same colour as an airman's kit bag, and were packed like one.!

Chapter 9
What are you doing in Fighting Kit?

The years 1920-1934 have often been called the 'Golden Years' of the R.A.F., which might be construed as years of easy living after the rigours of the First World War. This could be no further from the truth, in fact, the word golden when related to the financial state of the service, would be better substituted by the word 'leaden'. The R.A.F. struggled on minimal budgets imposed by a Government working to a 'Ten Year Rule', a condition imposed by the Lloyd George Government of 1919, which decreed in its wisdom that Britain would not have to fight a major war for a decade.

Agreed by Trenchard in his fight to keep the R.A.F. going at all costs, a cut of nearly £3 million in 1923 became for ever known as the 'Geddes Axe'. The net result of this Air Estimate pruning was to condemn the R.A.F. to second and third class equipment, the majority of its aircraft obsolete, outdated living accommodation and stringent economy for many years. The only first class commodity it possessed was its manpower. With that last quality it attained a standard of efficiency unsurpassed in the world of aviation achievement.

Unlike the majority of the world's Air Forces the R.A.F. was, despite its small numbers and dated equipment, almost continually on active service throughout the 'Golden Years' in brush wars and peace-keeping operations in Russia, Mesopotamia, Kurdistan and India, Iraq, Egypt, Aden, Transjordan, Waziristan and Afghanistan. This had the effect of producing a succession of experienced, able and keen air commanders, hand picked by Trenchard, who were determined to keep the R.A.F. in the forefront of military aviation development.

That the R.A.F. was successful in its operations was due to the determination of its air and ground crews to back Sir Hugh Trenchard and his devoted Air Officers, and the famous 'esprit de corps' which was beginning to be felt.

Of all the operational theatres mentioned the R.A.F. was most deeply involved in Mesopotamia, the land of two rivers, or Iraq as it became. Under Trenchard's plan that he could control Iraq from the air with a greatly reduced cost in manpower and materials, which appealed to the government, the R.A.F. took over the job under Sir John Salmond in 1921. The campaign lasted many years, had the most men and machines committed to it, and overall was the most successful. But it must be mentioned that the conditions of the time and the geography of the country ideally suited the advanced concept of control from the air.

Very briefly, the R.A.F. had to contend with Turkish inspired rebellions and holy wars between tribes in and around Kurdistan and Mosul from 1922 until 1926; the risings of Sheikh Mahmoud, ex-Governor of Sulaimaniya 1919 to 1931; risings by disaffected tribes in Southern Iraq from 1923; and troubles caused by Sheikh Ahmad of Barzan in Central Kurdistan 1925 to 1927.

Real in-the-field maintenance of a 203 Squadron Nieuport Nightjar used in the Chanak crisis of 1922 Dardenelles. MOD. (Crown Copyright reserved).

Method of carrying casualties by DH9 in Iraq during 1920's. Rushton.

A Crossley recovery vehicle being used to lift a pranged Audax of 20 Squadron for transport to workshops. Peshawar 1937. J. P. Murray.

Vickers Victoria probably of 216 Squadron, and normally a troop carrier, loaded with emergency bomb load comprising 12 x 100 lb and 4 x 20 lb anti-personnel bombs. Peshawar NWFP. J. P. Murray.

The force comprised, in 1921, No's 8 and 30 (DH9A) Squadrons at Baghdad, 84 (DH9A) at Shaibah, 6 with Bristol Fighters and 55 (DH9A) at Mosul. An Aircraft Park moved into the newly opened Hinaidi aerodrome in late 1921, joined by 6, 8 and 30 Squadrons. No. I (Sopwith Snipe) arrived from Ambala, India, and in early 1922, two Vickers Vernon Squadrons, 45 and 70, arrived in Iraq, moving into Hinaidi, which became the main central base near Baghdad.

Military strength was reduced to six battalions of Indian troops, three British regiments, two Royal Artillery batteries, sappers and the famous armoured cars which were soon to be wholly manned by the R.A.F. Last, but by no means least, there were three Iraq levy regiments mostly of Kurdish troops, one battalion of Arab levies and three battalions of Assyrian levies, who all did extremely well in the subsequent ground operations.

The aeroplane was the new, efficient weapon, terrifying to the ignorant tribesmen, able to reach the scene of an incident in hours against days of footslogging, and before guilty tribes had time to melt away into the wild hills.

Although the R.A.F. could never entirely replace the infantry for day to day occupation duties, it nevertheless lightened the load of the soldiers by the aircraft carrying essential stores, mail, food and water to marching columns or garrison troops and flying sick and injured back to base hospital.

Air reconnaissances were quite often able to inform the troops of an ambush and, by its swift appearance, more often than not be able to break up a potentially dangerous situation. When recourse was made to more positive action a punitive air attack usually resulted in complete rout of the hostile tribesmen.

The most casualties in Iraq were not from operational sorties, but from flies and mosquitoes and heat exhaustion. The majority of the R.A.F. could expect to be posted overseas to this theatre in the years before 1933; a tour was of five years and airmen posted to Iraq stayed only two summers in that country, and were then posted to India or Egypt for the remainder of the five years. For the men on the ground a tour of Iraq was one to which they could look forward to dust, fierce heat and icy cold, months of boredom and the occasional flurry of operational activity. The diseases that Air Mechanic Hague had known during his war in that theatre were still as prevalent, and all were subject to possible attacks of dysentery, bubonic and other crippling diseases.

Operations in a largely hostile country meant that air units had to operate from known and protected bases. Mosul, Kirkuk, Kingerban, Erbil and Sulaimaya were some which were used against Sheikh Mahmoud, the major thorn in the British flesh. Kirkuk, a stone built old Turkish town, was at this time a temporary airstrip which was eventually developed into a permanent aerodrome.

It was extremely hot on the plains aerodromes at Hinaidi, Shaibah, and Kirkuk, and a relief system was organised for the men in the summer season on a rota system for a period of rest in the hills — a system which was also introduced into India. One of the more popular stations was Mosul, which was sited in the cooler north of Iraq. To reach it from Baghad in the early 20's entailed a train journey, with all its crowded discomforts, to Sharyat terminus and then transferring to a solid tyred three ton Leyland for 90-100 bone shaking miles. Even with an open top the passage of warm dusty air brought little relief.

The road followed the tracks of an old camel caravan route and it was quite common to see, according to L.A.C. Marchant, bones of dead camels and occasionally those of a human, the possible results of Bedouin attacks on a caravan. Before the First World War

In 1925 AC Smith was crew on a Victoria which flew the then Air Minister from Hinaidi to Delhi in India. These were the passengers and crew on 23 Jan 1925. l to r; AC Davidson, Cpl Clarke, F/O Stewart, Sir Sefton Brancker, F/Lt King and AC Smith. R. O. Smith.

the railway had connected Baghdad but the Turks had destroyed the section from Shargat.

During periods of non-operations, life in Iraq soon settled into a pattern which became a basic routine in most overseas theatres, with variations on the theme dictated by local conditions.

In summer the day started with the bearers bringing a cup of 'gunfire' thick and strong at 0500 hours. No breakfast was taken for it was up to the hangar for 0530 to take advantage of the relatively cool and dense morning air. Sorties were flown until 0730 when the airmen stood down for breakfast. After the meal flying began again in rapidly rising temperatures and increased dust clouds from the slipstreams, until the flying ceased around 1100 and the aeroplanes were serviced. Special care was given in the inspection because of the inherent danger from wood shrinkage caused by the fierce heat, particularly if the aircraft were forced to stay out of doors for any length of time.

By cease work the temperature could be up to 120°F and the pith hat, or Bombay bowler, and spine pads were needed as the men walked, or were marched, back to their bungalows and 'tiffin', the midday meal. The afternoon was given over to universal siesta for those not on duty, until around 1700. This typical Eastern practice was followed by all until, wakened from a deep, sweat-soaked sleep under the mosquito nets by a cup of char, the erks were soon under the showers to freshen up before the evening meal. In the cool of the evening football, cricket, rugby and tennis was played, although the latter was predominantly an officer's prerogative.

The evenings were spent taking things easy and if the station boasted an open air cinema, a couple of hours would pass watching a flickering film, which might evoke a slight home sickness from the 'rain' appearing on the screen, but they were usually a good laugh.

*   *   *   *   *

Because of the distances involved long flights were common but quite often some of them became local sagas of adventure, hectic and exciting at the time, but now completely forgotten. One who had such an experience was A.C. Smith, who had settled in at Hinaidi in 1925. His story is given at some length to illustrate the conditions of the times.

Hinaidi in 1925 was a base aerodrome with nearly all the resident Iraq squadrons stationed there. In addition to housing six squadrons it was also the base for a General hospital, an armoured car company and an Aircraft Depot.

The Smith saga was a long flight from Hinaidi to India, which took two months, flying as escort, to the then Air Minister, Sir Samuel Hoare, who had flown out on an inaugural air mail route in a DH66. The aircrew of Smith's Victoria were F/Lt. King first pilot, F/O. Stewart second pilot, Cpl. Clarke wireless operator, A.C. Davidson fitter and Smith rigger. The aeroplane left Hinaidi 1st January 1927 and returned 1st March having flown via Shaibah, Bushire, Banda Abbas, Singah, Jask, Charbah, Karachi, Hyderabad (Sind), Jodhpur, Delhi, Ambala, Lahore, Peshawar, Kohat, Multan and Khanpur to Karachi and back to Hinaidi. This trip was memorable to Smith for several reason, a forced landing in the Sind which required an engine change; carrying Sir Sefton Brancker from Jodhpur to Delhi; meeting Stack and Leete, two ex-R.A.F. officers flying England-Australia in a D.H. Moth (A.C. Davidson rendered assistance) and being introduced to Sir Geoffrey Salmond, A.O.C. India. Quite a trip.

A Flight of 84 Squadron DH9As Iraq about 1925. F/Lt Rushton.

The starboard engine had begun to lose water just after leaving Karachi, sufficient to cause an emergency landing on Hyderabad racecourse. After topping up from their water drums they took off again but after only 45 minutes they were forced to land at Raragi. It was decided to try and top up the water tank in the air and all available tubing was collected and connected up to make a hose. With this the Victoria took off and at a few hundred feet the first pilot stood on his seat, reached up to the water tank filler and inserted the hose. The ground crew then passed up a large kettle and F/Lt. King poured the water down the hose. Water level was observed by a sight glass but it was noticed that the water level still went down after the first filling. F/Lt. King abandoned the idea, made a forced landing and the decision that a new engine was needed. A signal was sent to this effect by the wireless operator after rigging the telescopic aerial.

The engine failure was caused by bearing failure. The new engine had to be obtained from Hinaidi and a certain L.A.C. Jackson contributed his own small personal saga by bringing the engine, with a set of shear legs, by train to Basra, ship to Karachi, train to the nearest rail point and by bullock cart to the stranded aeroplane. After the engine was changed L.A.C. Jackson returned with the gear to Karachi. This small episode demonstrates the opportunity to use one's own initiative in Trenchard's, and subsequent, R.A.F.

While waiting for the engine to arrive the crews tried to move the Victoria with the help of local natives and started the port engine, but rapidly abandoned that idea when the power of the port engine overcame the pulling power of the locals on the starboard side. They dropped the ropes and ran. The fitter repaired the water leak and the ground crew removed the propeller, slackened bearer bolts and loosened all connections.

The engine was changed, in Smith's own words, '... Only two of the three shear legs were used ... The engine was moved by lifting it off the bearers towards the legs. A rope was tied from the top of the legs to a screw picket set into the ground some 30 yards away. The engine was hoisted up off its bearers, the rear rope was slackened and the other taken up. As soon as the engine was clear it was lowered on to bits of wood ... the new engine was installed by the procedure in reverse. . .'

They were on the ground nine days before taking off for Jodphur. Next day they picked up Sir Sefton Brancker, who slept nearly all the way to Delhi, so Smith and Davidson helped themselves to the good things brought aboard before they went stale! On the return trip at Jodphur they had their photograph taken with Sir Sefton.

L.A.C. Smith opined that the Victoria was easy to maintain, with bell crank levers fitted to the control runs at all turning points insteads of pulleys. Changing control wires was hardly known, although Smith had to exchange a broken swage rod in an engine bay with a spliced cable, working at night to finish the job. Burst tyres were frequent and with the weight of these aircraft, changing a wheel became a major operation. Smith enjoyed his tour with 70 Squadron with its high morale, '... It was nothing to see almost the entire flight personnel out in the hangar doing something to the aeroplanes in the cooler afternoons, not in summer, of course. . .'

*　　*　　*　　*　　*

For letting oneself go, Christmas was the big event for all servicemen overseas, boat parties excepted, the latter celebrating the homeward tour-expired. For Christmas the R.A.F. allowed a custom to begin to decorate huts, barrack rooms or bungalows and to compete for the best and original bar, and great was the enthusiasm thereof. These bars would be the subject of much design and discussion months before Christmas with many a 'scrounging' party organised to accumulate the necessary materials. As the erks had only about a week before the break to do the actual building of the bar this pre-planning was essential, and a number of erks found their true vocation as bar designers.

Each bar would be fully stocked, mainly with local brews, but would not be opened until the C.O. did his rounds of inspection to judge the best bar. On this inspection any C.O. who, out of courtesy partook of every drink offered him, had to have a very strong stomach indeed. He usually politely refused. After the visit the bar was opened and Christmas festivities had begun.

The next major event to follow the bar judging was the traditional Christmas dinner. The tables were usually arranged in long lines in the well decorated dining room, with the tables resplendent with tablecloths — the only time — and at each set place a bottle of beer, crackers, and maybe a few cigarettes. Once sat down the airmen were usually given a short address by the C.O. and the meal commenced. All officers and Senior N.C.O.'s who could attend, by tradition waited on the airmen. It was normally a happy meal with chat and wisecracks on all sides, autographing the menu, some songs, until at last the meal was over and the erks were left to themselves. Most of the men wandered back to their bungalows to sleep off the meal. The dinner was invariably first rate with full British traditional fare, from soup and turkey to coffee and cheese.

Part of the traditional celebrations included a comic football match between officers and N.C.O.'s and men. Dressing up for it was brought to a fine art, and with hardly the sight of a white women from one year's end to another, it was understandable that some good female impersonations were made, and this long before the beginning of drag. All kinds of garb was worn, or discarded, paint applied and most everything went provided it was in the fun of the thing. On the field of play kicking the ball was only incidental; it was handled in every conceivable way, with cricket bats, golf clubs, carried and even sat on. Clowning was the thing.

The evening might be devoted to drinking or a concert or both, with Senior N.C.O.'s being invited to the Officers Mess beforehand, an invitation that was reciprocated on Boxing Day. Members of the Corporals Club would be invited to the Sergeants Mess and vice versa. After the holiday it was 'back to normal' with a bang.

The intensive air operations that had characterised the control of Iraq by the R.A.F. was virtually over when, in November 1933, L.A.C. Marshall and Co. ex draft from U.K., joined 70 squadron at Hinaidi. Their reception in the country had begun, typically, almost before they set foot on land. '.. we paraded on deck with kit packed ... On the quayside a sight to make us blink met our eyes; a concourse of airmen were gathered dressed in overcoats, scarves, balaclavas, large flying gloves and any other clothing ... to keep them warm ... These chaps .. shouted up 'You wait 'till it gets hot' and other comments, and the married families, none of whom were landing at this God foresaken spot, were slightly alarmed .. When we went down the gangplank lugging all our worldly possessions .. we saw it was an elaborate hoax and they were sweating more than we were. ...' Such was the spirit of the R.A.F. in Iraq and India before the war, possibly the highest example of esprit de corps it has ever been.

The squadron aircraft in 1933 were still the faithful Victorias now supposedly nearing the end of their service life after many years of arduous operation. The engines, of which Marshall had accumulated much experience with 207 Squadron at Bircham Newton, weren't quite as efficient as those in the 3F's. They were, in effect, clapped out. '... Blowing valves, burst water jackets, excessive oil temperatures and bearing failures ... gave the engine fitters experience they had never dreamed of. These men became masters of expedience, knowing that upon their work often depended whether the aircraft would get back to base.'

Synonymous with the Iraq campaigns were those operations on the North West Frontier of India. Both were of a similar nature and as the two largest theatres of operations overseas required a steady flow of manpower. In India the R.A.F. was never in complete control as in Iraq, the Army Command was too powerful.

Active service was on the Frontier. It was in this area that the main actions took place, for along it lay Afghanistan, a turbulent seething area of tribes spoiling for a fight. Here were the wild Waziris, Afghans and Afridis; in the border areas were the proud Pathans, cruel, merciless fighters in war, reasonably magnanimous in peace.

Most of the operational aerodromes were in a thin line arcing in front of Afghanistan, some with names that were famous from Indian Mutiny days — Kohat, Nowshera, Miranshah, Risalpur. Other stations in India were Peshawar and Rawalpindi — both N.W.F.P. base units — Ambala, Lahore, Dum Dum (Calcutta) and Delhi. Others were laid down as the need arose.

* * * * *

When A.C. H. F. Whiting arrived at Ambala on 26th December 1921 after a long trip in H.M.T. Zeppelin he was billeted in quite comfortable barracks and was posted to 28 Squadron. Life at first was fairly easy and plenty of sport but the summer routine was drastically different from home:

Reveille at 0400	Breakfast 0600 to 0630
Parade for P.T. 0415 to 0445	March to work 0630
March to work 0450	Flying programme until 10.30
Flying programme until 0600	

The squadron with its Bristol Fighters moved to Kohat in the N.W. Frontier Province (N.W.F.P.) for active service against the restless tribesmen. Kohat was a garrison town and was strategically placed at the entrance to the Kohat Pass which linked it with Peshawar; it also had a rail link with Rawalpindi and a broad gauge rail to Bannu. Because of the close proximity of the insurgents — the tribal fires could be seen about six miles away — and a sympathetic bazaar only two miles down the road, night was always a time for alertness. This was the period when raiders, trying to steal arms and ammunition from

Westland Wapiti bomb load; four 100 lb HE's and anti-personnel bombs. J. P. Murray.

the camp, still greased themselves with cheetah fat to scare off dogs and make themselves a slippery handful. A three month detachment to Parachinar on the Afghan border made Whiting appreciate the delights of Kohat.

* * * * *

Serviceability standards of aircraft in the immediate post W.W.1 in India were shocking and dangerous despite the dedicated work of unit tradesmen. No less distinguished commanders than Marshals of the R.A.F. Sir John Salmond, Lord Douglas of Kirtleside and Sir Arthur Harris have mentioned the state of disrepair in India and Iraq. Aircraft were verging on the unsafe and at times were taking off on operations on the wheel rims. There were no spare tyres and because of tremendous shortages airmen were forced to buy canvas from local bazaars to repair aircraft fabric.

Engines were also dangerous, obsolete types were fitted with single ignition harnesses and few spares were available while at home thousands of spare parts were being held or sold. This state of affairs was attributed to the Army High Command who were keeping essential spares locked up in Indian depots under the guise of mobilisation spares.

Although there was a gradual improvement in the technical services of the R.A.F. as time passed, this theatre was to remain a backwater insofar as the supply of modern aircraft and equipment was concerned. Even when the R.A.F. proved itself, it was still neglected. The treatment did not deter the air and ground crews unduly, they simply got on with the job.

When the Japanese threat became apparent and there was a possibility that an enemy could force the Khyber Pass, then of course this area received the latest aircraft.

* * * * *

Along with 2,500 troops A.C. Nettingham went out to India on the Braemar Castle, taking 32 days to Karachi. A long rail journey of nearly two days took him to Peshawar where he joined 32 Squadron with Bristol Fighters.

After a short working-up period the squadron moved up to the Frontier at Dardoni where they met their first problem, a hurricane which uprooted the Bessoneau hangars and damaged a number of aircraft. The effects of the storm were far reaching for, because spare parts were unobtainable to repair the damaged aircraft, '... We had to change wheels and props after a machine had done a few hours to enable the squadron to carry out bombing raids on the tribesmen'. Exactly the conditions which had caused A.V.M. John Salmond to publicise the spares shortages in his book.

The camp was surrounded by barbed wire against hit and run raids by tribesmen after precious rifles and ammunition, but despite the close confinement the airmen managed to make a go of it, particularly with sport. They played many of the local regiments at football and, although wearing football boots, usually came off physically worse against the bare foot Ghurkas, Sikhs and Punjabis. On a local visit to Bannu to play the Tank Regiment they were ambushed in the Kohat Pass by tribesmen, and the two officers with them were held for ransom while the men, surprisingly, were allowed to go. It was a salutory lesson in those dicey times and all further visits outside the camp were stopped.

After a period the squadron returned to Ambala for a rest and a refit from the Stores Park at Lahore. The personnel were sent up to Murree for a break, which meant marching from Rawalpindi the 36 miles and a 7,000ft climb to Sunnybank in full equipment.

Whiting had the same experience, but they rested at Peshawar. By the late 1920's most of the men were being taken up by truck.

It was the practice in India to send batches of men up to the hill stations for a rest period, to recuperate from the effects of the enervating and dehydrating heat of the plains.

An important event in the history of the R.A.F. had taken place in 1925. After a period of spasmodic air operations against the tribes of Waziristan in support of the army, the Indian Government agreed to the R.A.F. operating independently on the North West Frontier, and gave it the job of bringing to submission the rebellious tribesmen. The R.A.F. did the job in two months with minor casualties and so successfully that other tribes outside the area voluntarily submitted.

The following verse, attributed to a W/Cdr. Pink, was written about that time. The tune, if any, is not known.

Waziristan 1925

Oh big 9A, oh big 9A,
What are you doing down Razmak way?
Why these bombs, this pomp of war,
Surely your home is in Risalpur?
Pomp be damned, you make me laugh,
There ain't no pomp in this small strafe.
I'm bombing hell from the local khan
To prove there's peace in Waziristan.

Oh smart Brisfit, oh smart Brisfit,
What are you doing in fighting kit?
I'm praying hard I'll avoid a konk
On offensive patrol from a sink called Tank.
Up the gorges and down Split Toi
Sniped to blazes, but atta boy.
They call it war on the banks of the Marne
But bless you, it's the peace of Waziristan.

If they ask me, what do I say
To the folks at home back England way?
Don't you worry, there's naught to tell
'cept work and fly and bomb like hell.
With hills above and hills below
And rocks fill in where the hills won't go,
Nice soft sitting for those who crash,
But war you call it, don't talk trash,
War's a rumour, war's a yarn
This is the peace of Waziristan.

About 1925 A.C. McConnell, a fitter M.T., disembarked at Karachi for an unpleasant initiation at a fly infested rest camp, probably Melir Cantonment, but eventually arrived at Drigh Road for the Repair and Overhaul Depot. This station was built about 1926 and is situated about eight miles from Karachi, on the edge of the Sind Desert, an area of high humidity and, because of its proximity to the desert, subject to dust storms. The accommodation, being the latest two storey blocks, was comfortable for the times. Service life at Drigh Road was rather monotonous, without the variety of life or scenery that so many serving on the squadrons had.

The peculiar attitude in India of non-fraternisation created much the same problems for the servicemen as those in Iraq; there was little mixing with fellow European civilians with their inverted snobbery; practically everyone was expected to keep to his own strata of society, and mixing with the Indians was just not done. The airmen were literally outside the pale, except to shopkeepers and the like, for obvious reasons.

The station employed local semi-skilled tradesmen and enlisted them in a unit known as the Indian Technical Aircraft Company. These men were paid very good wages and were employed in routine work such as valve grinding, piston ring lapping, tyre fitting and so on.

The erk's pay was at a favourable rate with a fixed rate of exchange which gave the men a few shillings extra per month. The chit system was universal and the men signed for everything and then argued with pay accounts afterwards when they received their credits.

McConnell had the rare distinction of meeting 'Lawrence of Arabia' who was posted in quietly and on the unit some time before the airmen realised that A.C. T. E. Shaw serving in E.R.S. was the great Lawrence.

After three years at the M.T.R.S. McConnell, much to his delight, was posted to 2 Indian Wing at Risalpur, where two new squadrons, 11 and 39 had been formed to operate a new aeroplane — the Westland Wapiti — along with eight Fitter D.P.'s in preparation for an operation that caught the world's headlines.

Risalpur was at that time a cavalry cantonment and the R.A.F. ex-cavalry barracks still held the smell of the horse. It was here that McConnell came upon another feature of overseas life, not done at Drigh Road, that of extra messing. Most unit personnel paid a small sum out of their pay to supplement the low service ration allowance towards extra items of food and some delicacies that they would not normally have. The practice often caused some arguments and suspicions as to where the money was being spent, particularly during periods when the meals were apparently more service issue than usual.

The drivers had the satisfaction of drives to the various aerodromes and emergency landing grounds, and through the Khyber Pass, but they drove only during the day because of the tenseness of the situation at the time. This tenseness, particularly in Afghanistan, finally blew up in 1928 with a major revolt by the Shiamwari tribe in the eastern part of the country, who rebelled against King Amanullah.

This uprising by the tribesmen and the investing by them of Kabul led to the first mass rescue, by an air force, of encircled people. The majority of Europeans had sheltered in the British Legation and the decision was taken to evacuate them by air, and all available troop carrying aircraft were concentrated at Risalpur; a number of these were called in from Iraq and Egypt. The air evacuation began on 23rd December 1928 and ended 25th February 1929.

During that period 586 people were air lifted, with over 24,000 lb of luggage, the aeroplanes covering 28,000 miles, most of it over mountainous territory, in their single engine DH9A's and twin engined Victorias and Hinaidis. There was only one forced landing, through mechanical trouble, and with no loss of life.

A DH 10 crashes at Ismailia, Egypt, probably of 216 Squadron about 1922. A. Welch.

To keep these aircraft in the air the ground crews worked long and hard. Refuelling alone was a time consuming job as at first all fuel was in four gallons cans and had to be filtered through chamois leathers. Night servicing was normal; among the essential back-up services was the M.T. which was kept busy in bringing up much needed stores and conveying the evacuees and their luggage.

For the operation the Army loaned a number of W.W.1 tanker vehicles, poorly maintained and with Indian drivers whose mechanical knowledge was abysmal. McConnell recalls, '... I remember one (driver) left the outlet valve open and flooded the drains with aviation fuel, thereby stopping smoking in the camp for several days. . .'

The evacuation was a complete success.

The air actions against truculent Waziristan and Afghanistan tribes continued sporadically through to the late 1930's, culminating with the Mahmud and Waziristan campaigns of 1935, 1937 and 1938 respectively. The actions were much the same as those in Iraq — containing raiding parties and/or punishing from the air those that did get through the net. Keeping a watching brief on the southern flank of the Frontier were the squadrons based on Quetta and Manzai and Tank.

The Indian Mutiny, although so long before, had left an indelible mark on the traditions of the services. The airmen carried rifles on the first parade of work day, but church parade was the most significant. Smith wrote, '... Church parade was an imposing affair. We went with a rifle and five rounds, a throwback to the Indian Mutiny days. After church we all fell in and marched past the C-in-C Quetta ... 'We' included different regiments ... last to go and least in number, the R.A.F. There were two full bands and I for one really enjoyed it. After the march past we (the R.A.F.) were conveyed back to the 'drome in lorries. . .'

Despite the problems, away from home for up to five years, the heat, cold, dust and diseases, the majority of erks considered their tour as the best part of the their service. For here was esprit de corps at its very best between all ranks. Even the knowledge of so long away from wives and families with little chance of bringing them out did not daunt this spirit, which seemed more deeply imbued in all pre-war airmen serving overseas. They relied on their comradeship, a few pints in the canteen with their special songs, a few hearty choruses of 'Roll on the boat' and an almost fanatical enthusiasm in their work. It was just as well, for these superb tradesmen had to maintain their obsolescent aircraft on a 'make do and mend' principle long after the machines were obsolete.

There was no Naafi at Quetta, the canteen being run by civilian contractors, and it was sitting in this place that Smith experienced an earth tremor just as he was putting his first pint of the day under the chair. Someone shouted 'Quake' and the canteen was emptied in seconds. It was a precursor of the terrible earthquake which practically decimated the Quetta R.A.F. and local inhabitants in 1935. On that Friday in May 54 R.A.F. personnel and 68 Indian other ranks were killed, with some 200 injured. The two squadrons 5 and 31, lost practically all their aircraft. The earthquake had a lasting effect on the survivors.

A practical problem that arose as a result of the shortage of N.C.O.'s on Quetta's establishment was that senior L.A.C.'s were detailed as guard commander on occasion. This short term policy created no possible doubts as to the erks fitness to take on responsibilities, as Trenchard's long standing policy had been designed to do.

During the early 1930's some squadrons had been re-equipped with the Wapiti, which was powered successively by Jupiter 9 and 10, Panther and Jaguar and achieved the unusual distinction of equipping all eight Indian squadrons by 1932, until the Hawker biplanes began to replace them in 1935. Although designed with India and Iraq in mind the designers forgot about, or ignored, the poor old erk by fitting crank starting.

This entailed a man standing on each lower wing root, bracing himself against a landing wire and turning the cranked handle while fitter or pilot primed with a Ki-gas pump. The effort involved in turning the low geared starters was considerable and very much unappreciated under a fierce sun and dust.

The last big operations on the Frontier was against the Faqir of Ipi who united the dissenting tribes into an anti-British consortium. The tribes comprised his own Bhitiani Mahsuds and Waziris, a formidable force which kept the Army and R.A.F. on the alert and active for two years 1936-38. The intensity of air operations caused casualties among the ground crew from exhaustion and sunstroke from operating on the open airstrips of

A Hawker Audax of 20 Squadron operating on the NWFP, India, has a heavy landing. J. P. Murree.

Miranshah, Manzai and Arawali. Continual air harassment and bombing soon induced the Mahmuds and Waziris to capitulate in 1937; the Faqir fled in 1938.

One of the dominant factors in helping the R.A.F. to maintain air control in Iraq was the R.A.F.'s own armoured car companies. The following may help the reader to understand a little known branch of the service which contributed considerably, and which developed eventually into the long range desert group type of warfare when the Second Great War burst on the deserts. The cars worked in close co-operation with the flying units and army patrols and were manned entirely by the R.A.F. They were the descendant of the R.N.A.S. units of the last war and in fact, the cars used were much the same pattern and design, being driven by a Rolls-Royce engine, had solid tyres at first, and mounted a turret equipped with a water cooled Vickers.

An armoured car veteran who arrived in Iraq as a comparative latecomer with a draft that had volunteered for these vehicles was L.A.C. Murray, who reached Iraq in 1937 to a memorable reception at Shaibah '... As we drew to a halt into the camp we were given a tremendous reception. Everybody had turned out to greet us, airmen, N.C.O.'s and officers and the native bearers. Most of the airmen were in fancy dress, we thought they were all nut cases.'

'We were soon whisked away to our quarters, our kit put away ... After a bath and change of clothing we had a slap-up meal. That evening in the canteen there was as much beer as you could drink, it was a wonderful welcome...'

R.A.F. Shaibah was a small station in South East Iraq, near Basrah, housing 84 Squadron flying Vickers Vincents, the armoured cars and a company of Iraq Levies. The total complement of R.A.F. was under 200. The station was heavily defended by a perimeter of a steel fence, in front of which were three belts of barbed wire; forming part of the fence were eight concrete blockhouses complete with machine gun mountings and sandbags and telephones. Within the perimeter were the canteen, cookhouse and dining rooms in the camp centre with the living accommodation around these. Because of its

A Rolls-Royce R.A.F. R.A.F. armoured car (ex-Fleet Air Arm) in Iraq during the 1920's. F/Lt. Rushton.

isolation there were a large number of amenities for the station personnel. An outdoor and an indoor cinema, a swimming pool officially the station reserve water supply, football, hockey and cricket pitches and tennis courts. During inclement weather indoor entertainment was provided by games rooms, billard tables, music and writing rooms, a thriving concert party and inter-bungalow competition of darts, dominoes and Ukkers (Ludo). The station was surrounded by desert.

Armoured car life was one of two extremes. At base discipline and training was rigorously applied with more than a modicum of bull thrown in. Out on patrol the reverse was the case. All concerned accepted the hard training gladly, knowing that as a fully trained and disciplined force they could afford to relax when out on the 'blue'.

The cars performed invaluable service in protecting convoys and were on patrol constantly. It was the kind of life where great reliance was placed on initiative; conditions were much worse inside the cars than any hangar. The country was rough going with much scrub, rock and sand. It needed a special car and Rolls-Royce had the answer. The engine was basically a 1913 modified 50 h.p. six cylinder Silver Ghost in a 1925 chassis, and both were to be extensively modified further to keep the cars up to date. Sgt. Rushton's photograph is of a 1925 car with solid tyres.

The engine had coil and magneto ignition; if one system failed the car ran on the other, one of the first fail-safe ideas. Water cooling was modified by the inclusion of a steam collector which condensed the steam and returned it to the cooling system, and proved most economical.

Each car carried 12 gallons of water in felt covered containers, one each side of the car. There were also six 'charguls' (one gallon canvas water bags tied with string at the top and used for drinking). These were stored three on each side. Sometimes the charguls were tied on the outside to cool the water, the canvas bags 'sweating' in the same way as a 'chatti'. Equipment for desert operation was comprehensive and included:

Two spare wheels, two sand mats, two 5 gall drums of petrol, two ramps, 40ft coil of hemp rope, steel towing cable, pick and shovel, signal racks, enamel utensils and cutlery, complete tool kit and semaphore flags. Two battery operated signal lamps were carried, one facing forward and the other to the rear.

Each car had a medium, water cooled Vickers mounted in the turret and a Lewis, with several thousand rounds of .303, a bag of Mills grenades and a Verey pistol with its cartridges clipped to the inside of the door. Each member of the crew carried a .45 Webley and a Lee Enfield, with the rifles held in racks.

The armament was the responsibility of the gunner and the ammo was checked several times during a recce, as the loss of a single round could result in a court martial unless a very good reason explained its loss, such as self defence from an attack.

*   *   *   *   *

After the Christmas festivities which had occurred just after the arrival of Murray's draft, the drivers took part in the training which made these units so efficient and so much admired. Firing proficiency had to be gained over 1,000 metres with rifle, Lewis and Vickers, including stripping and re-assembling the guns. Revolver practice with the issue Colt .45's was frequent and intensive. How to throw Mills grenades safely was an eye opener, judging from the number of dummy grenades which rolled back into the trench, until proficiency was acquired. Use of heavy mortars, for station defence, was included in the syllabus.

161

In addition to armament training there was car drill, carrying out different formations on the move, wheel changing drill (a trained crew could change a wheel in $2\frac{1}{2}$ minutes), flag signals for controlling the cars on the move and first aid. The last was extremely useful. Some time was spent on 'bulling' the cars and equipment; on top of these activities the company contributed to the normal station routine of billet, kit inspections and parades. Shaibah was an efficient station.

In 1938 No. 4 Company carried out their longest recce during L.A.C. Murray's tour. The route was from Shaibah to Dhiban, Mosul, Kirkuk, Rowandes to the Iraq-Iran border and into Kurdistan for a short distance and return, a total mileage of nearly 2,000 miles. While on the move in the desert the cars and support vehicles drove in fan formation extending up to a mile across to avoid each others dust. A stop was made each hour for a drink and to change drivers, a procedure not always adhered to when running behind schedule, '... through punctures, breakdowns and other mishaps...

'We stopped between 12 and 1 o'clock for tiffin, which consisted of bully beef and bread and a pint pot of tea; we would have the bread for the first two or three days as we could not keep it fresh ... after the bread ran out it was biscuits for the rest of the trip'.

Stopping for the night involved a definite drill. The cars and trucks, under a signal flag, closed up to a pre-arranged formation and formed a laager with the soft skinned vehicles in the centre. Before the men could eat, essential functions had to be done. The gunners swung the turrets and guns outward and readied them for action then dug a gun pit to take the Lewis and spare ammo and parts. The drivers serviced the vehicles, carrying out essential repair jobs such as changing the all too frequent burst tyres. On long patrols one support vehicle carried all the spare tyres and wheels only. The Aldis lamps were set up as ready made small searchlights, the wireless operators set up their mobile masts to transmit to base. If required the tents were erected. When any one man had completed his task he mucked in to help the others.

Supper was usually McConachie stew followed by tinned fruit. After supper, sentry detail was carried out on a basis of one hour each for all. Favourite drink of the airmen, indeed it seemed throughout Iraq, was McEwans Red Label, for on each patrol several cases were taken along.

At Kirkuk a mysterious stomach malady attacked the men, causing an enforced stay of two days. It was thought to be something they had eaten, which was correct. But had they known the truth there might have been one less cook to survive the patrol. Several weeks later the section cook confided in Murray, explaining that he had dropped a bone handled knife into the stew which melted the bone, so he had let it go and dished out the 'stew'! Wisely, Murray kept the confidence until after the cook went home.

The last part of the outward journey was sheer sensuous pleasure as the men feasted their eyes on grass, tree and bush and the rivers and mountains of the countryside through which they travelled, particularly the spectacular Rowandez Gorge. They stayed several days inside Kurdistan and then began the return journey.

Shortly after, a friend of Murray's went down with heat exhaustion and the section pulled into a deserted railway siding building, where the section worked on the sick man in an effort to revive him. Murray's account is interesting in that it showed both the elementary first aid treatment of the complaint and how determined his friends were to help all they could.

'They had my mate in this building on a makeshift table. They had signalled straightaway for an aircraft; four of the airmen were fanning like mad, they used their pith helmets for this and one kept sprinkling him with water. We worked in relays of four, about 20 minutes each team, the C.O. taking his temperature at intervals. This was the first object, get the temperature down, it doesn't seem much but its bloody hard work, which you find out when it's a matter of life or death. I don't know how many hours we kept at this, two, three or four, but a troop carrier arrived with a doctor and medical orderlies. We soon had him on a stretcher into the aircraft and away.'

*   *   *   *   *

Cpl. Murray stayed in Iraq until the outbreak of the war sent him into even more serious adventures with the Desert Air Force. His brother was a wireless operator on 20 Squadron at Peshawar during the last pre-war major operation, was also a keen photographer and, more important, kept his photographs. As a result we are able to catch a glimpse of life in the R.A.F. operating on the Frontier. It was a life of movement, flying with the squadron between the forward 'dromes, or moving by road through passes and places so well known from those days, Kohat Pass, Dera Ismail Khan, the road to the Khyber and the famous Pass itself with its forts at Jamrud, Shaai and Landi Khotal. Life on the few remaining aerodromes in India was more peaceful. Dum Dum aerodrome at Calcutta and Lahore were devoted to repair and storage. A squadron was stationed at Delhi and Ambala. For these units and the ground crew their time of warlike technical toil and tribulation was to come after 1939.

Egypt's almost perfect weather conditions and its geographical position made it an ideal base for the campaigns in Palestine and Mesopotamia. It was also used as a base for the Indian troubles until that Command laid down its own depots. Flying and technical training schools had been established and repair and maintenance depots laid down to supply the operational needs of the Command.

In 1917 No. 3 School of Military Aeronautics, a School of Aerial Gunnery, a Cadets Wing and a Wireless Observers School had been laid down at Helwan, Aboukir and Heliopolis respectively. In 1918 the R.A.F. established seaplane bases at Port Said and Alexandria; at the latter a Balloon company had its base.

Before this state was reached, however, the country had had to be pacified from the policital upsets caused by the war of 14-18. A few squadrons quelled the dissident Senussi tribes in the west before concentrating on driving the Turks out into Palestine. The battles of Gaza became as historic as those on the Somme, although with far less casualties and publicity and with more decisive success. All arms of the air services played a conspicious part in the fighting which eventually led to the collapse of the Turkish armies and Empire.

The post war period after the immediate crisis was resolved was one of turmoil and riot, as the Egyptians, not unnaturally, weren't too keen on Britain stabilising itself on her soil. Aerodromes were enclosed by barbed wire with searchlights at strategic points, and the airmen had to carry the bolts of their rifles in a pouch when the arms were not in use. Much the same as Iraq was to be.

In 1926 as part of Trenchard's policy of bringing the attention of the British public (and others) to the potential power of the R.A.F., a series of long range flights were instituted.

To 47 Bomber Squadron stationed at Aboukir fell the task of flying the second Cairo-Cape Town-Cairo flight in 1927. The aircraft used were Fairey 3F (Napier Lion) sent out by sea from U.K. and assembled in the depot at Heliopolis. To command the flight was

Air Commodore Samson, C.M.G., D.S.O., A.F.C., Air Officer Commanding Middle East. The aircraft crews were:

Pilots	Crew
Air Commodore Samson	F/Lt. D. L. Blackford-Navigator., H.Q. Middle East
S/Ldr. Maxwell C.O. 47 Sqdn.	F/Sgt. Evans 47 Sqdn fitter
F/Lt. MacDonald	F/Sgt. Johnson 47 Sqdn fitter
F/O. Bett	Either L.A.C. Holme or L.A.C. Hogan as reserve airman

Preparatory work on the 3F's was carried out by tradesmen from Heliopolis and Aboukir and included a great deal of modifications to fit the aircraft for their task. These major mods. were:

An extra water tank fitted to the floor of the rear cockpit
A redesigned radiator with revised packing glands
An extra 15 gall. fuel tank fitted under pilot's seat
Experimental petrol funnel for top centre section
A larger capacity oil tank
A three ply fuselage bulkhead to close off rear fuselage
Drinking water tank installed

70 Squadron Vernons arrive to transport the personnel of 112 Squadron to war. Aug 1939.

J. Cowburn

Chain swinging method with bag over the propeller to start a DH9A bogged down by the monsoon rains at Miranshah India in the 1920's. MOD. (Crown Copyright reserved).

There were many teething troubles, which had to be rectified such as oil pipe unions loose, radiators prone to leaks and difficult to remove, the propeller spinner fracturing, and a number of other minor faults. All aircraft were checked and modified to the same standard.

While this work and testing was going on advance parties along the route were laying out fuel depots and organising the aerodromes for the reception and servicing of the aircraft.

The flight was a success as was all the others that followed. The importance of these flights was realised when war broke over the Middle East, as was the almost continual operations throughout the area.

Egypt's role as the main training base since W.W.1 had been gradually replaced by its greater strategic importance as the Second World War drew nearer. The upsurging nations in the area and the rise of Italian military power in the Med: made it vital in the defence of Britain's interest in the Suez Canal. Italy's occupation of Benghazi and her attack on Abyssinia turned Egypt into an operational zone.

With the emphasis by the R.A.F. of maintaining control by air power in Iraq, a training airfield was necessary on which aircrews could practice their bombing techniques and this was established at Abu Sueir, in Egypt.

The crisis year of 1938-39 saw a rapid build up of British armed forces in readiness for the expected war. So vital did the British Government consider the importance of this strategic area and the urgent necessity to reinforce it that extra squadrons were rushed out, making up their establishments en route. One such squadron was 112 (Fighter) Squadron.

The unit was embarked in H.M.A.C. Argus for transportation to Alexandria, '.. along with its crated Gloster Gladiators and uncrated pilots ...' Its ground crew had not been fully complemented before it left U.K. and this was rather unfortunate for A.C. Cowburn and two of his course friends who had just completed a years Fitter Aero Engine course at Manston for they were posted direct, without embarkation leave, to the squadron via the carrier.

When the draft arrived at Portsmouth they found about 120 other ground crew posted in as part of the squadron. The trip to Alex: was as uneventful as sailing in a 20 year old Naval carrier as a working passenger could be. On arrival the two services carried out a joint exercise before the squadron disembarked. The ground crew assembled a Gladiator and tried it for fit on the aircraft lifts to give the Fleet Air Arm some useful data for the future. The aircraft incidentally, were well maintained Gladiators that had belonged to 72 Squadron, an elite fighter unit that had had its aircraft replaced by Spitfires.

The squadron disembarked and moved into Helwan where they received the traditional welcome from 80 Squadron, the resident unit, before settling down to the working up exercises. In the Naafi the new arrivals were introduced to a quaint Egyptian custom of debugging the wickerwork canteen chairs. '... the exercise became a necessary ritual. One lifted one's chair as high as possible and dropped it. This was done two or three times and each time a number of bugs would drop from the crevices in the chair and one would immediately stamp the same...'

The war was imminent and the strength of the squadron was raised to a war footing and it became a mobile unit. Fighter air exercises were increased and air-to-air and air-to-ground firing was the order of the day. With such intensity of flying there were the inevitable crashes. During this period the station had a visit from Iraq-based 20 Squadron with their venerable and decidedly ancient Vickers' Valencias. John Cowburn, now L.A.C., wrote that the first sight of these aeroplanes frightened him to death but he was to fly scores of hours in them during the early part of the war.

R.A.F. Middle East had yet another, but lesser known area, where there was trouble and their services were required. A first detachment went out to Somaliland in 1920 on H.M.A.C. Ark Royal to support a force of Camel Corps in their action to overthrow the Mullah at the centre of a local revolt. There were spasmodic outbreaks in Aden until 1928 when No. 8 Squadron was sent out, together with an armoured car section, to suppress the Yemeni and Suhebi tribes who crossed the border and advanced to Aden. Effective bombing which was carried on and off from the summer of 1928 to March 1929 resolved the situation and caused the sheiks to capitulate. A small outbreak in 1934 against Qtubi road guards was also put down by air action.

Aden, formerly the Royal Navy base and ideally sited to watch the Red Sea and Indian Ocean, became an important base for aircraft staging through to the Indian and Far East theatres, and also as an anti-submarine base in its own right. But it was one of the worse overseas bases so far as conditions of living were concerned, being barren and exposed to the hot winds both from the Indian continent and Saudi Arabia. Its barrenness reflected the heat from its stark hills and great sand wastes to make life there very unpleasant indeed. Peacetime period of service was six months only.

35 Squadron, along with 207, was detailed in September 1935 to proceed to Sudan to keep a watching brief on the Italian presence in Abyssinia. The move required much checking of stores which had been brought into the station, dismantling the Gordons at Sealand for shipboard loading, a short leave and a grand farewell—Naafi style. After ceremoniously burning the Naafi piano the squadron embarked at Liverpool on the S.S. Cameronia, an ex-cattle boat converted to a trooper, which set out to prove its ability to do everything but slow roll on the calmest seas. In the Bay of Biscay it nearly did that!

An eventful journey, which included the bum boats at Malta, jabs on deck and many games of Lotto, brought them to Port Sudan and a rail journey to a tented camp near Ed

Damer. The aircraft arrived a few days later having been assembled by the squadron fitters and riggers dropped off at Port Said. At all costs bull had to be maintained, with regular distances between tents and stones painted white. Life settled to a routine 0500 to 1100 with regular flights along the Eritrian border; in the back seat of one Gordon was L.A.C. Tansy Lee, who had become an air gunner with 35 and so achieved an ambition.

The heat was fierce and the ground crew had to be careful around midday, when the metal was so hot that an incautious hand could suffer severe burns. It was here that L.A.C. Coleman, while 'squatting the pole' was 'attacked' by a scorpion and made a record run to the Sick Bay for jabs.

'A' Flight of each squadron was sent to an airstrip at Kassala to fly alternate patrols along the Eritrian border to let the Italians know they were facing the cream of Britain's obsolescent aircraft. A more physical discomfort than the Italian presence were the 'Shitehawks', particularly crafty and persistent birds that could, and did, swoop on any erk who forgot to keep his plate covered when he crossed open ground from kitchen to mess tent. Whoosh! the food was gone along with the hawk. Another discomfort was the sudden arrival of dust devils, sometimes so bad that only the gasmasks the men carried could give relief, including eating their meals.

Christmas came, was celebrated in the traditional manner, and in April the squadrons were moved up to Gebeit, a wadi type area to continue the patrols — and to mourn the death of P/O Essam, a member of the Esso Petroleum Company and his passenger. The pilot was trying to do a climbing turn out of the hills, not so good with the ponderous, slow Gordon. The stay at Gebeit was further enlivened by a violent rainstorm which whipped the tents to all parts of the compass.

Shortly after the squadrons were ordered back to the U.K., returning by '... proper troopship, the Somersetshire, which was a cut above the old Cameronia and being travelled veterans we found the journey home more amenable than the outward trip. One thing we did learn was that an ammunition and bomb dump and petrol store we had been using on Barda Island, just off the coast in the Red Sea, and marked down for clearance, had been dug too deeply, and seawater had seeped in and ruined everything.'

The squadrons proceeded from the boat to Worthy Down, the new station, before going on leave.

35 and 207 Squadron were sent out to the Sudan for the Italian Abyssinia crisis of 1934/36. This is A Flight 35 Squadron with Fairey Gordons. 207 Vincents in rear.

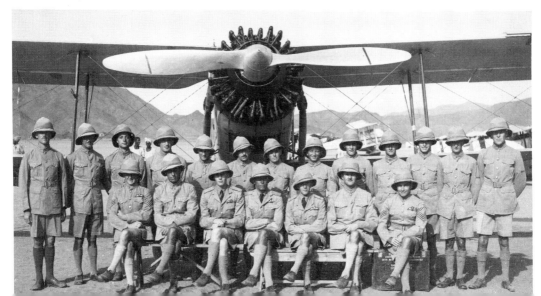

Chapter 10
Expansion

During the inter-war years the Royal Air Force, despite its problems of inadequate Air Estimates and the power struggle with the Navy and Army, contrived to make itself be regarded as the finest air force in the world. It achieved this deserved reputation not only by the efficiency of its operational units, its high quality of training, the calibre of officer and men, but by its participation in ventures which helped to advance the frontiers of aeronautical knowledge.

Not all ventures resulted in success, notably the Airship Service, but its possibilities were thoroughly explored. That this resulted in the loss of some of these craft along with their crews decided the Air Staff of the day that the form of construction and performance wasn't yet to the standard that made the airship a military proposition.

To tradesmen, as well as the air crew, an airship was a challenge, for the complexity of construction and method of operation was so different from aircraft. The amount of knowledge required just to understand the component parts of the structure was sufficient to daunt most trades and this, allied to a knowledge of gas filling and mooring procedures, made the airship rigger a man apart. All trades concerned in the servicing and maintenance of these ships were specialists.

The ships also required a large number of men for ground handling albeit most of them non-technical, but in the days when manpower in the services was at a premium, the use of a hundred or more men for mooring or ground manoeuvring was a luxury indeed.

By 1925 airship service was virtually over; it hung on for a few years with the civilianised R100 and service R101, the former successful, the latter involved in a disaster which spelled the end for the British airships.

It is probable that the airship contributed technically to aircraft design, for in their search for lightness of construction allied to strength the airship designers evolved quite advanced methods of strip metal construction and attachment of fabric to the transverse frames. Certainly, Barnes Wallis used a modified form of his geodetic airship construction for his Wellesley, Wellington and Warwick aircraft.

The R.A.F. participated in many international events, both to publicise the service and to develop aircraft. The most prestigious events were the World records, most of which the R.A.F. held, but more useful were some of the long range formation (very loose) flights.

In the field of pure technical advance the Schneider Trophy races contributed a great deal. High speed and manoeuvreability combined is an important asset to a service aeroplane and the speed contests ensured a continuous development along these lines. The machines and engines were specially built and, although seaplanes, the lessons gained were soon applied to land aircraft, and in fact led directly to the designs of new service monoplanes, particularly the Spitfire.

The accepted method of bringing a Schneider Trophy pilot ashore after flight, in this case from an S5 at Calshot in 1927. RAF Museum.

But it was a sad reflection on the times that a private individual (Lady Houston) had to finance the last, winning, entrant flown by the R.A.F. in 1931. The winning of the trophy outright must have been some vindication for all concerned, and a red neck for those who refused official financial aid. Selected R.A.F. tradesmen gained great experience on these High Speed Flights, some airmen attending courses at the manufacturers.

All areas of engine development for the series were exploited in the demand for engine power, and the chosen in-line liquid cooled engines developed dramatically. Ironically, the majority of the fighters of the day had radial air cooled engines. Both radial and in-line engines, however, were to benefit from these race bred engines. Some of these benefits became obvious with the arrival of the Pegasus, Hercules, Dagger, Kestrel and Merlin. While this technical development was taking place, in the quiet backrooms of Cranwell and Cambridge — sometimes not so quiet — a modest ex-apprentice, Frank Whittle (later Sir) was working on a novel form of aircraft propulsion, old in theory, new in practice.

There was also much development of better materials, steels, fabrics, alloys, paints, improving methods of construction, servicing and maintenance techniques and the other important aspects of flying such as instrumentation, wireless telegraphy and bomb aiming.

That essential, but deadly partner, armaments, was the responsibility of the Air Armament and Experimental Establishment (A.A. & E.E.) at R.A.F. Boscombe Down, who applied as much research to their work as other units. The brush wars going on in India and Iraq were only partially helpful to the A.A. & E.E. so far as bomb development was concerned, for the unit was always looking ahead to the possibility of a European conflict. Guns were also developed and at this establishment the final decision was made on such weapons as the 2-pounder (1 kg) carried on some Blackburn Perth flying boats, the Vickers gas operated 'K' machine gun used by air gunners, hydraulically operated enclosed turrets and the fitting of Browning guns to the wings of the new fighters.

Another example, in which Lady Houston's sponsorship helped aviation technology forward, was her backing of the R.A.F.'s attempt to fly over Everest in 1933, which was successful. The practical application of supercharging, heated flying clothing, oxygen supply at high altitudes and high altitude photography were all given a substantial boost. The aircraft were Westland Wallace with a special Bristol Pegasus S3.

The efforts of the Wallace stirred some interest in the Air Ministry for they commissioned the Bristol Aeroplane Company to build a special aeroplane, the Bristol 138, for an attack on the World's altitude record, in which it was twice successful, in September 1936 and June 1937. Two speed supercharging was the salient feature on this aircraft.

Britain was also supreme in flying boat operation, the constant long ranging flights in these craft with full service complement aboard, developed this branch of aviation so effectively that when the big Sunderlands entered service just before the war, the R.A.F. had a network of operational bases throughout the world which were to be invaluable in the coming U boat actions. Complementary to the flying boat flights were the long range land based aircraft flights which also had the same object, and had begun in 1926 on the Cairo to Cape Town route.

Where-ever possible selected tradesmen were carried, especially on the boats. As aircraft were improved by the results of these flights more and more squadrons undertook long range flights as part of their yearly exercise, which made a welcome break for the ground crew who participated, either by flying with the aircraft, or who were engaged in

Gloster Gladiator of 72 Squadron picketted out at RAF West Freugh after air firing exercises.

W. Hughes.

back-up work of servicing en route, until in 1933 this unique experience was becoming commonplace.

The R.A.F.'s effort helped the small aircraft industry by giving the designers and builders exercises in producing one-off aircraft, to small orders, to R.A.F. specification. Although the makers got precious little financial reward out of these orders they were at least enabled to avoid liquidation. The various economic crises had brought the industry to a parlous state and many of the well known manufacturers were relying more on major overhauls and modification work than orders to keep going.

On the carriers, too, great technical research by practical application was proceeding apace. The introduction of the steel deck, the laterally positioned deck arrestor wires, the steam catapult, all served to place the Fleet Air Arm well in front of its contemporaries. Because the F.A.A. believed, like the R.A.F., that only real practice makes perfect there were many bent aeroplanes as a result, and inevitably a number of lives were lost. Long range navigation over the seas was tremendously improved, particularly in the field of dead reckoning.

Down in the steel depths the tradesmen added their own smaller contribution by speeded-up repair methods and quicker drill in getting the aircraft up on deck and launching. All the information gained and valuable experience earned throughout the years of the first Furious, Argus, of Campania and the others, were incorporated in the breed of new carriers launched just before the war.

At the Royal Aircraft Establishment at Farnborough much research experiment and flight testing was progressing in every aspect of service aviation. Test equipment was being progressively developed to cope with the higher performance aircraft coming from the manufacturers, albeit mostly by one-off prototypes. A great deal of praise for this development must go to the manufacturers design staff. Many ideas started at this source, were tried out and, in conjunction with the experimental establishments were tested, rejected or developed. Their application paid off when from 1935 the industry consistently produced some of the finest aircraft in the world. Farnborough was responsible for great advances in wind tunnel design, decompression chamber techniques, aviation medicine, survival gear, in-flight refuelling and other spheres of exploration into flight.

At other units the radical, all-seeing eye, radiolocation, soon to be known as radar, was being developed by a team under the brilliant Dr. Robert Watson-Watt. Along with radar, other forms of radio detection and control under the equally brilliant Dr. R. V. Jones, which were also to revolutionise air warfare, were on the drawing board. The associated equipment of radio telephony, direction finding, navigation techniques and instrument flying were exhaustively researched.

Aircraft servicing, and the time taken to carry it out, was subjected to close scrutiny by top engineering officers and the results of their work was to produce a major change in this field towards the end of the war. In the lower echelons all technical tradesmen were encouraged to put forward ideas on any items of equipment that they felt might be improved and were given a suitable monetary award for any idea put into use. Also, long obsolete ground equipment was brought up to date to become more suitable for the new types of aircraft coming into service.

In practically all the development and experimental work the ground crew were involved, either by direct squadron trials of new aircraft and equipment, or in the manufacture of specialised items, or by direct testing at the Experimental Establishments.

Selected tradesmen were sent on specialist courses. The gunnery practice camps at West Freugh, Aldergrove and Catterick, were kept increasingly busy all the year round as operational units arrived to do their two week course in live gunnery and bombing, the culmination of a year's intensive training, when the aircrew had a taste of the real thing.

Time was a valuable commodity for the expansion of the R.A.F. for much needed to be done to bring the service onto a comparable basis with that of the new Luftwaffe, which had had the advantage of starting from scratch, with new ideas based on its Spanish venture, and equipment developed from that participation. The Royal Air Force, knowingly, was about to get involved, but there was still much to be done in the next few years.

The rise of National Socialism in Germany had caused considerable disquiet to a minority of forward thinking people headed by Winston Churchill, who saw in the New Order the probability of a major European conflict. This view, compounded by Italy's foray into new Empire building under Mussolini, and Japan's conquests in China caused this group, combined with increasing numbers of people in the street to exert pressure on the Government and finally, as a result of their own intelligence, the government of the day was forced to strengthen its own defence and make initial preparations for a war.

At last, after so many years of tight budgeting the strings of the Treasury purse were released and the R.A.F. and other services had the money they needed for so long. A review of the Air Estimates show how little had been spent and how much was needed to bring the R.A.F. up to some kind of parity with European countries. In 1928 the estimate was £16M; 1934 £20M (including Civil Air Estimates); 1935 £26M; 1936 £39M; 1937 £86½M; the first year of the war the cost rose to £200M.

Most of the money was spent in purchasing new types of aircraft from an aircraft industry that had never been allowed to gear itself to meet a sudden increase in production, and it took several years before expectation was coupled to realisation.

Despite the money and carte blanche the R.A.F. had the same difficulty as the other services, that of priority. With all three depending heavily on industries ill prepared to supply them there was sustained bar and lobby diplomacy to get priorities on such essential contracts as new aircraft, airfield buildings, uniform and accoutrements, general equipment and so on, without the added demand for essential strategic materials required for aircraft and weapons.

With Britain's world-wide interests at risk, overseas bases had to be strengthened and re-equipped and a move was made by sending reinforcements in 1935, many of them the new expansion airmen. But in terms of new equipment priority was given to the U.K. when the new monoplanes began to roll off the production lines.

The strength in manpower of the R.A.F. at 1st January 1934 was:

3,334 officers	11,000 reservists
25,170 other ranks	83 cadets
1,794 apprentices	

and the Expansion Scheme of 1934 as it became known, originally proposed another 2,500 pilots, 27,000 other ranks. The initial scheme was planned to 1936 and the trade structure was re-arranged to take into account the numbers and new technology of the monoplanes. The structure was formed into five groups, plus a separate small group for the medical and dental branches. Recruiting was under two parallel schemes, direct entry and apprentices.

The new entries of 1934 were primarily direct entry airmen, for the full technical weight of the increased output of apprentices and boy entrants was not expected to be felt until March 1937. To get the required numbers of tradesmen through schools and into service, and get the benefit of them, the initial period of engagement was limited to six years; such was the high standard of the pre-expansion fitters and riggers and other associated trades that it was considered that direct entry men could not benefit the R.A.F. within six years.

The recruiting authorities decided that men of some mechanical experience, engineers labourers, garage hands, etc., or men of superior intelligence (?) would be recruited, firstly as A.C.H.(G.D.) for training as Fitters Mate, a new trade, whose course would be of five weeks duration. On the results of examination on completion, those most suitable for fitting duties would be selected for a further eight months training in two new Group 2 trades, Flight Rigger and Flight Mechanic.

Overall, the scheme was a great success and it recruited many thousands, among them the author. The timing of the scheme was fortunately early enough to ensure that all the newly forming squadrons had adequate manpower when the crisis resolved itself into war. It was also nicely timed to meet the new generations of modern aircraft just beginning to enter service.

The men who swarmed to enlist in the Royal Air Force during the years from 1934 had much in common with their fathers in 1914. All were volunteers. Now given more opportunity to join the exciting young service they came in droves. In fact so great in numbers that the men had to be sent home to await recall. But the R.A.F. still insisted on a high standard, and after a gruelling medical exam and a written paper many were turned away; their turn came at the outbreak of war when the standards had to be lowered, albeit slightly.

The lessons of W.W.1 had been well learned and recruiting was a smooth, efficient process, the R.A.F. making the most out of the complexity of trades and professions that

Refuelling a 35 Squadron Vickers Wellesley of A Flight at RAF Worthy Down about July 1937.

MOD. (Crown Copyright reserved).

Servicing a Hawker Hart in the hangar at the end of the biplane era. About 1936.
MOD. (Crown Copyright reserved).

applied and fitting the majority of round pegs snugly into round holes.

The expansion scheme brought its own problems, particularly after 1938, when the imminence of war brought a flood of recruits pouring into the service with their attendant problems of accommodation and training. The magnificent force that Trenchard and his Marshals had built with just such an exingency in mind responded smoothly. The cadre of highly trained and skilled ex-apprentices and Group 1 direct entry trades were the first to receive promotion and move on to use their superlative experience to form and operate the rapidly blossoming squadrons, depots and units.

A crash building programme for hangars, barracks, including the well designed H Blocks, and other buildings, had been instituted in 1934-35 but despite great efforts on the part of some contractors, a number of stations were slow in nearing completion. The result was that by 1939 some barracks were double banked for accommodation purposes, some barrack rooms designed to sleep 16 men to peacetime standards held 40 in two-tier bunks. This state of affairs lasted for some time into the beginning of the Second World War.

Because of the high intake of volunteers the recruit depot facilities at Uxbridge were soon saturated and alternative recruit depots were opened at Orpington, Cardington, West Kirby and Squires Gate. The author well remembers the crowded conditions even in September 1935, living in huts in East Camp, Uxbridge, queues everywhere, whether for food, jabs or pay. A number of contemporaries experienced similar conditions; they varied only in particular from the author's personal involvement.

Uxbridge, by late 1935, was adjusting itself to the increased intake of recruits and life was hectic. Every day the square resounded to vocal commands, stamping feet, the slap of hands on rifle, the thump of butt on ground and the occasional melodious taps of a side drum beating in time with a metronome. The drill corporals became hoarse, the recruits sweated.

Meal periods were like scenes out of an American prison film; it was a refined version of those meals described by Air Mechanic Cornish and all the others. The airmen were ushered eight to a side of the long tables and at a command all sat down and were told to be quiet. This quietness was broken when trolleys, laden with large galvanised iron trays filled with foods, were wheeled from the kitchens and the trays placed on a long serving table running the full length of the dining hall. When the staff had gone the order was given to serve and apparent chaos broke out as the two men at the head of each table began to serve out 16 meals for the hungry men at their table.

*   *   *   *   *

A.C. Lee was posted to the School of Naval Co-operation at Lee-on-Solent from Uxbridge in November 1934. The station was used for both land and sea aircraft, Fairey 3F land and seaplanes, Walrus and Supermarine Seagull V, with two Queen Bee radio controlled target aircraft. As an A.C.H.(G.D.) the 'all purpose' trade, 'Tansy Lee' was drafted to a Wading Party whose job was to launch and retrieve the sea going aircraft.

In the summer the job was a sinecure when, after the aircraft were away the party relaxed on the pebbly beach, albeit in their heavy gear. Sunbathing and playing the mouth organ was favourite. Operating in winter was a trial of endurance of body and mind, the vicious cold water striking through the protective gear. On these occasions the

AC Moore seated in a training Bristol Bulldog airframe at RAF Henlow, a Technical Training School for fitters and riggers. Author.

men were issued with a large tot of Navy rum'—God, it nearly set your hair on fire—' from Sick Bay. This, coupled with 'running on the spot' restored circulation.

Tansy applied for air gunner training and while waiting sat and passed the L.A.C. and Sgts. Educational Qualification. It must be mentioned that A.C.H.(G.D.) were not below educational standards. Far from it, if anything their standard was probably higher up to 1935; those that the author knew were all men of good family background.

While on the wading job A.C. Lee had an experience that has stayed forever in his mind, '... when a large armoured Thornycroft high speed launch bearing R.A.F. roundels pulled up to the slipway and three airmen appeared on deck, an A.C.I., a Corporal and a Sergeant. The A.C.I. gave the orders and he it was that was ... pick-a-backed to the slipway. He was scruffy! His buttons were undone ... and were absolutely green, his tunic and slacks were oiled and dust stained ... He marched off up the slipway with just a nod to us, who stood there eyeing him curiously. Despite his appearance, he had a purposeful and authoritative air ... and just the hint of a wild gleam in his eyes. Several of the older bods ... said 'Hello! hello! wonder what he wants this time? — they had obviously seen him before. ... Naturally we were curious and asked who he was, and back came the reply, "Aircraftsman Shaw from Calshot" It was several minutes later that the familiar sounding name suddenly rang a bell, "Cor, stone a crow! It's Lawrence of Arabia" muttered one erk in an awe struck voice ... I had stood within inches of him and tried to weigh him up. I never saw him again, yet that once chance meeting made a lasting impression on me which I still recall vividly today'.

Aircraftsman Shaw was killed a few weeks later at Bovingdon on his Brough Superior motor cycle, in an unwitnessed accident.

*　*　*　*　*

The next step for those Fitters Mates who had passed out was to Henlow, in Bedfordshire, an old station that had been made ready for the increase in trainees by the building of new wooden huts. The u/t Flight Mechanic were accommodated in the old station as No. 5 Wing and the u/t Flight Riggers in the new huts as No. 2 Wing. The courses were of approximately eight months duration and were very thorough. As was to be expected from training schools life was at a constant pressure of studying, intermingled with guards, fatigues, drill and inspections.

It was here that the enthusiasm for aeroplanes which had led so many along this path began at last to be satisfied. At Manston they had been surrounded by Wapiti, Siskin, Atlas, Demon, Osprey, Moth and Tutor, all immobile. Now the trainees were deep into the technicalities of airframe and engine fitting, repairing, handling and servicing and enjoying every minute of their training. First came basic workshop practice, followed by simple rivetting exercises which led to built-up repair exercises, which involved tubes and plates and simulated the repair to various types of steel fuselage construction. Splicing wire cables was a basic operation.

Together with the practical side there was the theoretical 'gen' to assimilate and lectures took the trainees deep into nuts, bolts, threads, taps and dies, drills, taper pins, with clearance angles, pitch diameters, root thread, morse taper, carbon and alloy steels, non-ferrous metals and their heat treatments. Moving on to the 'Pickle Factory' the trainees would at last be working on actual aircraft, dismantling and erecting D.H. Moth, Bulldog, Atlas, Gordon and Hart. Fitters stripped and assembled Pegasus, Lynx, Lion and Jaguar.

Maintenance on a Bristol Pegasus of a Vickers Wellesley of 35 Squadron at Worthy Down 1937. F/Sgt Driscoll, LAC's Gardner and Hillier. Author.

The trainees also played hangar draughts (moving aircraft in and out of hangars). Some of the lucky ones were given their first flight, the author among them.

At Henlow, the author and a few hundred other airmen, witnessed a rare public punishment, that of two airmen being dismissed the service with ignominy, or 'drummed out', for being convicted of stealing. The Wing were paraded in a three sided square with the band in attendance. The two convicted airmen with their escort and the Station Adjutant and other officers, marched on and the Adjutant read out the charges and findings of the Court Martial. The Adjutant then stepped forward and ceremoniously cut off the badges and buttons of the two unfortunate airmen. These two and their escort were then marched away to the acompaniment of a beat on the side drums.

The scene created a long lasting impression which it was designed to do. It may have appeared medieval but the reasoning behind the act was sound for, if stealing from comrades who had little anyway, was lightly punished, then it could become rife and a man would not be able to trust his neighbour. In a fighting service the elements of trust was important for all.

Most airmen had the same favourable view of Henlow as the author, who considered the eight months as one of the better periods and the standard of technical training extremely high. The syllabus was comprehensive and more than adequate for the majority of tradesmen when they reached their service units.

There must be many ex-Henlow erks who feel a twinge of nostalgia now and again for crowding into Birch's cafe on a wet, muggy afternoon, with steam and conversation rising on all sides over the tea and toast, or going for a swim in the quarry behind the camp. They must remember the hot summer days, dismantling and erecting assorted aircraft at the 'Pickle Factory', the stir of interest that went around when an operational aircraft landed, evenings in the Naafi scratching along on beans on toast or a bar of Duncans. They might remember the highlights, Sports Day, the A.O.C.'s Inspection, Empire Air Day and, blessed event, Passing Out.

1936 saw the introduction of sophisticated monoplane aircraft into the R.A.F., commencing with the Avro Anson, followed by Vickers Wellesley and Wellington, Bristol Blenheim, Fairey Battle, Armstrong Whitworth Whitley, Handley Page Hampden and Westland Lysander. For the ground crew these aeroplanes were completely new concepts of aeronautical engineering from the traditional biplanes; they were faced with a bewildering array of new technical systems and applications to master, and just had to get down to the new techniques of hydraulic and pneumatic operations, stressed skin construction, increased use of electrical application, variable pitch propellers, coolant systems and supercharging and many others that now made up the new breed of aircraft.

A few lucky airmen from each squadron or unit to be equipped with one of the types were detailed for manufacturers courses. The author was so detailed for two weeks at Fairey Aviation Co. at Stockport in 1938 and found it excellent.

The basic servicing of aircraft did not change with the advent of these aircraft, only the methods altered. The increased complexity demanded the employment of tradesmen who required more specialist training and servicing equipment and this was forseen by introducing in 1938 several new Group 1 trades; Fitter 2 Airframe, Fitter 2 Engine, Fitter Armourer, Instrument Fitter, Wireless Fitter whose syllabuses reflected the greater technical skills needed for the new aircraft and equipment. Likewise manufacturers were

Armourers bombing up a Harrow with 250 lb bomb.

pressed to supply quickly the specialist equipment. The courses were each of about a year but early in the war the courses were drastically shortened and additional training schools opened. For example, the Fitter 2 A course at R.A.F. Innsworth was reduced to four months.

* * * * *

A.C. Venton was posted from Manston to the F.A.A. base at Gosport to No. 1 Coastal Artillery Co-operation Unit (C.A.C.U.); the station also housed a Torpedo Development Unit, using Swordfish and Vildebeest, and also trained F.A.A. aircrew in deck and catapult operation. The C.A.C.U. was equipped with three Hawker Osprey and two Fairey 3F's, the five aircraft being later replaced by Ansons.

Gosport was a good station and under a modern and enlightened C.O., the erks had ample free time and the C.O. saw to it that there was plenty of opportunity to meet officers and aircrew socially during off-duty hours, by dart matches, socials and just plain drinking sessions. All this made for a happy station and with the munificient pay of 5/- — 5/6d (25 — 27p) a day an L.A.C. could be self-supporting, in an age when price rises were measured in one tenth of a new penny.

Routine was fairly typical in that, despite the reasons for expansion, there was still not the urgency of crisis to accelerate the flying programme, and work proceeded very much on the lines that had been formulated during the years of economy. Aircraft were still kept inside the hangars when not flying and the weather was still an important consideration affecting the flying programme. Because of this it was not unusual for aeroplanes to be pushed in and out several times a day.

Casualties among ground crew did not always result from the effects of flying crashes, airmen were killed from associated causes. For example, Venton describes two similar incidents with Swordfish at Gosport, '... One erk was walking between two hangars when a Swordfish suddenly appeared coming in to land too low, and he was unable to dodge it. Part of the undercarriage fairing caught him and severed his head from his body like a knife, leaving splotches of blood where it hit the ground. This occurred next to our hangar and as we marched across the tarmac back to dinner we went past these pools of blood and the body being carried away. I don't think many went to the cookhouse that day.

'Two or three days later another airman was scalped when attending to the smoke flares on the aerodrome, this time also by another Swordfish, which landed over him...'

These incidents show some of the occupational hazards of ground crew operation, along with death or injury from revolving propellers (more common on the crowded flight deck of a carrier), skin diseases from handling oils and greases and dopes, occasional injury from dropped unsafe bombs or inadvertantly fired guns, to name a few. Although this paragraph seems to imply that these were frequent occurrences, it was not so.

* * * * *

The developing crises from 1933 had brought the strong conviction that womens services were once more going to be needed — at least that was the opinion of a knowledgeable section of the community.

From 1934 to 1936 proposals for the formation of a joint womens service, although considered, were rejected on grounds of finance and were also 'neither desirable or necessary' (favourite rejection phrase of the War Office) by a body who could have applied the quote to their own title, The Womens Reserve sub-committee of the Manpower sub-committee of the Committee of the Imperial Defence. But 1938 became the year of turnabout and culmination.

Under constant pressure from the press and such responsible organisations as Womens Transport, Womens Legion, Emergency Service and First Aid Nursing Yeomanry (F.A.N.Y.), the Cabinet finally approved a War Office scheme for a Womens Auxiliary Corps, later changed to Auxiliary Territorial Service (A.T.S.). The Air Ministry was fully informed and had a sitting member when the scheme was devised, but the R.A.F. was fully committed to expansion and was less than interested.

The original A.T.S. operated on a geographical basis, each county raising one unit. One company of the unit was designated an R.A.F. company but remained under Army control, its members distinguished by wearing a special badge. Whereas the army companies were formed as trade companies — of cooks, clerks, drivers, equipment assistants and orderlies — the R.A.F. companies were composed of girls specially selected for their suitability for officer and N.C.O. status, for it was the intention of the R.A.F. to use them for training a nucleus of the necessary leaders in the event of war — the Trenchard influence. Originally, the decision was made to recruit photographers, draughtswomen, tracers and aircrafthands (the latter including waitresses, cleaners, messengers, teleprinter operators, fabric workers, etc.) into the R.A.F. companies, but this was a recruitment not pursued after the formation of the A.T.S.

The peacetime establishment of an R.A.F. company was around 65, which comprised 50 volunteers and the remainder the Commander and her Assistants and Senior and Section Leaders.

Final reward for the years of endeavour, accelerated because of the rapidly worsening threat of war, was reached when, in May the Air Council approved a womens service and on 28th June 1939 the Womens Auxiliary Air Force was formally brought into being. After the W.A.A.F. was formed the R.A.F. companies were invited to rejoin the W.A.A.F. Its first Director was Miss Jane Trefuses-Forbes, with the rank of Senior Controller (Air Commodore), who did a magnificent job in bringing the W.A.A.F. from its slightly chaotic beginning into a highly skilled and efficient service in its own right.

The W.A.A.F. mobilised on 28th August 1939 and recruiting began for other ranks in the trades of telephonist, teleprinter operator, radar plotter, M.T. driver, clerk, equipment assistant, cook and mess staff. The war establishment of the W.A.A.F. was in the ratio of three women to two men of similar trade. On 1st September postings began to get the girls onto stations as an organised force. The girls were originally drafted in groups of not less than 10 with an officer or N.C.O. in charge and lived out, going to their unit in civilian clothes. The girls were accommodated in station 'married patches' where vacant, or requisitioned houses in the area. Billeting was avoided where possible.

In addition the W.A.A.F. had their own toilet facilities, the use of lecture rooms, workshops for trade training and other buildings for meals. The company or section of the W.A.A.F. provided its own kitchen staff and medical orderlies.

This brief account of the W.A.A.F. beginnings is intended only to carry to the beginning of the Second World War. Their importance in that event was quickly realised and utilised, and they came rapidly into prominence, first on radar and as balloon operators. Very soon they took over other responsible trades such as parachute packers, then became aircraft ground crew until eventually their trade structure was almost as large as the airmen.

Whoops! A Nimrod pilot makes a hash of it landing on HMAC Courageous. RAF Museum.

The concept of week-end service had been brought to fruition by the raising in 1924 of the Auxiliary Air Force (A.A.F.), a territorial organisation comprising a number of squadrons and army units. These units were maintained by the County Joint Association on which the R.A.F. and Army were represented.

As the scheme developed, other squadrons were raised and named after city and county. Each squadron was controlled and manned by a nucleus of about 40 regular officers and airmen, who were skilled tradesmen and competent instructors.

The Auxiliary Air Force was open to all trades, clerks and A.C.H.(G.D.) and attendance was on selected evenings, week-ends and a yearly camp of 8-15 days. All those who joined were liable to call up into the regular R.A.F. in event of emergency. Like candidates for the apprentice and boy entrants schemes, only British subjects could join, for an initial term of four years. At the end of that period an auxiliary airman could re-engage for one, two, three or four years at a time. If an airman wished to opt out he had to give three months notice and pay a sum up to a maximum of £5.

During the first year airmen were required to attend a minimum of 25 instruction and 10 drill parades, each of one hour duration. For second and subsequent years the parades were 15 and six respectively but still an annual camp was required. However, uniform and equipment was supplied free of charge and the men received £2.10s (2.50p) bounty per year. These men were dedicated and enthusiastic.

On annual camp the airmen were integrated into the routine of the particular station and were subject to all the disciplines, fatigues, drills, etc., but rarely did any guard duties. The prime object was to give them aircraft operating experience under normal squadron routine. The airmen usually made the most of their two weeks, the older hands, ex-airmen, reliving their past and bragging a bit, the younger near-civilian types getting more than a glimpse of how a working station operated. Some regarded this period as their annual holiday, all benefited, including the R.A.F., for many of the youngsters enlisted for regular service as a result.

After the 1938 crisis the squadrons were put on a war footing and brought up to establishment and the personnel became 'hostilities only'. The squadrons went into action still under their auxiliary title.

In the five years of Expansion the R.A.F. grew in manpower to 186,000 officers and men, including 68,000 reservists. It had many problems to overcome in a short space of time. Practically the entire strength of obsolescent aircraft was being replaced by complex modern aeroplanes with their attendant servicing and maintenance re-organisation, new squadrons were being raised monthly and thousands of young men were flocking in to be trained. To accommodate airmen and squadrons, new airfields, storage and repair depots and training schools had to be built. Existing airfields were camouflaged.

For the first year or two of expansion, the old pre-war aura of sedate routine retained its influence. Working days remained the same, 0830 to 1630 with an hour plus for lunch, very little night flying, good week-ends off and a fair measure of parades, inspections and bull. But perceptibly the tempo of life increased as air and ground crews became familiar with their new aircraft and routine, new squadrons had 'shaken down' and the politics of Europe became more unsettled.

The influx of recruits inevitably raised another problem. Many of these young men realised that war could be in the offing and decided to get married much earlier than they otherwise would have done. But they were up against the regulations of the R.A.F. concerning marriage and at this time the R.A.F. had much more serious problems on its collective mind. Many of the airmen who married did not comply with the minimum marriage age of 26 and as a consequence had to marry on their service pay, thus laying themselves open to a tough time, living on a borderline of near poverty.

The average erk expected little promotion in the years 1919-1934. There just weren't sufficient establishments to warrant a large body of N.C.O.'s. It was possible for a tradesman to make Corporal within 12 years (this engagement period was mainly for apprentices) and then spend the remaining 12 years to pension (if selected) in that rank.

The early system of promotion which was adopted was that vacancies in a unit for a Corporal would be filled by that unit and if one was not available, or suitable (in the same trade), the unit applied to the Air Officer Commanding (A.O.C.).

Senior N.C.O.'s were promoted under a dual system by:

1   An unforseen casualty, death, deserter or discharge by purchase. The promotion was authorised by A.O.C. of the station concerned.
2   Ordinary vacancies, time expired, relief and other reasons. Promotion was authorised by the Depot or unit who had previously posted the N.C.O. and from its own promotion roster.

Warrant Officers were promoted by the Air Ministry in conjunction with their parent unit.

The role of the N.C.O. of the future, and his possible commissioning in the event of the service expanding, was taken a vital stage further in the 1920's by the introduction of an Allied Trade Test. This test required the budding senior N.C.O. to have a comprehensive knowledge of workshop practice, stores procedure, administration and disciplinary matters. The N.C.O. had to have this qualification before confirmation in his rank.

All the quality, training, the experience, the maturing by campaigning in Iraq, India and other, minor conflicts, with the initiative developed by the economic shortages were now put to the test. Most of the ex-apprentice erks mentioned in this book served in the various theatres of war and some, by virtue of their pre-war training and service, were quickly commissioned, fulfilling Lord Trenchard's far sighted aim at having a nucleus of trained men for the responsible positions in a war-expanding service. The large number of direct entry airmen who did an equally fine job as Senior N.C.O.'s somewhat negated the Trenchard theory of specialist selection.

Bombing a Fairey Battle. Airmen are wearing respirators for this 1938 exercise. Flight.

Chapter 11
From The Ground Up

The war was here. At 11 a.m. on 3rd September 1939 it was announced over the radio by the Prime Minister and almost immediately the Air Raid Imminent siren was sounded; it symbolised what the population was going to endure, for in this war air power was to be the dominant and decisive factor. This first alarm, however, was a false one and except for isolated incidents was not to be heard in earnest until May 1940. Once more the Allies had it all to do again, a war that had been predicated only a few years after W.W.1. But by the 'scrap of paper' of Neville Chamberlain's final realisation in 1938, a year's grace had put the R.A.F. in a bearable position.

The post war media was quick to label the eight months of non-operations from September to May 1940 'the phoney war'. To the civilian population, brought up to expect the horrors of Guernica and Warsaw, this period with the lack of large scale air raids was disconcerting but they were grateful, for it enabled uninterrupted production of much needed arms and equipment. Until the bombs began to fall.

For the R.A.F. the phoney war was never on and was to prove a blessing in disguise. The period was used by both air and ground crew to gain experience of operational techniques and boost output of men and machines from training schools and maintenance units. While the combat damage was relatively light the ground crew who saw off the aircraft by day and night and received them in the early hours were also gaining useful experience. Those ground crew on the flying and technical units would profoundly agree that there were more than 24 hours in a day, but the introduction of shift systems was soon to ease the long hours of work.

Most of the operational units were up to full war establishment, a state that gave some erks unpleasant living conditions on stations that were designed for smaller peace time establishments of biplane aircraft. Initially, the aircraft were picketed out in a dispersal line that followed the line of the airfield boundary, and nicely placed for any sabotage.

Additional to the long hours of flying programmes and those spent in the unheated, poorly lit hangars was that of dispersal guards which befell the main hangar tradesmen. Stamping up and down in an icy wind and warmed only by an inadequate leather jerkin and a few woollies, with the aircraft silhouetted against a moonlit sky, the duty ensured that the night would be one of tension and cat naps. Further duties would keep the erk also doing fire picquet, main guards, room orderly, and hangar key orderly to add a little variety.

Down among the fighter boys all the displays, affiliations, dispersals and detachment exercises of peacetime and the gunnery practice camps, were now brought to fruition. Night flying had been mastered, the squadrons were up to war strength and ready to go. In the familiarisation flights necessary with new aircraft a few had been bent, with resultant hospitalisations and a few funeral parties.

L.A.C. Hughes who served on 72 Squadron describes how a typical fighter squadron was divided into Red, Blue and Yellow sections, each with four aircraft plus several spare, and new erks posted in were directed to sections as needed. Fighter aircraft, particularly Spitfires, had a short endurance and on landing were expected to be turned round at high speed. This was done at first by refuelling up to three aircraft at a time from special bowsers. Armourers replenished ammo if the guns had been fired and checked the guns, fitters and riggers checked engine and airframe, with ancillary trades trying to do their bit at the same time. There might even be a queue waiting to get into the narrow cockpits. On completion of servicing the starter trolley was plugged in, the pilot's chute either put into the seat or placed on the tailplane according to whim and hood and windscreen cleaned. The group refuelling was later abandoned in view of its vulnerability.

At the end of the winter the squadron picked up its tents and moved again, to Acklington, north of Newcastle and a unique experiment. The airfield surface was so soft that, to maintain operations the Spitfires were changed for the old Gladiators, with their lower wing loading. Mud was the great enemy of the fighters and the Spitfire, with its narrow track undercarriage and thin section tyres, was prone to troubles in mud. When the period was over the Spitfires were returned. After this Corporal Hughes was posted to another fighter squadron which attained its fame on the prowess of one of its Commanding Officers, S/Ldr. Douglas Bader.

All fighter squadrons are not single engine types. The exigencies of war decreed that with the shortage of aircraft other suitable types be impressed and the Blenheim Mk1, the short nose version, was utilised. 145 Squadron was based at Croydon where at first the conditions were atrocious and very little flying was done.

Conditions normal. Laying some much needed duckboards at Carew Cheriton home of the 5 Coastal Patrol Unit Tiger Moths in the winter of 1939/40. K. Riseley.

L.A.C. Venton found the other ranks living in the hangar, no beds, furniture or heating until other accommodation was found. The beds supplied were the old Air Force three planks and a straw palliasse. The hangar doors were jammed permanently open and the snow drifted in as they worked. Little flying was done in the winter and the aircraft were kept in the hangar until the powers-that-be decided they should be dispersed, implementing the order at night. There being no tractor, all the aircraft were pushed around the perimeter track by the ground crew.

As an example of the paucity of suitable aircraft at the war's beginning No. 5 Coastal Patrol Unit based on R.A.F. Carew Cheriton was equipped with Tiger Moths, armed with a Verey pistol. To this unit of a difference had come L.A.C. Riseley from Shiny Twelve Squadron — and what a difference. Conditions on this new unit were perhaps worse than Venton experienced at Croydon.

'... We were billeted in the pigsty of an old farmhouse on the far side of the 'drome. No beds, no lights except by tins cut in half to place candles, lying on duckboards and trampled by rats all night for several months ... It did nothing but rain, rain, rain ... and we slogged through mud all day ... The hangars were of canvas. ...'

The unit operated under these conditions until buildings gradually improved until July 1940, when it was disbanded. Riseley went on to a Fitter 2A's course at R.A.F. Kirkham.

After the course Riseley was posted to R.A.F. Scampton where he quickly met a piece of the war, and was instrumental in putting out a few incendiaries that had landed on the hangar roof. Running out of sandbags he had carried up the ladder Riseley used his overcoat, much to the annoyance of the Stores Sergeant when he went to change it. Two weeks later Riseley was promoted Corporal, probably a happy coincidence but possibly influenced by his work on the hangar roof.

'Working on the operationally damaged Hampdens of 82 Squadron would often mean being at work continually for three days and nights, kipping down where ever it was possible for an hour or two ... Food was brought to us in the hangar to save time, as were a dozen or so camp beds to rest on. ...'

The Women's Auxiliary Air Force expanded rapidly after the war began. Into the original trade entries in 1938 of cooks, clerks, drivers, equipment assistants and orderlies, they accepted in August 1939 telephonists, teleprinter operators, plotters and mess staff. By the end of the war the airwomen had been involved in 89 trades and had done a job of work that commanded respect, male chauvinists included.

Their first major contribution was in the communication and plotting fields and the western world knows how much they did in the Battle of Britain, including dying. As clerks they were first class. The pay scales in 1940 for other ranks, roughly two thirds that of airmen, included the same conditions as for erks.

In another important field, that of parachute packing and maintenance, the women's touch made them irreplaceable. Very rarely indeed could a faulty chute (itself a rarity) be caused by incompetent work. This delicacy of touch and attention to detail made them an asset in the instrument and electrical trades.

When the girls finally invaded the bastion trades of the erk, that of aircraft servicing and maintenance, they had to prove themselves against some very 'anti' tradesmen, whose caustic criticisms was often both unnecessary and wrong. Out on an airfield they shared the same weather conditions and long hours as the men; they were given preferential treatment only in the matter of accommodation. They all tried hard and in that peculair women's way succeeded in gaining the admiration of the working tradesmen, not for their charms but as hard working tradeswomen.

Great emphasis was laid on flying training and a number of extra O.T.U.'s were formed, mainly for multi-engined conversion and where an aircrew finally came together as a team of pilot, observer and wireless operator/air gunner, training on the aircraft they were to fly on ops. One such was 17 O.T.U. at R.A.F. Upwood. The conversion aircraft was the Blenheim in both marks, and the Anson was used as a navigational trainer. As the intensity of flying built up a two 12 hour shift system was introduced. Prior to this it was a common occurrence to start work early, work throughout the day, have an early tea and go out on the flare path for an all night stint, finish at dawn, go back to the billets to clean up, have breakfast and start work again. The fatigue factor dropped considerably when the shifts were introduced, although it was rather strange to have breakfast at five p.m.

With the pilots coming fresh from the training schools casualties were to be expected and Blenheims got rather strewn over the surrounding countryside. Writing about crashes may be deplored, except by the media who exploited their dramatic appeal, but they were a fact of life in the wartime R.A.F. and cannot be glossed over. They were inevitable with the pressure on the aircrews, and the type of construction usually ensured unpleasant results with a very high death rate and injury per aircraft caused by high velocity impact, fire and the results of jagged edged metal.

To see an aeroplane burning after a crash and know that humans are inside, possibly friends, and knowing that nothing could be done to help often engendered a helpless feeling of inadequacy in technical achievement. A burning aircraft was always a bad sight and became worse at night, the darkness accentuating the horror.

* * * * *

In Europe the first winter of the war was probably the coldest. On the bare, windswept airfields of bomber country in Eastern England, the freezing wind whistled almost unobstructed, causing hands already cold to go numb after a few minutes contact with metal at a temperature many degrees below zero F. How welcome was the Naafi wagon not only for the tea but for the chance of a few cigarettes for sale.

The mechanics on the squadrons tried various methods to lower the viscosity of the engine oil to assist cold starting. Using a mobile heater to heat the oil and then transfer it into a fighter aircraft's tank helped a little until unexpected scramble exercises put paid to this time consuming method. In France canvas 'tents', with a safety heater inside, were placed over the radial engines of aircraft such as the Blenheim. The tents also assisted in keeping the ground crew fitters sheltered while they serviced. Later, hot-air vans were used to pump heated air around the engine and cockpit.

The congealed oil created its own problems. Trolley accs trying to start cold engines soon became 'flat', starter motors could not take the strain. A method of oil dilution was introduced but there was the danger of excessive dilution to the detriment of wearing surfaces. Before starting, props had to be turned by hand through at least two revs to break the cold seal of the oil in the cylinders. Once started, engines had to be excessively run to warm up and on fighter units and other aircraft on stand-by duty engines were started regularly to keep them warm. The introduction of high viscosity oil virtually cured the problem.

As L.A.C. Hughes observed '... ground running was not very popular with Chiefie ... ham use of the primer could mean soaked plugs and nil compression, and ham use of the throttle when it did start, with failure to observe minimum oil temperature restrictions, could result in a burst surge valve or, worse still, a leaking cooler. A run also meant a fuel top-up right away because of the chance of a red take-off or scramble and the inherent short range of the fighter...'

With the requirement that aircraft should be dispersed in the open and so have their flying surfaces prone to icing up on the ground, a solution was sought to prevent this. The manufacturers designed canvas covers to fit engines, cockpit/cabins, mainplane and tailplane, even prop blades, but they were not much use in icy weather for the often damp covers would freeze nearly solid, and trying to undo the lacing could be very irksome when an impatent Flight Commander was trying to get his aircraft into the air on a bitterly cold morning.

An anti-freeze solution that was tried was a low solution mix of glycol and water which proved fairly successful and paved the way for the introduction of Kilfrost, specially designed for the job. Kilfrost was in both paste and liquid form and the former was applied by hand to an approximate thickness of $\frac{1}{8}$th in (3mm) to the wing and tailplane leading edges. It was quite effective but, as Hughes found '... fighter pilots were not keen unless it was thinly and evenly applied because they recorded that it sometimes had an adverse effect on the handling' To apply the paste by hand to give the smooth aerodynamic surface took some time. Liquid Kilfrost was applied as a spray by a stirrup pump, usually from a bucket,and effectively removed most frost and snow deposits quite quickly.

Later aircraft incorporated built in systems for removing, and preventing, the formation of ice, usually by a rubberised de-icing 'boot' fitted to the wing leading edge, which either pulsated to remove the ice or pumped warm air through a perforated boot.

On the outbreak of war the Royal Navy wasted no time and immediately went looking for trouble, accompanied on some occasions by a carrier. Aboard that carrier all would be ready, squadrons worked up, modified to date and armed, with bombs ready. Such it was with 818 Squadron, flying Swordfish from H.M.A.C. Furious, in which was serving L.A.C. Ward. Life in the carrier was to be very exciting indeed for him, with a full measure of 'Join the Navy and see the World'.

The first encounter of the Furious was into the Skaggerak but no enemy ships were encountered. However, your friendly German bomber welcomed them with a near miss astern which jolted the aeroplane that Ward, an airframe mechanic, was working on off its rear trestle. This episode was naturally reported by Lord Haw Haw as a sinking.

From their base at Helston in the Orkneys, which they shared with the civilian contractors, even to a 'hole and pole' type latrine, the carrier carried out convoy duties across the North Atlantic, This entailed standing air patrols by the Swordfish, which meant plenty of deck operation and servicing. In January 1940 Ward was given the doubtful blessing of a posting to the ship's H.Q. Flight, which meant he was permanently accommodated in the ship, remaining there when the squadrons disembarked and working in the cramped hangar on major repairs and inspections.

The Norwegian campaign in April 1940 saw them operating from ice covered decks, not very nice with the possiblity of slipping into a revving propeller or even an aircraft sliding on the brakes. That, the cold and fog, plus the attacks from enemy aircraft, made conditions rather dangerous. To an inexperienced eye the flight deck was a nightmare of

WAAF airwoman driving a bomb train, just part of the quantity required for one four engined bomber squadron operation. Whereabouts unknown. RAF Museum.

noise and danger. It was. Aircraft were ranged at the rear with engines running and crews aboard, codelights were flashing, hand signals a necessity above the noise. A 35 knot wind over the deck added more danger. With eyes everywhere the launching party moved aircraft into the take-off position, lay flat under each wing to hold a wheel chock. A signal from the deck officer, chocks away and another aircraft dipped over the bows and slowly climbed away. Facing them was several hundred miles of sullen sea in which accurate navigation and the regular steady revolutions of the engine and all systems working was a life line back to the carrier.

On normal operation on the flight deck the deck handling party was sub-divided into specialist parties and watches, such as lift party responsible for bringing up, and down, aircraft on the lift; pin party who were responsible for folding and unfolding the aircraft mainplanes; ranging party who placed the aircraft in correct sequence as decided by the deck officer; chock party who chocked the aircraft wheels; barrier party who raised and lowered the crash barrier during landing on operations, and the steam catapult party who specialised in securing the aeroplane to the launching gear. There were ratings whose job was to remove the aircraft's hook from the arrester wire and other specialised jobs, the whole flight deck party working as a well regulated and cohesive team under the direction of the deck officers.

Ward and a fellow fitter were put ashore at Tromsoe Fjord to give some assistance to the Norwegian Air Force, and from its shores they saw the Furious steam out to sea — a nasty experience — but finally caught up with her at night after being picked up by a destroyer and transferred to H.M.S. Devonshire.

On the North Atlantic run again Ward had an experience so unique, he would never forget. No, not blood and gore! At Greenock they took aboard gold bullion in boxes, each box of which was checked every yard of the way. Ward was posted to a door of the magazine. '... When the job was finished I had to go along to the Paymaster's office and sign a paper stating the number of boxes I'd counted. I was then told I had signed for £18M worth of gold bullion. What a signature!...'

On the return trip from Halifax the ship carried bullion of a different kind, 30 second-hand Northrop and Brewster Buffalos, which the erks assembled on the dock side. The aircraft were well lashed down and inspected twice a day for security; the engines were also turned by hand. The Furious landed its precious cargo at Gladstone Dock, Liverpool and it was transferred to R.A.F. Speke, all without damage. Shortly after they were notified that some of the aircraft were damaged and investigation at Speke revealed half the Buffalos had damaged tail wheels, incurred by the handlers who had not lashed down the aeroplanes properly on their removal to Speke.

L.A.C. Ward had another diversion, this time into the Arctic Circle again in company with H.M.A.C. Victorious. When the new Albacores joined with the Swordfish for a raid on Petsamo loss and damage to these slow aircraft could be expected. And it was. One of the Swordfish returned with parts of its undercarriage shot away but made a successful landing and was eventually put under repair by H.Q. Flight. Ward had the job and it was his first major repair since he had left Henlow.

'... This was a taper pin and sleeving repair. Later on I saw this aircraft in workshops at R.N. Donibristle when on a week's course on the new Fairey Fulmar, which were coming into service in 1941. A gang of civilian fitters were working on this airframe and so I asked what they intended to do with that repair, and was told that they could not fault it and so were leaving it. I was very pleased with that little job. ...'

*　　*　　*　　*　　*

Among the essential units formed as a result of war were the Repair and Salvage Units (R.S.U.'s) the personnel of which often had one of the war's most unpleasant duties. Theirs was the job of recovering those crashed aircraft which could be moved and were considered repairable, or were in a position where they could be an obstruction, or would constitute a objectional sight to the local population. Or were still on the secret list. Theirs was also the problem of recovering the remains of any unfortunate aircrew who had been unable to abandon their aircraft—never a pleasant sight.

An R.S.U. also carried out the repair work and quite often arranged the employment of civilian repair parties, removal of serviceable components and disposing of aircraft as required. Part of the unit detailed to collect crashes comprised several R.A.F. self-contained teams each with its own transport and trailers and all equipment necessary for staying several days on site. Long hours with no respite was the norm and each team included a full range of specialist trades, with a larger number than usual proportion of A.C.H. (G.D.) erks to assist in the rough work. And a medical orderly if required.

The main areas of operation were the South and East side of the country where many returning bomber aircraft force landed and, during the Battle of Britain, was a fertile area of friend and foe. It was also one of particulary harrowing intensity as they worked to clear up the litter of that vital battle. Surprisingly enough they salvaged quite a number of bombing and training aircraft, for in spite of the fierceness of the battle, bomber and trainer units carried on throughout.

On being ordered to proceed to a crash a team would set out on a map reference over a route usually bereft of signposts. On arrival in the area the N.C.O. i/c would contact the local police and be guided to the crash site to meet either a mass of twisted duralumin and steel stewn across the field, a badly bent aeroplane on its belly or worse, a large hole in soft earth where an aeroplane had dived vertically. According to the state the N.C.O. made his dispositions of transport and men.

If it was a buried aircraft it had to be dug for if possible in order to identify the type and pilot, if with the aircraft. During the Battle of Britain, because ground staff were overwhelmed with this work, and if the hole did not constitute a hazard, it was sometimes just filled in and its location and dates, etc. logged. There was a danger to the team from the possiblity of earth collapse as they dug and, of course, the real horror of coming across a piece of aircrew. But it had to be done for the record — and to give the aircrew a Christian burial. A bent aeroplane was usually guarded by local police, army unit or even the team, and was dismantled as quickly as possible, for repairable aircraft was the object of the exercise. It had to be moved back to base on 'Queen Marys' where equally hard working erks would repair and return the aircraft to operational status.

Across the Channel where mighty armies were poised in massive inaction the Advanced Air Striking Force (A.A.S.F.) and R.A.F. Component of the B.E.F. (R.A.F.C.), two major forces comprising the British Air Forces in France shared even worse winter conditions than their comrades in the U.K. The A.A.S.F. comprised 10 squadrons of Battle and Blenheim day bombers and the R.A.F.C. consisted of a mix of five squadrons of Lysanders, four of Blenheim recce and four of Hurricanes.

In addition to coping with the harsh winter, one of the coldest known in France, with serious technical problems at minus degrees F., there was the uncertainty of French military tactics to consider. For as a major Ally the French should have issued clear directives to enable the R.A.F. to make definite dispositions. Unhappily, this was not the

Refuelling a Blenheim Mk I. From the primitive camouflage and erks carrying gas masks this may be in France on a fighter version of the aircraft – a front gunpack seems to be mounted below the fuselage. Alternatively, it may be happening during a UK exercise. 230 Octane was introduced late 1938. RAF Museum.

case and the French apprehension of the Luftwaffe had a detrimental effect in the later real war.

But this is no war history. Down on the ground the ordinary erk had to endure one of the worst recorded winters without any special cold weather clothing — as did the troops. The woollies knitted by so many dedicated ladies were really much needed and became a vital factor to the men's comfort. Cold weather operations were still in their infancy from a peace time routine of restricted flying in these conditions. All the major forces were crippled by the winter but as spring arrived so air activity increased. Here the R.A.F. were disadvantaged by putting slow and obsolete Battles into the air for Me 109 practice. Many a ground crew sent off their Battles and that was it. It was a bad foretaste of what was to come when the May 10th breakthrough occurred and the Germans advanced in force.

*   *   *   *   *

For back-up servicing of the fighter squadrons in France when the phoney war ended a number of Servicing Flights were formed and to No. 15, assembling at Henlow, was posted Cpl. Venton in April 1940. This unit was in a hurry and comprised about 30 airframe and engine mechanics, 20 M.T. drivers, radio men and a few A.C.H. (G.D.) who formed a Fire Crew. The two officers in charge, a S/Ldr. and F.O. tended, Venton thought, to be standoffish but when the going got rough did a thoroughly good job, except at the end.

The move to Le Havre from Henlow irritated Venton, who couldn't understand why, as the unit was a highly mobile one geared to operate quickly in the refuelling and re-arming role and find suitable airfields for the fighters to land for servicing, they should go off in the kit that they did '... complete with greatcoat, useless webbing, tin hat, full pack, rifle, two blankets, gasmask, etc...' some of that equipment was to come in very useful despite his protestations that it was useless gear.

From Le Harve to their first site took three days and two nights, feeding on bread and 'McConachies', stopping twice a day for essentials. At Beaumont Le Roge the Servicing Flight began operating a convoy comprising pick-ups, fire tender, radio tender and 20 new American White lorries, with all necessary gear for servicing aircraft. On a farm where they were billeted the magnificent draught horses had priority of accommodation.

Prior to the breakthrough the Flight had not been too busy, although it had been visited by the Luftwaffe. As with all units the German military attack transformed the preconceived theories of war with its Blitzkrieg, and the Flight was soon on the move in its designated role which, however, did not last long. For the Flight convoy was cut off from relevant news and immersed in the tidal flow of humanity on the choked roads. From this point the Flight was involved in a minor saga and adventure with deadly undertones.

Under chaotic conditions the Flight moved around the area seeking to give assistance, with little success. They found the refugees were creating much towards their own damage and demoralisation, looting houses, shops and farms. The morale of the Flight in this atmosphere, coupled with non-co-operation from their Allies, began to deteriorate. At three French air force stations they found aircraft either grounded under orders, or the station preparing to move south. During stops it became noticeable that suspicious looking characters gathered around and watched all movements. With rumours of 5th columnists in mind the airmen kept a close grip on their weapons.

On one occasion the Flight saved a Hurricane by chance when they saw it standing in a field. The pilot attracted their attention, told them the undercarriage was damaged and he had run out of fuel. '... On inspection it turned out to be the plug end of the starboard radius rod had pulled out, shearing the rivets. Luckily we were carrying some fuel with us but we had no rivets or spares of any description. I hit on the idea of removing some nails from a nearby fence and using these as rivets. Some of the lads put their backs under the plane to take the weight while I knocked the stubs of the rivets out and inserted the nails and burred them over. The pilot was delighted and had no qualms about taking it off, which he did safely, but I don't know what happened when it landed. ...'

The Flight was now on its own with orders to make for any Channel port that was open. They had difficulty in finding the road to St. Nazaire and were just about at the end of their tether, and had almost resigned themselves to capture, when a detachment of Sappers found them and guided them into port. Passing through the town they saw the effect of the bombing and looting, the Naafi being fair game.

The erks left the trucks with all their equipment and arms although Venton persuaded those with revolvers to retain them. The remnants of the Flight managed to board a small coaster after much 'to and froing'. There was no water or food or other facilities and many of the troops were British soldiers; accommodation was rough plank bunks, three tier high, nailed around the side of the hold. The coaster sailed at dusk and most of the troops were soon asleep, and awakened as the ship was entering Portsmouth harbour. No reception. They waited in the hold all the hot day without food or water until the evening. '... On the quay the Church Army had set up a canteen and dispensed hot tea and sandwiches, and I shall always remember them for this. We were given a postcard on which to write home ... The people of Portsmouth gave us a rousing welcome ... walking besides us carrying our bundles or kitbags ... I shall never understand the reason for the welcome as we were certainly anything but returning heroes...'

The heroes had to pay their own fare to their homes, where they were sent after processing at R.A.F. Cosford. Here Venton and his friends came up against a hard face of service life. After each being given a £1 note, an approximate size pair of boots and a jacket, it was the pay that aroused resentment. When in France the erks had been paid 100 francs a week, the rest put in credit and the R.A.F. Form 64 (Pay Book) marked accordingly. The last payment had been made just before the run into St. Nazaire and the paybooks left in care of the pay clerk in one of the lorries. When they had been abandoned so had the paybooks. The Accounts Branch had refused to pay without proof (where were the officers?) and the requisite duplicate records had apparently gone down with the Lancastria, when it was sunk during the evacuation with a loss of over 4,000 lives.

*   *   *   *   *

The defeat and Blitzkreig of the Battle of France led to the Allies adopting total war as practised by the enemy. The bomber squadrons, relegated to night attacks and relying mainly for successful sorties on targets which were visual, such as coke ovens, marshalling yards and steel furnaces, began to attack less specialist targets which had been difficult to find at night with the existing standard of navigational aids and techniques. The era of mass bombing was beginning, and more and more night raids were to be geared to numbers of aircraft available rather than quality of precision bombing.

As a result every available aircraft on a squadron detailed for a raid was somehow pressed into use. The ground crew now really felt the strain, for unserviceable aircraft had to be made operationally serviceable at whatever cost. That is, those that could be repaired within the station capability. It is quite possible that as a result of the pressure on the technical branch to get aircraft ready that inspection standards may have slackened somewhat on the odd squadron.

A mainstay of Coastal Command escorts to the lifeline convoys converging on and leaving the U.K. was the long range Short Sunderland flying boats. They were based in small units around the Allied war theatres close to convoy routes, and when due for major maintenance were flown into U.K. to a base geared for that work. Such a base was R.A.F. Pembroke Dock, home of Base Servicing Party commanded by S/Ldr. Wicks M.B.E., where Sunderlands completed a major overhaul in 10 days. Constructional work took a little longer.

After arrival from its home base, the aircraft would be taken out of the water, an extremely skilful operation usually under the charge of a F/Sgt. with the civilian operator of the electrically controlled cradle as his No. 2. The cradle ran on a slipway ramped into the sea to a depth of about four feet ($1\frac{1}{2}$m) with one man, clad in a waterproof rubber suit and heavy boots, on the cradle to assist with heavy chocks. The flying boat was usually moored on the nearest buoy to the cradle. A pinnace stood by and the beaching gear was towed out by dinghy.

The beaching gear consisted of a couple of twin-wheeled beams carrying cork flotation pads and a four wheel steerable tail trolley, likewise floatable. The beams were attached to the boat from the dinghy as was the tail trolley, and in a choppy sea with an icy wind blowing, was rather unsettling, as the erk often had to put his arms into the sea up to his shoulder to get the pins in, as the author discovered. When the beaching gear was attached, ropes were secured to the wing floats and drawn up to the slip each side of the cradle, which had been taken below water level.

The pinnace was now secured by a line to the nose of the aircraft and when all was well the boat was slipped from its moorings, a moment of peril, for until the Sunderland was placed in a position opposite the cradle which would allow it to be drawn up, the pinnace was the only means of preventing it drifting away.

This is where the skill of F/Sgt. 'Chimpie' Darlington came to the fore. For, by giving the correct orders at the right time and being one move ahead of the whimseys of tide, current and pinnace, and with perfect co-ordination from pinnace commander, the boat was kept under control and drawn nearer to the cradle, where the gangs could do their final job and gradually bring it on the cradle with the ropes, the pinnace keeping it firmly in line. When the Sunderland was eventually on the cradle our shivering friend in the rubber suit placed the chocks beneath the wheels of the gear, and the cradle slowly moved up the ramp to the quayside where the boat was manhandled to where-ever required. For his gallant services in operating in three feet of water for about 20 minutes our deep sea diver was awarded a tot of rum.

The Sunderland was taken into the hangar where small gangs of erks completely stripped the boat, removing all armament/radio and instrumentation, all flying control surfaces (leaving only the basic wing) the engines and props. The airframe was thoroughly checked and all items replaced, or previously reconditioned items were used, as in the case of engines and props. When all was satisfactory the boat had a water test on the hull, it was given a thorough anticorrosive treatment, lowered into the water and given an air test. The work took 10 days, and the transit crew arrived back from leave to take it off.

The working ground staff operated on a 12 hour day with extra time in the summer; they got half a day off a week and tried to spend it in the nearest town. The only cinema was invariably booked up as Pembroke Dock was also an army garrison town. Post Dunkirk there was much friction between army and R.A.F., the erks having to endure the 'Brylcream Boys' taunt so, as can be gathered, there was much local fisticuffs until eventually everyone became more understanding of each other's problems.

*　*　*　*　*

In July 1938 an article in a Stockholm newspaper maintained that Germany was gaining a foothold in Iceland both by commercial treaties and by annual visit of its Navy. On 2nd April 1939 the Emden visited Reykjavik, carrying a glider expedition, S.S. men and genealogists for the ostensible purpose of investigating German ancestry in Iceland! It seemed painfully apparent that German air bases on the island could be directed against Allied shipping convoys and fishing fleets, and to facilitate egress to the North Atlantic for the German Fleet.

As a result the island was occupied by British forces on 10th May 1940, and the following August 98 Squadron, flying Battles, was sent there followed by 269 Squadron with Hudsons, 330 Squadron, a Norwegian unit, with Northrop floatplanes, and some Whitleys and Sunderlands. The R.A.F. had two main bases, at Reykjavik the capital, and at Kaldadarnes about 40 miles (64km) to the East, where 269 Squadron was based. The choice of Kaldadarnes as a site for an airfield must have caused some heartburn for it was considered difficult to supply over a narrow rocky road from the capital, isolated, and a

A group of Servicing Flight Waafs who did a sound job of servicing No. 1 Parachute Training School's Whiteleys and Dakotas at RAF Ringway 1943/45. Author.

possible area of attack by parachute troops, but it was an all weather airfield and vital to the Battle of the Atlantic.

Against the British there was a strong anti feeling brought on, so it was said, by the conduct of Canadian troops of the original occupying force and compounded by a prevalent pro-German feeling and, at a later date, by the conduct of American troops. Whatever the reason, the life of the average other rank was made uncomfortable by the American ability to prise open doors with his dollars, and his use of hotels and bars which were put out of bounds to British troops.

Living at Kaldadarnes on a windswept plain, bordered by a river, was communal, so much so that the erks lavatory was a 22 seater where any notions of modesty were soon dispelled. Accommodation was in 'Tingloos', corrugated iron clad Nissen huts banked up all round with packed earth to keep them on the ground during the winter winds. Except for an issue bed and table all furniture was do-it-yourself.

The Hudson squadron was a strike unit and there was maximum effort of heart bursting activity on receipt of a 'U boat sighted' signal. While the aircrew were being briefed the ground crews were running around whipping off engine covers, lugging starter trolleys in sweat soaked sprints from aircraft to aircraft. The armourers were busy fusing the depth charges. As soon as the aircrew were aboard bursts of engine noises around the field indicated quick run-ups, then chocks away and they were off, as hard as they could go. The literally exhausted ground crew sought a few minutes rest in the crew room.

In 1942 the British suffered a shortage of fresh food as the Atlantic war of attrition caught up and main dishes were made from McConachies meat stew, tinned potatoes, hard biscuits, margarine and jam. Manna to some theatres of war. Our American allies were living on chicken and complaining of 'buzzard again!' On their tables were cream, sugar, fruit, tomato ketchup, etc. However, the Americans threw open their P.X. canteen to the R.A.F. and it was a revelation to British eyes grown used to strict economy of rations. There were American cigarettes in abundance at ridiculously cheap prices.

At Reykjavik was 1407 Met Flight which daily sent out a Hudson into the Atlantic to the extremes of its range to bring back valuable weather information. Preparing an aircraft for a weather recce, particularly in winter, was somewhat involved and illustrates the cold weather problem.

The aircraft had to take-off an hour before dawn each day and the ground crew had to be in the hangar two hours before. To warm the engines into a state suitable for start up, a mobile de-icing van which carried a hot air blower unit with three large diameter flexible hoses, was used. One hose was placed in each engine cowling to warm the cylinders and sump, the third into the pilot's cockpit. Output from the M.T. van was poor and was supplemented in winter by two small mobile American versions which were most efficient and probably developed from the North American winter requirements.

After an hours warm up during which all pre flight servicing was done the aircraft was taken out and started to warm up the engines. The Wright Cyclones were prone to catch fire through the air intake and it was a bit dodgy as the fire had to be extinguished quickly. As well as having extinguishers handy a number of 'split-arse' caps were scorched in the process and doing this at night, with the prop turning a few inches from the erk's head, could be irksome!

There were a number of unfortunate crashes with a disproportionally high death rate, and the place of burial in a hillside cemetery above the city was bleak, bare and windswept.

The crosses and the coffins were made in workshops and painted air force blue. The ceremony was long and the cemetery, facing out to the sullen sea, was a torment to the living and, standing to attention with a sub-zero wind whining across the sea, featureless landscape around, one felt almost sympathy towards those being laid to rest. The funerals were often attended by civilian undertakers in full evening dress and white gloves, an incongruous sight.

Onset of winter was preceded by weeks of rain, on the cessation of which the snows started and packed down to become a thick coating of ice throughout the winter, and forever dangerous. Part of the winter weather was winds so strong that Whitley aircraft secured with half a dozen six hundredweight (305kg) concrete blocks were blown backwards, and their propellers turned by the force of the wind. The whirr of empty petrol tins over one's head made one think twice about enjoying the primeval forces of nature and get out of the way. Iceland was considered by the Air Ministry to be a one year station for ground crew and six months for aircrew. The Atlantic Star was issued to the aircrew only.

*   *   *   *   *

In the last days of 1941 Margaret Trimble had endured an initiation into the W.A.A.F. at R.A.F. Innsworth which failed to dampen her enthusiasm. The new girls had shivered in their wooden huts over the New Year; no warmth from a stove without fuel during their kitting up period before they were posted to Morecambe for recruit training. Thankfully, the hotel accommodation was better, but on a freezing, windswept promenade, dangerous with its icy surface, many minor injuries were sustained.

Mid January, and A.C.W. Trimble was posted to R.A.F. Oban, a Coastal Command station operating Sunderlands from the Sound of Kerrara, arriving at the seemingly pre-arranged time for service posting-in of 23.30 hrs., to the sound of screaming wind and heavy seas. Again, the W.R.A.F. billets were in the Oban hotels and there was a wide range of tradeswomen employed on the station. Teleprinter operators, telephonists, clerks, parachute packers, sparking plug testers, M.T. drivers, cooks, A.C.H. (G.D.'s), pay accounts and equipment assistants — the trade structure was well represented. Some of the tradeswomen were ferried daily by pinnace across to a workshop on the Isle of Kerrara.

Cpl. Trimble's tour of Oban was marred by a tragic event. As she said '... On a sad day in August 1942 one of our kites crashed into a mountainside (in Sutherland, near Wick) — the late Duke of Kent along with all but one of the crew were killed, they were well known to us all. ...' A course for Equipment Accounts became necessary when the Admin Branch was made redundant and Cpl. Trimble had to pass out with a minimum of 80% at R.A.F. Penarth in order to retain her tapes (the author had a similar experience). Her success was followed by a posting to R.A.F. Wilmslow, a W.A.A.F. recruit training school.

Although she enjoyed the job and especially its proximity to her home, as soon as she reached 21 she applied in January 1944 to go on Overseas service, having the necessary quaificiations; over 21, single and a good service record; she finally left for Cairo in July 1944.

*   *   *   *   *

Definitely one of the most vital trades in modern war is that of the armourer, especially on the bombing squadrons of W.W.2. There were many technical trades in that war which

F/Lt Rushton, ex-ranker, and his team of armourers load a Wimpey at R.A.F. Lindholme 1940/41. F/Lt Rushton.

required special skills and high intelligence and no doubt, while not disagreeing with the above statement, these would contest a place in it.

On the bombing squadrons the armourers work required them to be strong and tough in addition to possessing high technical skills, for handling the bombs of that war was still a distinctly 'dicey' prospect. On the early bombers the bomb loading gear was designed to be manually operated and was slow and hard work as a result. When bombing squadrons and their establishment of aircraft increased to war footing and began regular operations, the armourer became one of the hardest working of the trades.

Typical of the bomber squadrons of the mid-war period was 419 (R.C.A.F.) Squadron, flying Wellingtons, to which Cpl. Morgan was posted. The aircraft could carry 4,000lb (1,800kg) bomb load in a variation of 1,000lb (450kg) 500lb (225kg), 250lb (112kg) bombs and 4lb (2kg) incendiaries (90 off to a container). Sea mines were also carried. An increasing complexity was the various devices with which they were fitted, anti-handling, delayed action, different fuses; safety measures; different constituents of the explosives. When the four engined heavies came into service bomb sizes went up to 8, 12 and 22 thousand lb (3636, 5454 and 10000kg).

N.C.O.'s in the trade had the added responsibility of releasing any hung-up bombs and on the Wellington this involved a great sweat. Morgan had his moments when a bomb or incendiary container had jammed in the bomb doors. He said '... Then one diced with one's life, for one could not hydraulically pump a Wellington's bomb doors down an inch at a time and then jack up a bomb trolley right underneath as one could a Halifax, to prevent the bomb from dropping ... Incendiaries especially got stuck in their container. Then, sweating blood and with one's heart in one's mouth one went into the cockpit and whoosh! they flew open (the bomb doors), and personally I was fortunate for I only had to deal with some incendiaries that went off. These were nose heavy and when dropped would land nose first and would go off. Then it was a mad rush to get out of the kite, catch the burning incendiaries quickly and fling them away from the aircraft. This in the dark was quite nerve racking I can tell you. ...'

When the squadron converted to Halifax, although the bomb load was heavier, the work was less strenuous because of the up-to-date design of the bomb loading gear. But the mid-upper turret required accurate gun alignment to avoid the gunner shooting off bits of the aeroplane.

Promotion was invariably followed by a posting and more responsibility, and Sgt. Morgan found himself in charge of a bomb dump, undoubtedly one of the most potentially dangerous of jobs. '... This meant fusing the bombs and getting them out to the 30 aircraft on operations ... One particularly dangerous bomb that I fused was one with an anti-handling device and a delayed action of up to 168 hours, which was dropped on German factories ... and bomb disposal units would not be able to defuse ... The anti-handling device was used in conjuction with a fuse in the nose of the bomb, so that if the bomb was moved even a degree, mercury would run causing contact and it would blow up ... Once dropped Jerry had to leave it ... for they were set from 6 to 168 hours, depending on the target'.

'This fusing was a dangerous job, for the bomb dump at Snaith, near Doncaster, had blown up twice in the same year ... and over 40 armourers had been killed ... Normally, if a tail pistol cross threaded as you were putting it in you took it out again, but with the No. 39 anti-handling fuse a quarter of a turn backwards, or anti-clockwise, meant that you blew yourself up. So it was decided that only Senior N.C.O.s would fuse these bombs in future, and when I did I cleared everyone else away, for even talking about the 'flicks' would distract one, as only one part turn to the left meant self-destruction. It's no wonder my hair's white.

'Another dangerous job was testing sea mines for mine laying, especially acoustic types, for to test one one had to check for a positive circuit and in this five second period I had to stop all aircraft engines and even lorries, for even changing from low to high gear could produce enough increased change in tempo of electrical energy to set the mine off. A sharp tap with a sledgehammer would not set the acoustic mine off, but if one increased the strength of hitting with even a toffee hammer from a light tap to a frenzied, quicker, heavier tapping the mine would go off. Hence the increased revs of engines could have the same effect.

'Armourers had such dangerous jobs and so many died through bomb explosions that at one time we had to wear red bands on our arms, and when we approached aircraft to bomb up other ground crew trades cleared off.'

* * * * *

It had been the practice on pre-war squadrons to allocate one rigger and one fitter to a particular aeroplane, to which was also detailed a pilot. Ancillary trades usually had several aircraft to one tradesman. This was the system that worked quite well in the more leisurely days and in fact increased the esprit de corps by the pride of having one's own aircraft. The aeroplane had more personal attention and was certainly better groomed. A bond was also created between air and ground crew, subject to the acceptability of each other, which consolidated the trust so essential in an air service.

When the aircraft was due for an inspection it went into the hangar with its ground crew who carried out the work, up to major inspections. It was proved by war that no unit could afford the luxury of one aircraft per ground crew, although fighter squadrons hung on as long as they could.

A modified flying training school type of servicing was introduced, loosely called the garage system under which the squadron Servicing Flight, mainly staffed by Group 1 and 2 trades, accepted all inspection and minor repair work and issued aircraft to the flights as they became serviceable. Major repair work went to Maintenance Units. The scheme wasn't too popular with some pre-war erks, particularly the fighter squadron types, but that was progress. In any case, when the Battle of Britain was being fought the old system would have been useless with ground crew teams losing up to several aircraft per week.

The whole system of aircraft servicing and maintenance was regularly scrutinised and during the war it was safe to say that no breakdown occurred in the method, only its logistic which, like everything else was subject to the exigencies of war. A Wing Commander A. E. Harrop eventually developed the ultimate Planned Servicing system which became the standard serving procedure for the post war R.A.F.

One school in the U.K. which produced more than its share of trouble for the enemy was that at R.A.F. Ringway, the famous No. 1 Parachute Training School, known throughout the Allied world for the excellence of its 'products'. The venerable Armstrong Whitworth Whitley started the ball rolling, but the bulk of the drops were done by the ageless and famous Douglas Dakota.

The Whitleys were reliable, much loved, elderly and slow aircraft. With an honourable and little publicised record of operational flying in the early years of the war, they had been retired to training duties. The author went for a trip in a Mark 5 to Cottesmore, then a base for American DC3's. As we taxied around the perimeter we could see the looks of utter disbelief on the faces of the Americans. 'It can't be', 'What is that?', was written all over them as the black, ungainly droop nosed aircraft went past, only its Merlins giving off their crackle of defiance. Very quickly we had a small audience and it was patently clear that some were getting a distorted idea of their Allies aircraft status.

Marshalling of the aircraft was carried out on the cab rank principle once flying had begun in earnest. The aircraft followed the leader round an enclosed tarmac, stopping to pick up their human freight. Life was hectic at busy times, the norm, with six aircraft taxying in and out of the confined space, props whirling a few feet from the tail of the aircraft in front, troops marching out to various aircraft. On these days, and there were many, alertness was a prime factor and it is good to record that there were extremely few taxi accidents, with no injuries.

All the parachute packers were W.A.A.F. and there is no recorded case of a parachute failing to open through being incorrectly packed; everyone had complete confidence in the girls who packed hundreds of thousands of chutes and they built up a reputation that was the envy of all. The troops loved them. Out on dispersal they shared the same conditions as the men.

*   *   *   *   *

The war in the Middle East was one of three major land campaigns and as in earlier chapters, the experiences of a few participants are described to give some personal insight into the conditions for the erk. The Middle East area of command ranged loosely from

Gibraltar in the West, along the Med: to Palestine in the East, North to Greece and South to West and East Africa.

The North African campaign was confined to the Mediterranean coastal strip, because inland was a vast desert with no communication network. The only metalled road on the coast was a single one linking the coastal towns, some with port facilities. The so-called desert was vividly described by F/Sgt. Ken Marshall, '... it was gravel desert in some places, so interspersed with rocks that only with great difficulty could wheeled vehicles be driven ... In the lower parts ... the winter rains had washed the silt down which had formed into mud flats, dried rock hard in summer and an impassable bog after rain. On all the higher regions were ... wadies washed away when the torrential rains ran away to the lower surfaces ... Over the flatter parts the camel thorn flourished and when driving over this it was a bumpy ride ... during all this time the wind blew faintly or not at all at dawn, gradually increasing as the sun got up and dying down at sunset. Normally this gave us no bother but with ... wheeled vehicles the surface broke up ... it only needed a very minor wind to raise the dust and if it blew with any force ... everything disappeared in a blinding pall ... Airfields were areas of hard packed sand and level scrub as near a road or track as possible'.

Returning to camp after a day out in Cairo L.A.C. John Cowburn found the camp in a state of 'yonks'—war had been declared — and other ranks of 112 Fighter Squadron busy belting up .303 (was this job of filling up ammo belts the origin of the terse instruction-belt up?) in readiness '... for a war that didn't reach us until June 1940' Almost immediately the camp went on hard tack, bully and biscuits but catering gradually improved.

The squadron liaisoned with 70 Squadron still, in 1939/40, flying the venerable Valentias that Ken Marshall had known in 1934. Cowburn said that had he known he was to fly many war hours in this mobile wind drag he would have been frightened to death. The Valentia soldiered on reliably, but oh! at what risk. The squadron formed a special K Flight from its flights to go to Port Sudan to be ready for Italy's entry into the war, and Cowburn volunteered for it. The trip to Port Sudan was most interesting and included both train and paddle steamer; he learned the procedure of making tea by the bucketful from the engine boiler.

At Port Sudan the erks were under canvas on a site about two miles (3.2km) from an airfield a few days before Italy's entry into hostilities. On that day the sirens sounded at dawn (0430hrs) and the camp was bombed, making everyone run for cover, many without shoes on the hard, coral-like ground which had been reclaimed from the sea. Savoi Marchetti 79's bombed '... with amazing accuracy from 15,000ft (500m). Only snag was the bombs landed with precision almost between every set of pickets where an aircraft had been tied down ... The 14 Squadron Wellesleys had taken off earlier to do sub: patrols. ...'

One bomb landed on the camp from a Caproni 81 which was turning over the area when it released its bomb load. Cowburn's Gladiator, piloted by P/O Hanlyn, had been first off and shot the Caproni down. 'I was thrilled it was my Glad ... As a result of the run for cover many bare feet were badly cut and there was a long queue outside the sick bay tent ... One poor wretch of a Sudanese was at the rear ... with a gaping hole in his back. He was looking in at the police post when the bomb exploded about 50 yards (45m) behind him. The shrapnel hit him and he slumped onto the table. The Cpl. S.P. told him to stand up and then he saw what had happened. The Cpl's run would have beaten any world record ... the poor Sudanese ... died on the way to hospital.'

14 Squadron's Wellesleys proved to be tough, the geodetic construction able to absorb much punishment from their Italian adversaries. One incident occured on the squadron which in retrospect may even have appeared funny, and concerned a Wellesley which had returned late and was being refuelled in the dark. A squadron 'erbert' who was holding the refuelling nozzle and couldn't see how full the tanks were, asked for a light '... He was passed a hurricane lamp (sealed torches and any other sophisticated equipment was non-existent). The 'erbert' held the hurricane lamp above the tank orifice and there was the obvious boom. He was blasted clear luckily but the aircraft was a write-off. Just one more that the Iti recce reported as shot down next day.'

The occupation of Eritrea by the British in May 1941 ended the R.A.F.'s offensive role in the Sudan and K Flight were recalled back to Cairo, where it was presumed that the ground crew would form the nucleus of 250 Fighter Squadron. K Flight's erks had a 'red paint' night out in Cairo in anticipation of an easier time in Palestine with the new squadron. That lasted two days. At midnight on the second day they were on a train heading for Sidi Haneish in the desert to man the Hurricanes of 73 Squadron whose own ground crew were trapped in Tobruk.

Cowburn records '... The acclimatisation to Curtiss Tomahawks was very interesting and all sorts of gadgets were produced by the ground staff to make for easier servicing. One item I particularly remember of the aircraft was a mass of wires in loom form. When changing engines (and this was often, due to overboosting) all these wires had to be individually dealt with. We had a Curtiss representative permanently with us and when the replacement Kittyhawk was produced a multi-plug was provided to join all wires. An engine change could then be carried out in 2-3 hours. . .'

Engine fitters servicing an Avro Lancaster. The naughty erks should be wearing their overalls.
RAF Museum.

Crashed Blenheim Mk4 at Apapa Lagos 1941. The Sergeant is the one doing the work! R. Venton.

When Italy entered the war it had the effect of closing the Med: to the reinforcing of the R.A.F. with badly needed aircraft. Only long range bombers were able to fly the hazardous routes to Gibraltar and Malta, to refuel. The initial demand in the desert was for fighters and bringing these by sea was proving too expensive in ships and lives.

The air chiefs brought into operation a previously planned scheme to bring aircraft into the campaign theatre by the 'back door' via Takoradi in the Gold Coast, West Africa, where they were brought as deck cargo by sea. When the scheme got under way an R.A.F. Section, with assistance from local labour, assembled the mainly Hurricanes and Tomahawks and fitted them with long range tanks. When sufficient numbers were ready a Blenheim, acting as navigating aircraft, led the fighters via Lagos, Kano, Maiduguri, Fort Lamy, Ati, El Geneina, El Fasha, El Oberd, Khartoum, Wadi Halfa to Suez and the Canal Zone where they were serviced and made operational.

The first party of R.A.F. arrived in Takoradi on 14th July 1940 where they got to work on organising living quarters and technical facilities, admin, accommodation and wireless communication. The main party of 350 officers and men arrived on 24th August and small parties were soon on their way to the staging posts. The first batch of six crated Blenheim 4's and six Hurricanes arrived on 5th September.

Cpl. Venton was posted to Uxbridge in August 1940 to miss his draft to Takoradi by 24 hours; he might have been in the main party had he made it; he finally left at the end of October. At Freetown they transhipped to a real trooper for the run to Takoradi. Within a few minutes of landing Cpl. Venton was informed he was on his way to Lagos to allegedly fill a F/Sgt.'s vacancy. Apparently Senior N.C.O.'s were in short supply and Venton was on his way with hardly time for a cuppa, going by B.O.A.C. Lockheed aircraft. The move pleased him as it was supposed to be the best staging post on the route.

At Lagos the Technical Officer was a much respected F/O Cumber, predictably and unofficially known as 'Q'! There was a period of a few weeks before the scheme got really going, which gave Venton a chance to get some much needed technical equipment together. '... Between us we had only one Flight Mechanics toolkit. Luckily ... there was a small Goverment dockyard and we were given the use of it. We set to work making a set of spanners ... and screwdrivers, while our caterer scoured the few stores in Lagos for tools and found some pairs of pliers ... with these we managed for many months before we received proper toolkits ...'

On each staging post the small party of erks refuelled and serviced the aeroplanes, helped by a few locals, and comprised two airframe and engine mechanics to each flight, with a proportion of each of the ancillary trades; as time passed they were reinforced with more tradesmen. First aircraft through were the Tomahawks and Hurricanes fitted with essential desert equipment, '... we also persuaded the local Works and Bricks depot to make up some wooden trestles to fit under Hurricane and Blenheim mainplanes ... they made us some heavy concrete blocks to picket the aircraft ... necessary because of the hurricane force winds ... Even with two of these at the wing tip and two at the tail, I have known a Hurricane to be shifted a few dozen metres by the wind (shades of Iceland!)

'The climate at Lagos was atrocious. The humidity was high and the temperature rarely dropped below 90°F even at night. Cigarettes were always sold in tins as a packet would be sodden and unsmokeable in three days. Such things as envelopes and stamps were protected on the gummed side by sheets of greaseproof paper. Our blue (uniform) which we never used, simply rotted away. Malignant malaria was a scourge, it was normal for all units to be one third under strength at all times through this illness, and it always recurred every six months or so. ...'

To increase the flow of aircraft the carriers Argus and Furious were pressed into service to bring in aircraft to Takoradi. On the Furious Cpl. Ward and his fellow mechanics worked flat out for 36 hours to assemble a batch of Hurricanes which were flown off the Furious. Ward says the F.A.A. was impressed with the R.A.F. pilots' efforts in taking off from the deck without previous experience.

A major problem, when it occurred, was a crash on the narrow runway. First priority was to get the aircraft off to enable a convoy staging through to land. Most of the crashes were comparatively minor and the usual method to remove single engine fighters was straight local manpower. For larger aircraft a couple of M.T. vehicles were used as well. There were two fatal accidents during Venton's stay, one to a Bombay when a starboard wheel burst a tyre and caused the undercarriage to collapse which in turn caused a fire with four crew deaths and passengers injured. The fire tender was a native, manual, hand-drawn cart, totally inadequate, and the Lagos fire brigade was too far away. The other was a Tomahawk which went into a swing on take-off and — most unpleasant — when Venton reached it the Polish pilot was dead and the magnesium of the engine burning furiously.

The humid climate caused engine troubles, and to make a set of sheer legs for engine changing three trees were cut down and block and tackle borrowed from Takoradi. In March 1941, Venton, with a few erks was moved up to Minna, an emergency airstrip, about 300 miles (483km) north of Lagos, to service a few machines that had landed and to organise refuelling arrangements for convoys, particularly for Tomahawks with their short range. During his short stay they were notified a V.I.P. was passing through who proved to be General de Gaulle. After refuelling, and before boarding the aircraft the General thanked them and shook their hands, an appreciated little touch.

* * * * *

One of the most disheartening campaigns was that of Greece and Crete. It was one of disconsolate retreats and defeat, despite the best kind of British courage—brought about by the German Army coming to rescue an incompetent Italian Army who had been enmeshed by the 'inferior' Greeks. The R.A.F. units, which had been drawn off an already weakened desert force to back up the army, had little opportunity to distinguish themselves before they were on their way as the full force of the Wehrmacht and Luftwaffe exploded against a pitifully too-small British force and disorganised Greek Army.

Blenheim and Hurricane squadrons were decimated and every scratch airfield was bombed and straffed. Lines of supply and communication were shattered, reinforcements virtually ceased. The whole retreat was one of trying to get available aircraft off, and refuel, re-arm and service those that returned. With no alarm system it was too often a race by all against an Me109 or Ju88 to the nearest shelter, slit trench or piece of rock. M.T. lorries suddenly became very precious as the only means to reach the coast where, hopefully the Navy was waiting. On the retreat the men got what food they could and hardly any sleep as the night was the safest time for travel and the Germans were fast advancing. The R.A.F. often operated in small groups of two or three lorries heading for the beaches around Nauplia and Athens. In effect it was another Dunkirk on a smaller scale. Those that reached the area within the stipulated time were lifted off by native caique or the Navy.

Tired, hungry and some dispirited, they slept where they sat for the short trip to Crete. Once on that island there was some attempt at keeping units together but it was not very successful. It was then a case of waiting for ships to take them off to Egypt and preparing for the expected German air attack. Bands of British defenders waited apprehensively, nerves taught, as they gripped inadequate weapons, determined to give everything.

At about mid-afternoon on 20th May 1941 a large force of German paratroops dropped around Heraklion and Retino where British troops and airmen were concentrated in some force. Fierce fighting took place and despite swift, vicious and professional attacks by the paras the German casualties were very serious, almost critical. Here and there army Bofers opened up, doing considerable damage against the huge mass of airborne troops and gliders. Some Army and R.A.F. units were still disorientated after a nerve stretching escape from Greece, aggravated by enemy bombing on Crete for days. In the confusion many small actions went unrecorded. In a Cretan valley a group of R.A.F. tradesmen, left to fend for themselves, took on the firepower of the paras who were using captured weapons against them. The fierce fighting culminated in a 1914-18 type charge up the valley side by the R.A.F. who captured the enemy position, arriving with a decimated force. Bands of airmen — and other troops — captured in the chaos, managed to escape and make their way to the coast where Naval vessels might pick them up. Their luck had to endure beyond the range of Ju87's and 88's which accounted for many ships. The R.A.F. lost over 360 men out of a total of 618.

A number of groups of R.A.F. other ranks reached the Middle East ports, leaderless, with no knowledge of what to do, where to go. As a result of their experiences in this direction some erks lost interest in the war and looked forward to their demob with even greater anticipation. The Greece and Crete campaigns caused much recrimination between all three services, with the Navy and Army particularly hostile to the R.A.F., and once again a post Dunkirk atmosphere pervaded when R.A.F. ground staff were not safe in town against soldiers and seamen ignorant of the true state of affairs and not enlightened by their superior officers.

The survivors were given well-deserved leave and posted to new units, or to units which badly needed their experience. At this time the R.A.F. faced a problem which was causing concern to high command — the maintenance system in use could not cope, and too many aircraft were 'locked up' in depots awaiting servicing for which there was insufficient facilities and manpower — as a result of all the 'minor' campaigns recently fought, East Africa, Greece and Crete, Iraq and the recent retreat in the desert from Rommel. There were only the depots at Aboukir and Abu Sueir and one R.S.U.

A change of command ensued and A.V.M. G. G. Dawson, the Chief Maintenance and Supply Officer, ruthlessly and efficiently altered the whole structure, upsetting many people in the process but getting the job done. One of his better moves, after a visit to Takoradi, among others, was to send home airmen who had contracted malaria more than twice. He set up a new (No. 206) Group and enlarged existing R.S.U.'s; created new units such as a Base Salvage Depot and shook up the little empires that had accumulated.

Servicing a Mk 2C Hurricane on a forward airfield on the Indian-Burmese border. RAF Museum.

One of his original schemes was to use Egyptian technical labour to the maximum from the small garages and workshops that abounded in Cairo, and opening up the caves of Ture-el-Asment from which the rock for the Pyramids had been cut. These were converted to modern, bombproof, overhaul and supply depots with all services laid on. Much repair work, hitherto considered only for U.K., was done. That dynamic approach and the results were indicated by a great increase in output from the M.U.'s. All the engine overhaul units had full back-up facilities of welding, blacksmiths, machine shop, plating shop, stores, propeller repairs, instrument and electrical equipment.

* * * * *

The growing numbers of ground staff apparently giving in too quickly to enemy ground attacks on their airfields, and of cases of ground crew other ranks left leaderless, which had started in France and had snowballed in the fighting in Greece, Crete and the desert, had repercussed back up to the top echelons of command. It caused sufficient concern for a special meeting to be convened by the Chief of Air Staff on 11th August 1942 to discuss R.A.F. discipline and the solving of what appeared to have been a major problem of other rank behaviour in war. The meeting was convened by the A.O.C.'s-in-C of all Commands, together with Air Members for Personnel and Training, the vice Chief of Air Staff, the Inspector General and the Commandant of the Staff College.*

The C.A.S. told the meeting that discipline in the R.A.F., adequate at home, was feeling the strain of difficult conditions overseas, and the Inspector General told the meeting of his concern at serious weaknesses in discipline abroad which he had found on his tour of the Middle and Far East. He said this was apt to break down under fire. In such conditions there was no proper control of the men. N.C.O.s were not used to taking charge and the men were not used to obeying them, the officers appeared to take no part in control, and as a result a unit was apt simply to melt away under bombing or gunfire.

The Inspector thought the reason for this weakness was that officers and N.C.O.s did not regard themselves as having definite responsibilities for the discipline and welfare of a certain number of men, while the men did not know whom they should look to for orders. He had noticed that N.C.O.s regarded it as none of their business to report complaints to officers, who never heard the complaints and as a result became out of touch with their men; the men had no-one whom they could regard as their officer, and who they knew was responsible for their welfare. He thought the remedy lay in improved organisation and establishment of a proper chain of command and responsibility; he also attached importance to outward signs of good discipline and respect for officers, e.g. men being marched to work by their N.C.O.s and paying proper compliments to officers.

After a preliminary discussion the C's-in-C gave three main reasons, none of which cast reflection on courage or behaviour of other ranks. These were:

Lack of proper organisation —
> No clearly defined change of command, officers and N.C.O.s unaware of disciplinary responsibilities and men didn't know whom to look to for orders.

Lack of training —
> Technical training had taken priority. No real training included in their duties as N.C.O.'s and on qualities of leadership.

Frequent postings —
> Frequent postings abroad made it impossible for officers and N.C.O.s to get to know each other and for units to attain cohesion and esprit de corps necessary for good discipline.

The C's-in-C went into a long discussion in which the posting question seemed to be the major issue, probably as this would affect their own Commands. They agreed overseas postings had reached enormous proportions and added to the problem by its transient nature, for once a man was warned he was on the Preliminary Warning Roll (P.W.R.) officers lost interest in the man (and the man usually lost interest in the unit). An idea by C-in-C Army Co-Operation Command that complete units should be posted — as Army regiments — was well received but rather difficult to put into practice. A.M. Sir Arthur Harris did not care for 'specialists' being posted overseas to jobs in which their specialist knowledge would be lost and opted that overseas commands ought to accept a higher proportion of men straight from training. The reverse view could, of course, apply from overseas commanders.

* Air 2/4899 Public Record Office

The conditions created for the incidents referred to might have initially begun in France 1940, where there were some cases of officers, N.C.O.s and men making their own way to the evacuation points. It happened in Army units also and, in the totally unprepared state for Blitzkrieg warfare is understandable. Malta was mentioned at the Air Ministry conference but seems to have been caused by the intense bombing and strafing with nowhere to run.

Greece and Crete are other obvious theatres where an air force with insufficient, out-of-date aircraft, backed up by penny packets of ill-spared reinforcements, unbriefed and manned by many men who had recently taken part in a traumatic retreat in the desert, were facing highly trained, well equipped and numerically superior forces who believed in total war.

R.A.F. other ranks had not been trained to defend airfields, were taught only rifle drill, and firing that rifle on the range at 25 yards (20m) during their recruit training. Subsequently they might fire an annual 15 rounds, make one bayonet charge on a dummy and, when war arrived fire a Sten and maybe even get to throw a grenade. Their whole training was geared to make them service tradesmen. Lessons of Poland, Norway and France when ground crew came under attack, albeit mostly from the air, and the para: attacks on airfields in Crete, became the object lessons that against seasoned troops the airmen were virtually powerless despite any reserves of courage and determination. Gut power was no substitute for inadequate weapon training and a service life geared only to servicing aircraft.

There were very few courses for newly promoted N.C.O.s, with the exception of one that ran at R.A.F. Cosford in 1941, an excellent course which taught Corporals all aspects of R.A.F. Admin and Organisation, how to drill and control men and look after them. This course stood the Corporals in good stead and gave them sound basics. Unfortunately it was discontinued and so a useful asset was denied Junior N.C.O.s. No weapon or tactical training was given.

By virture of its organisation there were no 'permanent' bodies of men in the R.A.F. as in the Army with its regiments or the Navy with the ship's companies, where a man could serve all his time. The R.A.F. way of service produced a restless, moving body of men subject to individual posting any number of times in their careers.

But it was a traumatic experience for men, untrained in ground defensive tactics, to be bombed and chased by the efficient German force, yet trying to keep aircraft serviceable during a retreat. The German Air Force was Army orientated and so were trained to infantry standards. That some men were unable to cope was to be expected, it happens in all wars, but even with the greater number involved in this war, the percentage of low morale was low.

The result of the C's-in-C meeting was centred mainly in a solution to produce a scheme whereby 25% of tradesmen were held by Commands for one year, with an additional 25% for 6 months for O.T.U.'s. to minimise posting between Commands and to regulate the postings overseas. A great effort was made and in late 1943 the scheme was stabilised.

Most probably as a result of the C's-in-C concern over the defensive capabilities of the ordinary airman when his airfield was under attck, the R.A.F. Regiment was brought into being. Initially recruitment was by ordinary tradesmen and A.C.H. (G.D.)'s with an emphasis towards armourers; later, as the war was seen to be running strongly for the Allies, many intended aircrew who would not now be trained were diverted to its ranks.

208

Training of Regiment personnel in the Middle East was carried out at R.A.F. Kabrit in the Canal Zone and the syllabus was for a combined Navy/Army operations course to near Commando standards, with instruction on light field weapons of 6 pounder (2.72kg) guns, 3in mortars and heavy machine guns. The course also taught the refuelling of the types of aircraft in use in the Middle East. A Squadron normally comprised A, B and C Flights trained to infantry standards, a Support Flight which handled the heavier weapons and an Admin/H.Q. Flight. The squadron had 40 vehicles, and trades included Medical Orderlies, Clerks, Equipment Assistants, M.T. Fitters, Cooks and Armourers.

Cpl. Wally Jones of 2824 Regiment was posted with it to R.A.F. Silver Fox, near Aleppo in Syria, to guard radio equipment being sent into Turkey.

The squadron also spent some time on a satellite airfield, Bab-el-Howa (Valley of the Wind), on the Turkey/Syrian border. The airfield was truly a dummy, and included plywood fighter aircraft, which it was the squadron's job to move around at irregular intervals, and to show themselves to create an 'operational blurr' for the enemy P.R. aircraft.

In early 1944 the squadron advance party was serving at Taranto in Italy, from where it was detailed for Greece, sailing in H.M.S. Ajax of River Plate fame, which itself was protecting a large convoy. They disembarked at Piraeus and moved to Kalamachi airfield, where they received and unloaded DC3 aircraft bringing in squadron personnel and equipment. The Greek Civil war began while they were at Kalamachi, between E.L.A.S. (Communist) and Government forces. The squadron went on to airfield defence, guarding perimeter and entrances with E.L.A.S. putting guards also at these points.

In the early stages of the civil war the R.A.F. H.Q. at Athens, the Hotel Brittanique, fell to the E.L.A.S. forces after a spirited defence by 2933 Squadron of the R.A.F. Regiment, backed up by admin: personnel not trained in defence. E.L.A.S. took an estimated 500

S/Ldr Chester: contribution in snow landing. The Authors aircraft.

prisoners and marched them some 300 miles across Greece. They were subsequently rescued by British parachute troops at Miagara, their E.L.A.S. guards fleeing when confronted by the paras:. On release most of the R.A.F. prisoners were sent home, suffering from malnutrition and exposure after their bad treatment under the Communists.

* * * * *

By an unwanted coincidence Venton was once again posted to West Africa, in mid-1944, this time to 95 Squadron flying Sunderlands out of Bathurst, known by the troops as the 'arsehole of the Empire'; it was unclean and stank.

At this stage of the war there was little for the boats to do but this didn't last, for when a Free French squadron moved into Freetown 95 Squadron was detailed to do their aircraft inspections, which meant an increase in the working hours of the men. This situation contributed to a most rare event — a strike by the erks. Other contributory factors were war weariness, the locale and the nearing end of the war. The 'Strike' lasted just over a day during which a number of airmen were arrested and the Station Commander read the Riot Act and the Articles of War. After that the men went back to work and the nett gain of the protest was a reduction in the working hours of 15 minutes.

In March 1945 Authority decided to write off four clapped-out Sunderland Mk I's and this was done by taking the boats out to eight fathoms of water, knocking a few holes in the hull and sinking them. The first also supplied the opportunity to get in some belated machine gun practice. Sgt. Hughes who was at nearby Yundum had the frustrating experience of overseeing the dumping of cased props, machine and workshop tools and mobile fire appliances into the sea about five miles out from Gambia. A large number of two and four engined aircraft were also destroyed.

In June Bathurst was closed down and the men flown off in batches to Freetown and the boat. Venton went with the last flying boat with 30 men and their trip was an event. Weather was very bad, an engine sprung an oil leak and was shut down and the weather worsened until they became lost. Eventually the captain did an emergency landing in a creek, which sprang a leak in the hull. The Navy came to the rescue after a night of baling out and took all aboard. The aircraft captain took off on three engines with the airmen's kit and made it to Freetown. This rather hairy 'do' was compensated by a decent trip home.

The contrast between Venton's men and those on the boat returning home from South Africa was startling. They appeared the picture of health and with smart, clean uniforms. '... We were almost the exact opposite, yellowed with Mepacrine, emaciated by malaria and fever with worn, ragged uniforms still showing signs of our adventure. Some of the men had lost their hats, and all the kitbags were stained and soaked with salt water. They must have wondered just what had joined them. For the first few days they avoided us like the plague, but after a time we made friends among them and one told me that before we were put on board the ship's M.O. told them a party of men from the West Coast of Africa was joining the boat and they should be avoided at all costs, as they were probably riddled with infectious diseases! Not a very nice way to ensure a welcome.'

* * * * *

The conditions for the erks in the Middle East had been rough and tough. For those enshrouded by the Burmese jungle and swamped in the monsoon mud of its plains life was yet still bearable compared with the fighting troops. The average erk's life in Burma was one of either moving backward, keeping a constant sharp lookout over their shoulder, or forward.

In the initial fighting for Malaya as Jap troops landed for their advance to Singapore, many ground crew were engaged as infantry in the defence of Kota Bharu, the local airfield, often fighting at very close range among airfield buildings. They did not run but unfortunately were overwhelmed by the sheer efficiency of these ruthless troops. Some ground crew, assisted by local natives, managed to slip away into the landscape. At Singapore the battle raged for the island and the airfields at a pace too fierce to last and many ground crew were killed fighting as impressed infantrymen.

The fear of the rapidly advancing Jap, their cruel behaviour, caused initially a great panic. There was a shortage of food and clothes; their bodies wasted by the high humidity and heat the O.R.'s were weakened by this demoralising life, but none gave way. They retreated in good order, giving the troops as much support as their resources allowed, until these ran out.

The monsoon period was one of great hardship in the Burma and Far East campaigns and the rains were of particularly high density and with the usual high humidity. It was the one period where, unless there was an allweather airfield, flying activity was nil. And during that nil period the ground crew were expected to thoroughly overhaul aircraft that had been subjected to hard use.

In some areas the mud had the consistency of glue and on drying set like concrete; this was particularly noticeable in Burma where the intense rains, another weather problem to overcome, stirred up some of the 'best' mud! If an aircraft left the hard strip or runway it was almost certainly lost if no heavy tractors or heavy M.T. was available; it was virtually impossible to move them by manpower, however many Chiefie managed to round up. This problem was finally conquered by the introduction of perforated steel planking (P.S.P.).

Peculiar to the Far East, the high rotting factor was noted and a watch was kept for attacks by various insects on wood and other materials, including glues, particularly applicable to aircraft like the Mosquito with its wood and glue construction. Many a tasty khaki uniform was gratefully devoured by the Burmese insects.

Sgt. Jim Wilkins had his share of the so-called Forgotten War. He had been posted to India in 1942, doing the slow, laborious journey in a coal burning trooper which called in for coal at Freetown, Durban, Mombasa and Bombay. He was posted to 177 Squadron flying Beaufighters at Feeny, as a Corporal, and stayed with it until he was promoted to Sergeant and then, as often happens was posted, to Chittagong to take charge of 83 Refuel and Re-arm Party.

This unit, one of several similar, was created to service aircraft which were giving close support to the Army's forward troops, using the 'leap frogging' technique. Personnel consisted of one of each basic trade plus the M.T. drivers. As the soldiers captured a mutti strip, and on a signal from them, the Party would drive to the strip with their convoy of four petrol bowsers, four three tonners and the command Jeep. Here they would refuel, re-arm and service the Hurricanes, Thunderbolts and Spitfires which were pressing the Japanese. Occasionally, other aircraft were serviced. Any battle damaged aircraft·that crashed on the strip was simply dragged off and left.

211

As another mutti strip was taken so another party would leapfrog the unit already in operation, to be ready to service aircraft and even carry out minor repairs. These tactics were as Sgt. Price has described in the Middle East and was done in the dry season, working from dawn to dusk. Life on the strips was primitive to say the least. Food was mainly bully beef and biscuits and its variations, living in bamboo 'bashers' previously occupied by the enemy. After checking for booby traps an important act was to put each leg of their charpoys in a can of paraffin to stop the bugs. Another was to dig fresh latrines. Both sides used whatever supplies each had left behind, particularly petrol.

Wilkins says, '... the danger of Jap encirclement was always there to add to the shellfire, bombing and low level attacks. At least twice we were surrounded and it was only the great efforts of the Green Howards that enabled us to break out. Several times the enemy were less than three miles away. On one air attack I dived under the nearest vehicle for protection; when it was over I crawled out from beneath a full fuel bowser!! On a number of occasions we were on the strip so quickly, before the Air Support Signals Unit, that I had to direct the fighters in by Aldis lamp. ...'

This hectic, exhausting life, in an unhealthy country, living on poor repetitious food and at full stretch resulted in Jim Wilkins and his men going down with malaria and dysentry, not uncommon ailments in Burma. Another, more insidious casualty, was the

Re-arming a Typhoon.
R.A.F. Museum.

disappearance of several airmen, which Wilkins put down to them throwing caution to the winds to visit the local brothel and simply vanishing, either being killed and robbed by the locals or captured by the Japanese.

When the grey teeming rains swept their watery veil across the country the active close air support was curtailed and 83 R. & R. P was withdrawn to its wet season base at Chittagong. But there was no let up, for the semi-permanent runways ensured a swarm of aircraft which required servicing, among them DC3s, B29s, Commandos, Mosquitos, Thunderbolts, Beaufighters and others, even a regular service Anson from Comilla with the papers and Indian Burma newsreel of the outside world.

83 R. & R. P. was the first unit into Ramree Island, whose runway the Japs had left in a tank trap condition, a DC3 pilot skilfully putting them down. With but 20 alive out of the 1,000 garrison the scenic area was grim but Sgt. Wilkins commandeered gravestones from the local cemetery and with the aid of the Army levelled the runway to allow the first squadron of Spitfires to land. At Ramree Servicing Commandos took over the refuelling and re-arming duties and Sgt. Wilkins was deservedly Mentioned in Despatches. He was posted back to his squadron, now at Chittagong.

Before he really settled down he volunteered for a most unwarlike job which gave him a therapeutic break from the tensions of war in Burma. A Works and Bricks party was formed from N.C.O.s and men with basic civilian trade experience to convert the newly captured Rangoon Law Courts into H.Q. Burma. The painter erks complained about the indiscriminate use of flame throwers by the Army when flushing out Japs from the building! The war ended soon after.

* * * * *

The work of the M.T. drivers in these small and large campaigns has hardly been recognised. In most accounts the driver has been considered with as much interest as the vehicle he was driving. They had to be at the wheel all the time and either know the route or follow carefully those who did. They were responsible for the safety and maintenance of the vehicle and when destination was reached had to service it before finishing work. Some of the desert convoys numbered hundreds of vehicles, but large or small convoy, they were a target for the fighter bombers. In Burma they had all the terrible conditions of terrain and weather to contend with. In many cases a crosscountry operation was dependant on their driving skill across bad country. They shifted thousands of tonnes throughout the war and they were the essential back-up to all operations, from moving bomb trolleys (usually by W.A.A.F.) to the mail vans. Many of the drivers were W.A.A.F., their reward, it could be said, is that they were taken for granted.

The second worst event that can happen to a serviceman is to be taken prisoner. Surprisingly, a quite large number of R.A.F. were Prisoners of War (P.O.W.) and taken in France, Greece, Crete, the Middle and Far East, particularly Singapore. The standard of life in captivity was related to the Hague Convention for P.O.W.'s; Japan was not a signatory and regarded surrender as a cowardly act.

With a few exceptions, practically all escapees from German custody were officers. Very few O.R.'s were able to escape, which might imply that the officers were better at it, because the officer's background and information available might have contributed, but the major reasons appear to be that the officers were not allowed to work, had more facilities and cash and more time to plan and prepare escapes, and more direct help by MI9.

213

The O.R.'s were employed on farms, coal mines, industries, transport, where-ever they could relieve the local manpower situation without noticeably contravening the Hague Convention. They had the bare minimum of food, very little cash, were under constant guard and whacked out by hard work by the time they returned to camp. Very few had the qualities that might be needed to escape from a working party deep in the heart of enemy country, such as knowledge of languages, local geography, way of life of the enemy. This did not deter those that did try and a few succeeded, but the odds were greater against them than the officers.

Senior N.C.O.s gained a few privileges and were also kept together, and to ensure that at least this privilege would be available, no aircrew was of less than Sergeant. Strangely, the Luftwaffe did not do this and many of their aircrew were of Corporal rank. In the very early days of the war a number of R.A.F. airmen gunners were captured.

P.O.W.s of the Germans generally had a tough but liveable time, those in Italian hands were subject to degradation. But all were civilised and protected to some degree by the Hague Convention and the delivery of Red Cross parcels. Those unfortunates in Jap hands had no such protection, the Japs neither recognised the Convention or that servicemen should allow themselves to be taken prisoner, and treated them sadistically. More seriously than the physical debasement with its universal lack of nourishment that they suffered, was that many P.O.W.s were mentally affected by their inhuman treatment. It seemed unbelievable that a nation could do this to its enemy.

Books written by P.O.W.s of the Germans and Italians were usually small epics of courageous adventure, those written by P.O.W.s of the Japs were horror stories. Towards the end of the war as the enemy felt oncoming defeat the P.O.W.s suffered in proportion, many by starvation. When the P.O.W.s were released by the army the soldiers were horrified by the condition they found the prisoners in. It made the soldiers very angry.

The Gloster Meteor heralded the first operational use of the jet aircraft by the R.A.F. and was followed by the end of the war, which was also the end of an era for those ground crew who had been brought up on the propeller driven aircraft. The R.A.F. was to go through the agonies of demobilisation, but had made provision in the lessons learned from 1919 by introducing a two year conscription service to ease the R.A.F. through demob and rebuild.

Demob itself was much more organised, with an administration more suitable to move the very large numbers into civvy street. The erks, pre-war and hostilities only, poured through the demob centres, collected their civvy suit and clothes in the cardboard box and departed eagerly, cheerfully, and apprehensively, to re-adjust to an interrupted life.

It would be many years before the majority had the luxury of nostalgia, most were too busy making a living, building a family and 'getting on' in life. When they did, what must their thoughts have been? Many and varied no doubt, but few would think that their own service in the ranks had contributed much. But it had, and collectively a great deal. Through the R.A.F. Association and personal friendships and reunions the memories would flood back.

Perhaps in the more adult reasoning they might agree that they had done 'their bit'. They surely had, for by their well trained hands the aircrew—God bless 'em—would not have been able to perform so efficiently the selfless and dedicated deeds that enabled the Royal Air Force of W.W.2 to be the war winning force it became. Everyone, except the inevitable scroungers, should be proud.

And what of the erks we have followed in this book. To follow their fortunes would unnecessarily extend it. The few incidents described can only be a fraction of the thousands waiting to be told; if the erks could only record them before it is too late, if only for posterity and to tell the historians how much they contributed. Suffice to say that our erks were moved around as is the way of the R.A.F. and saw service in various theatres. Nearly all were promoted.

All ground crew, direct entry and apprentice, airmen and airwomen, took on their responsibilities in the manner expected and exemplified Per Ardua ad Astra. If there were one or two hiccups on the way, well, they were ordinary people.

Index